Virginia Woolf

Twenty-First-Century Approaches

Edited by Jeanne Dubino, Gill Lowe, Vara Neverow, and Kathryn Simpson

EDINBURGH
University Press

To the scholarly generosity of the worldwide Woolf community

Edinburgh University Press is one of the leading
university presses in the UK. We publish academic
books and journals in our selected subject areas across
the humanities and social sciences, combining cutting-
edge scholarship with high editorial and production
values to produce academic works of lasting
importance. For more information visit our website:
edinburghuniversitypress.com

First published in hardback by Edinburgh University Press 2015

Edinburgh University Press Ltd
The Tun – Holyrood Road
12(2f) Jackson's Entry
Edinburgh EH8 8PJ

Typeset in 10.5/13 Adobe Sabon
by Servis Filmsetting Ltd, Stockport, Cheshire,
and printed and bound in Great Britain by
CPI Group (UK) Ltd, Croydon CR0 4YY

A CIP record for this book is available from the British Library

ISBN 978 0 7486 9393 1 (hardback)
ISBN 978 0 7486 9394 8 (webready PDF)
ISBN 978 1 4744 1413 5 (paperback)
ISBN 978 1 4744 1417 3 (epub)

Contents

Acknowledgements

First, we would like to thank all the contributors to this volume for sharing with us their intellectual and creative responses to Woolf's life, writing and thought. Their commitment to this project and willingness to engage with all the various (and sometimes protracted) processes of bringing any publication into being means that this certainly is no 'solitary birth' but one co-evolving and rich in multiplicities and new configurations.

Second, we'd like to extend a heartfelt thanks to Jane Goldman and all involved in organising the Twenty-first Annual Conference on Virginia Woolf, to the participants at the conference for papers which stimulated our ideas for this collection, and to Derek Ryan and Stella Bolaki for their finely edited *Selected Papers* – another source of inspiration for us.

Some essays included here have developed from previously published works and we would like to thank Edinburgh University Press, and Wayne Chapman and Clemson University Digital Press, publishers of *Contradictory Woolf: Selected Papers from the Twenty-First International Conference on Virginia Woolf*, edited by Ryan and Bolaki, for permission to re-use certain sections. Edinburgh University Press has published versions of the essays by Claire Davison and Nuala Hancock; and Clemson University Digital Press, versions by Davison, Jeanne Dubino, Diane F. Gillespie, Vara Neverow, and Kathryn Simpson. We would also like to thank those permitting access to the Hogarth Press papers in Special Collections at the University of Reading Library; the Manuscripts, Archives and Special Collections (MASC) at the Washington State University (WSU) Libraries; the Monk's House Inventory at Scotney Castle in Kent; the Leonard Woolf Papers at the University of Sussex Special Collections; and the Random House Group Limited for permission to reproduce the dust jacket for by Viola Tree's book.

Thanks must go to the editorial and production staff at Edinburgh University Press who have worked so positively with us throughout this process, namely Jackie Jones for her enthusiastic response to our proposal and for ongoing support, the indefatigable James Dale, who has provided invaluable editing advice, Rebecca MacKenzie for her work on the book cover, and Dhara Patel, for her editorial assistance. We also wish to thank Sarah M. Hall for her careful copy-editing.

We would like to thank friends, partners and families for their love, support and patience throughout (and, of course, for proofreading, catering and general taking care).

Last, but by no means least, we'd like to thank each other for the hard work, dedication, and support that we've all brought to this project. Working together, and from across the ocean through the waves of email (and the added marvels of Skype and Dropbox), has indeed been a great pleasure!

Contributors

Eileen Barrett is a professor of English at California State University, East Bay. She teaches critical theory, modernism, women and literature, pedagogy, and gay and lesbian literature courses. She is co-editor of four volumes of Woolf criticism, including *Virginia Woolf: Lesbian Readings* (New York University Press, 1997) and *Approaches to Teaching Woolf's Mrs Dalloway* (Modern Language Association Press, 2009). Her current project pairs Woolf with James Baldwin.

Kristin Czarnecki is an associate professor of English at Georgetown College in Kentucky, where she teaches classes in composition, modern British literature, and multiethnic American literature. She has published articles on Virginia Woolf, Samuel Beckett, Jean Rhys, and Louise Erdrich. Her most recent publication is *Virginia Woolf, Authorship, and Legacy: Unravelling Nurse Lugton's Curtain* (Cecil Woolf, 2013). Currently she is working on further comparative studies of Woolf and Native American women writers.

Claire Davison is a professor of Modernist Literature at the Université Sorbonne Nouvelle – Paris III. Her recent publications and ongoing research, including her co-edited *Ford Madox Ford, France and Provence* (Rodopi, 2011) and her monograph *Translation as Collaboration: Virginia Woolf, Katherine Mansfield and S. S. Koteliansky* (Edinburgh University Press, 2014) focus on intermedial modernism, Anglo-Russian and Anglo-French literary networks, and modernist soundscapes. She is also a freelance translator.

Jeanne Dubino is a professor of English and Global Studies at Appalachian State University in North Carolina. She edited *Virginia Woolf and the Literary Marketplace* (Palgrave Macmillan, 2010) and co-edited *Virginia Woolf and the Essay* (St. Martin's, 1997) and *Representing the Modern*

Animal in Culture (Palgrave Macmillan, 2014), to which she also contributed essays. She organised the Seventh Annual Conference on Virginia Woolf (1997), and is serving her second term as the secretary/treasurer for the International Virginia Woolf Society.

Diane F. Gillespie, Professor Emeritus of English, Washington State University, is author of *The Sisters' Arts: The Writing and Painting of Virginia Woolf and Vanessa Bell* (Syracuse University Press, 1991) as well as numerous essays on modern British women writers and painters. Her most recent publications include chapters for Maggie Humm's *Edinburgh Companion to Virginia Woolf and the Arts* (Edinburgh University Press, 2010) and Helen Southworth's *The Hogarth Press and the Networks of Modernism* (Edinburgh University Press, 2012). Gillespie also is editor of Woolf's *Roger Fry* (Shakespeare Head Press, 1996) and *The Multiple Muses of Virginia Woolf* (University of Missouri Press, 1993). She co-edited *Julia Duckworth Stephen: Stories for Children, Essays for Adults* (Syracuse University Press, 1993), *Virginia Woolf and the Arts: Selected Papers from the Sixth Annual Conference on Virginia Woolf* (University Publishers Association, 1997), and Cicely Hamilton's play *Diana of Dobson's* (Broadview Press, 2003).

Nuala Hancock is a writer and researcher whose work explores the interrelated fields of architectural and garden history, art and literature, museum studies, and Virginia Woolf. Her most recent publication, *Charleston and Monk's House: The Intimate House Museums of Virginia Woolf and Vanessa Bell* (Edinburgh University Press, 2013), centres on the correspondence between biography, space, and place.

Gill Lowe is senior lecturer in English at University Campus Suffolk. Her research interests are life-writing and early-twentieth-century literature. She teaches courses on narrative, modernism, autobiography and the short story. She edited the juvenilia written between 1891 and 1895 by Vanessa, Thoby and Virginia Stephen: *Hyde Park Gate News, the Stephen Family Newspaper* was published by Hesperus Press in 2005.

Ann Martin is an assistant professor in the Department of English at the University of Saskatchewan. Her scholarly publications include *Red Riding Hood and the Wolf in Bed: Modernism's Fairy Tales* (University of Toronto Press, 2006) as well as articles on Canadian, American, and British modernisms. Her current project focuses on the motif of the motor-car in interwar British fiction.

Vara Neverow is a professor of English and Women's Studies at Southern Connecticut State University. She wrote the introduction and annotations for Virginia Woolf's *Jacob's Room* (Harcourt, 2008), serves as the managing editor of the *Virginia Woolf Miscellany* (2003-present), was president of the International Virginia Woolf Society (2000–2005), and organised the second Annual Conference on Virginia Woolf (1992). Her recent scholarship focuses on Woolf's exploration of sexualities.

Derek Ryan is lecturer in Modernist Literature at the University of Kent and author of *Virginia Woolf and the Materiality of Theory: Sex, Animal, Life* (Edinburgh University Press, 2013). He co-edited *Contradictory Woolf: Selected Papers from the Twenty-First Annual International Conference on Virginia Woolf* (Clemson University Digital Press, 2012), and co-edited a special issue of the journal *Deleuze Studies* themed on 'Deleuze, Woolf and Modernism' (2013). Currently, he is completing a book, *Animal Theory: A Critical Introduction* (Edinburgh University Press, 2015), and co-editing, with Linden Peach, the Cambridge University Press edition of Woolf's *Flush: A Biography*.

Kathryn Simpson is senior lecturer in English at Cardiff Metropolitan University. Her main research interests are in modernist writing, particularly the work of Virginia Woolf and Katherine Mansfield. Other research interests include the work of contemporary writers Sarah Waters and David Mitchell. She is author of *Gifts, Markets and Economies of Desire in Virginia Woolf* (Palgrave Macmillan, 2008).

Abbreviations

AROO	*A Room of One's Own*
BTA	*Between the Acts*
CE	*Collected Essays* (4 vols)
CSF	*The Complete Shorter Fiction*
D	*The Diary of Virginia Woolf* (5 vols)
E	*The Essays of Virginia Woolf* (6 vols)
F	*Flush*
JR	*Jacob's Room*
L	*The Letters of Virginia Woolf* (6 vols)
MOB	*Moments of Being*
MD	*Mrs Dalloway*
O	*Orlando*
PA	*A Passionate Apprentice*
TG	*Three Guineas*
TTL	*To the Lighthouse*
TW	*The Waves*
TY	*The Years*
VO	*The Voyage Out*

Introduction

*Jeanne Dubino, Gill Lowe, Vara Neverow,
and Kathryn Simpson*

Our vision for this project has been to bring together a collection of articles taking diverse twenty-first-century academic approaches to Woolf studies. The publication emerges from the collaborative effort of four editors: two from the UK and two from the US. Representing recent trends in scholarship about Virginia Woolf, the volume offers multiple angles of interpretation and enquiry. It examines patterns in Woolf's life and work that are unstable, multilateral or evolving; fractured but also fused; contradictory yet connected. Many of the essays examine unresolved dissonances, binaries and doubles, ruptured meanings, and oppositional factors, and focus on ambivalence, antithesis, and paradox. Each essay takes a distinctive perspective and examines unresolved or previously unexplored tensions, whether in the contexts of Woolf's own experience or in the framework of her literary, political, and intellectual work.

The essays are organised into five interconnected sections. Beginning with essays exploring the private and personal, the focus then moves outwards to consider linguistic investigations, wider cultural concerns focusing on commodification and constructions of identity, and a scrutiny of ideas of being (human or nonhuman). The collection concludes with a fresh perspective on firmly established themes in Woolf studies – gender, sexuality, and the nature of the other – offering new and illuminating lenses through which to read her work in the twenty-first century. Woolf's own assertion in her 1924 diary entry that 'we're splinters & mosaics; not, as they used to hold, immaculate, monolithic, consistent wholes' (*D* 2: 314), fully validates our investigation of the splinters and mosaics in Woolf's life and work. As this introduction will establish, these approaches are embedded in contemporary scholarship, such as Bryony Randall and Jane Goldman's edited collection *Woolf in Context* (2012). Gabrielle McIntire's *Modernism, Memory, and Desire: T. S. Eliot and Virginia Woolf* offers the reader an intensive co-analysis of literary expression and issues of authorial identity in the chapter 'Virginia Woolf, (Auto)biography and the Eros of Identity: Reading *Orlando*'. McIntire's analysis is representative of the sophisticated ways in which Woolf's personal experiences and creative expressions are currently being interpreted by scholars who cross the boundaries between the text and the author, casting aside the mantra of the intentional fallacy. Similarly, each chapter in this new collection explores liminal and ambiguous elements that permit realignments and reconfigurations. These investigations contribute not only to Woolf studies but also, potentially, to a broader audience of readers interested in such inter-disciplinary fields as auto/biographical studies, psychology, linguistics, publishing, commodity studies, animal studies, ecocriticism, and queer studies.

The eleven essays included in the volume are subdivided into five sections: **Self and Identity; Language and Translation; Culture and Commodification; Human, Animal, and Nonhuman;** and **Genders, Sexualities, and Multiplicities.** These categories are representative of recent developments in modernist studies and, more specifically, Woolf and Bloomsbury studies. Studies of Virginia Woolf continue to proliferate, each one adding new facets to our understanding of her relevance and her influence. Recent book-length biographical studies of Woolf include Alexandra Harris's *Virginia Woolf* (2011) and Julia Briggs's *Virginia Woolf: An Inner Life* (2005). Maria DiBattista's *Imagining Virginia Woolf: An Experiment in Critical Biography* (2009) also examines Woolf's life. Finn Fordham's *I Do, I Undo, I Redo: The Textual Genesis of Modernist Selves* (2010) and Carl H. Klaus's chapter, 'Never to Be Yourself and Yet Always: Virginia Woolf on the Essayist's Problem' in *The Made-Up Self: Impersonation in the Personal Essay* (2010) are of relevance here.

Contributing to this sustained continuum of auto/biographical scholarship on Woolf's life and creative expression, the first article in the **Self and Identity** section focuses on how an individual is fashioned and presented. Gill Lowe, in '"I am fast locked up", Janus and Miss Jan: Virginia Woolf's 1897 Journal as Threshold Text', examines the young Virginia's conscious resistance to the construction of personality. Lowe shows that Virginia is in abeyance, averse to creating a personal narrative in this journal. Virginia uses the trope of the key, associated with Janus, the double-faced god. She acknowledges that by writing the journal her life is 'locked & put away' (*PA*: 134). Lowe uses twenty-first-century neuroscientist Antonio Damasio's theories about the 'self-as-object' and the 'self-as-subject' to analyse how the fifteen-year-old Virginia systematically resists subjectivity in this early journal.

She deliberately uses strategies to protect herself: assiduously avoiding the first-person singular and creating a surrogate self, 'Miss Jan', so she may express her views covertly. In 1897 Virginia is in stasis, at a threshold but not yet prepared to cross into autobiographical consciousness. Lowe's own earlier work, including her edition of *Hyde Park Gate News: The Stephen Family Newspaper* (2005) and her paper for the 2011 Glasgow 'Contradictory Woolf' conference, '"Observe, Observe Perpetually", Montaigne, Virginia Woolf and the *Patron au Dedans*', are similarly interested in investigating consciousness, subjectivity and the creation of crafted identities.

The second essay, 'Elusive Encounters: Seeking out Virginia Woolf in Her Commemorative House Museum' by Nuala Hancock, shows the influence of location on Woolf's sense of self and how we may interpret that sense of self. The article examines Monk's House, its contents and its garden to show how, by studying these places, one may read and better understand Virginia Woolf's lived experience and her creative expression. Hancock analyses, in particular, the dissonance between the enduring qualities of Woolf's material things, and the ephemerality of her living; the paper considers the concept of what Hancock terms 'palpable absence' (see p. 43 this volume). Hancock takes a phenomenological approach based on her expert and intimate knowledge of the spaces in Monk's House and its garden at Rodmell, East Sussex. She considers furnishings, textures, decoration, colour, light, mood, and ambience. Relevant contemporary scholarship on Woolf's personal life and evolving identity includes Hancock's own volume, *Charleston and Monk's House: The Intimate House Museums of Virginia Woolf and Vanessa Bell* (2012). Contextualising Hancock's approach are volumes such as Ruth Hoberman's *Museum Trouble: Edwardian Fiction and the Emergence of Modernism* (2011) and Anthea Arnold's *Charleston Saved: 1979–1989* (2010) as well as Maggie Humm's edited collection, *The Edinburgh Companion to Virginia Woolf and the Arts* (2010).

An overview of recent scholarship on Virginia Woolf shows a strong interest in the contexts and practices of publishing, the influence and evolutions of periodicals, and the politics of the literary marketplace and of the Hogarth Press. Significant publications include Kathryn Simpson's *Gifts, Markets and Economies of Desire in Virginia Woolf* (2008), Alissa G. Karl's *Modernism and the Marketplace: Literary Culture and Consumer Capitalism in Rhys, Woolf, Stein and Nella Larsen* (2009), Jeanne Dubino's *Virginia Woolf and the Literary Marketplace* (2010), and Helen Southworth's *Leonard and Virginia Woolf: The Hogarth Press and the Networks of Modernism* (2010). Book-length monographs highlighting the importance of research on the Woolfs' involvement with publishing include Patrick Collier's *Modernism on Fleet Street* (2006) and Paul K. Saint-Amour's *Modernism and Copyright* (2011). Such investigations into publishing are continued in the second section of this volume, **Language and Translation.**

Diane F. Gillespie, in '"*Can I Help You?*"': Virginia Woolf, Viola Tree, and the Hogarth Press', focuses on two works by Viola Tree that were published by the Hogarth Press: *Castles in the Air: A Story of My Singing Days* (1926) and *Can I Help You? Your Manners— Menus—Amusements—Friends—Charades—Make-ups—Travel— Calling—Children—Love affairs* (1937). This paper considers the ways in which both Woolf and Tree learned the rules of polite society, then how to negotiate and, ultimately, to challenge traditional expectations of behaviour. Gillespie shows how both writers, while behaving courteously towards others, were able to undermine accepted conventions. She shows too how the apparently domestic concern of etiquette had much wider social and intellectual application. As Gillespie convincingly demonstrates, both women were ultimately interested in 'how to live effectively'. She explores Woolf's engagement with Tree through multiple lenses of analysis, drawing on Woolf's autobiographical reflections in 'Am I a Snob?' as well as the underpinning concepts of gender and pacifism in *A Room of One's Own* and *Three Guineas*.

In the second essay in this section, Claire Davison's 'Bilinguals and Bioptics: Virginia Woolf and the Outlandishness of Translation' takes as a starting point the idea of the 'outland', an archaic term designating an outlying territory and associated with ideas of foreign territory, alien cultures and linguistic dislocation. Davison explores Woolf's outlandish translation and its 'transformative, performative' potential. In particular, this stimulating and innovative analysis explores Woolf's engagement with the 'quintessentially outlandish literature of Russia' via a 'bioptical' gaze. Woolf's border-crossing comparative reading across and between languages, in reading 'through a French–Russian–English optic', paves the way to a radically new way of thinking about Woolf's participation in translation and about Woolf as a translator. Woolf's awareness of the 'dynamic interface between languages' emerges as a marker of the avant-garde, in both aesthetic and conceptual terms; in fact, Davison suggests that Woolf evokes millennial third space thinking. Woolf's participation in the processes of translation reveals her as a reader thoroughly attuned to the liminality and prismatic nuances of language in translation. This work is part of a renewed interest in Woolf and Russian literature, indicated by Galya Diment's *A Russian Jew of Bloomsbury: The Life and Times of*

Samuel Koteliansky (2011), Roberta Rubenstein's *Virginia Woolf and the Russian Point of View* (2009), and *Translations from the Russian* by Virginia Woolf and S. S. Koteliansky, edited by Stuart N. Clarke and introduced by Laura Marcus (2006). Davison's own related book, *Translation as Collaboration: Virginia Woolf, Katherine Mansfield and S. S. Koteliansky*, was published by Edinburgh University Press in the spring of 2014. Burgeoning interest in language studies more generally is evidenced by such works as Judith Allen's *Virginia Woolf and the Politics of Language* (2010) and Emily Dalgarno's *Virginia Woolf and the Migrations of Language* (2011).

Rapidly evolving scholarly interests in culture, time, and place and the influences of history, location, technology, and commodification in Woolf's novels and essays are manifested in multiple publications, including edited collections such as Pamela Caughie's *Virginia Woolf in the Age of Mechanical Reproduction* (2000), and Michael Whitworth and Anna Snaith's *Locating Woolf: The Politics of Space and Place* (2007); and monographs such as Lorraine Sim's *Virginia Woolf: The Patterns of Ordinary Experience* (2010), Bryony Randall's *Modernism, Daily Time and Everyday Life* (2007), Rachel Bowlby's *Carried Away, the Invention of Modern Shopping* (2000), and R. S. Koppen's *Virginia Woolf, Fashion and Literary Modernity* (2009). In '*I'd Make it Penal*': *The Rural Preservation Movement in Virginia Woolf's* Between the Acts (2011), Mark Hussey discusses how what appears to be progress to some is viewed as ruination by others. What critics uncover repeatedly are the rich contradictions at the heart of Woolf's thinking about the changing experience of modernity, particularly in relation to the commodities and luxuries increasingly within her reach and the guilty pleasures and profound anxieties that her increased wealth brings.

Such tensions and contradictions are explored in the two essays in the section entitled **Culture and Commodification**. Ann Martin's chapter, '"*Unity – Dispersity*": Virginia Woolf and the Contradictory Motif of the Motor-car' dovetails with Hussey's discussion of the 'particular misery' Woolf experienced as suburban life spread out to the Sussex Downs. Martin in part explores a related point of contention in the concerns Woolf raised about the devastation of the rural landscape caused by the motor-car. The conflict between technological and mechanical development and the preservation of the existing framework of daily life – what was deemed progress and what was considered irrevocably detrimental – is embodied in this increasingly popular vehicle. Focusing primarily on the motif of the motor-car in *Mrs Dalloway* and *Between the Acts*, Martin aligns her argument with recent scholarship that considers modernism in the evolving cultural interpretations of technology and its impact on society. Martin's argument is situated in relation to the work of critics such as Garry Leonard, particularly his article, '"The famished roar of automobiles": Modernity, the Internal Combustion Engine, and Modernism' (2009), and Edna Duffy's *The Speed Handbook: Velocity, Pleasure, Modernism* (2009). At first critical of the motor-car as a costly machine that generates noise, filth, and offensive smells with the potential to cause damage, once Woolf has experienced the pleasures of the open road in her own car (particularly the Lanchester 18, 'a luxury *marque*'), her views began to shift. Experiencing the comfort, speed, and ease of travel she also becomes immersed in a community more 'mobile' in many ways. In this lively and refreshing consideration of Woolf's engagement with commodity culture and fashion, Martin considers the ways that this newfangled fuel-powered vehicle both constructs and defines the self according to existing social structures and notions of 'authenticity', even as it simultaneously reveals the performative dimensions of such identities and, indeed, their temporary and provisional status. As Martin argues, 'Woolf uses the motor-car to figure moments of temporary social unity which involve diversity and difference' (95) and which are always poised to disperse.

In '"Am I a Jew?": Woolf's 1930s Political and Economic Peregrinations', Kathryn Simpson examines the troubling and contradictory attitudes to Jews and Jewishness found in Woolf's writing, particularly of the 1930s (namely, *The Years*, and two short stories, 'Lappin and Lapinova' and 'The Duchess and the Jeweller'). Her paper builds on work published in the *Selected Papers* from the Twenty-First Annual International Conference on Virginia Woolf at Glasgow University (2012). Taking on board Zygmunt Bauman's assertion of the Jew as a 'semantically over-loaded entity' (2000: 39), Simpson examines how expressions of antisemitic revulsion and hostility are offset by defensive manoeuvres that align Jewish persecution and exclusion with the ostracisation of other groups. That Woolf's Jewish characters function metaphorically to reveal deep-seated cultural and personal anxieties is a key focus. As she suggests, '[t]he wandering meanings of the Jew in Woolf's writing seem to mirror her own peregrinations in relation to personal and political boundaries of belonging' (112). Simpson considers these anxieties as they surface in relation to Woolf's concerns about the damaging effects of commercialisation of literature alongside her own complicity in playing the literary market for her own profit. Simpson's essay makes a contribution to ongoing and recently reignited discussions of Woolf and antisemitism, which include Maren Tova Linett's *Modernism, Feminism and Jewishness* (2007), Karen Leick's 'Virginia Woolf and Gertrude Stein: Commerce, Bestsellers and the Jew' (2010), and the special section of the *Woolf Studies Annual* devoted to Jews and Jewishness (2013).

The fourth section of the volume, titled **Human, Animal, and Nonhuman**, explores topics affiliated with the rapidly growing and evolving field of critical animal studies (inclusive of human–animal relations) as well as the evolving investigation of ethical subjectivity across disciplines. In this large field of study, a range of scholars scrutinise the divide between the human, the animal and the nonhuman, fusing science with philosophy as well as feminist and critical theory. For instance, the contributors to Carol J. Adams and Josephine Donovan's edited collection *Animals and Women: Theoretical Explorations* (1995) explore how such factors as entrenched speciesism, the licence to kill, and the ethics of care relate to hierarchies that privilege humans over animals and males over females. Colin Allen and Marc Bekoff's *Species of Mind: The Philosophy and Biology of Cognitive Ethology* (1997) approaches the minds of nonhuman beings, countering anthropomorphic views that creatures are lesser beings than humans through studies that recognise animal thought processes. Rosi Braidotti's recent publication *The Posthuman* (2013) pursues related lines of enquiry, but focuses, as indicated by her title, on defining the posthuman historical condition and arguing that for 'posthuman theory, the subject is a tranversal entity, fully immersed in and immanent to a network of non-human (animal, vegetable, viral) relations' (195).

In the particular area of Woolf studies, Christina Alt's *Virginia Woolf and the Study of Nature* (2010) and Bonnie Kime Scott's *In the Hollow of the Wave: Virginia Woolf and Modernist Uses of Nature* (2012) both testify to the importance of these areas of study as does the special Fall 2013 issue of the *Virginia Woolf Miscellany*, edited by Kristin Czarnecki and Vara Neverow, which focuses on the topic of Virginia Woolf and animals. This issue includes Jeanne Dubino's article, 'Virginia Woolf's Dance-Drama: Staging the Life and Death of the Moth'. Derek Ryan's recent publications also make substantive contributions to this emerging field including his book-length study, *Virginia Woolf and the Materiality of Theory: Sex, Animal, Life* (2013b) and his article, '"The reality of becoming": Deleuze, Woolf and the Territory of Cows' in the special issue of *Deleuze Studies*: "Deleuze, Virginia Woolf, and Modernism" (2013a), which he guest-edited. Ryan is also the guest editor of the Spring 2014 *Virginia Woolf Miscellany* which addresses the special topic of 'Woolf and Materiality', and is completing a book-length study, *Animal Theory: A Critical Introduction* (due 2015).

Jeanne Dubino's 'The Bispecies Environment, Coevolution and *Flush*' and Derek Ryan's 'Posthumanist Interludes: Ecology and Ethology in

The Waves' bring fresh perspectives to rapidly emerging critical area of study. Dubino explores the growing awareness that interdependency is just as essential to human survival as to the survival of other living beings, and ultimately to the planet itself. As she observes, it is 'through interacting with other people, species, and groups, and through changing in response to these interactions' (131) that our very existence is sustained. Taking into account the gendered divide between the feminised domestic and the masculinised wild, Dubino investigates the complexity of the intertwined existences of living creatures, integrating the human and nonhuman. She analyses four types of bispecies interactions: predator-prey, competitors, host-guest, and mutual beneficiaries, and considers the significance of the environments in which these complex relationships take place. Dubino scrutinises the financial investment inevitably racked up in the human–animal companion relationship. Her close analysis of coevolution in *Flush* reveals the subtle and not-so-subtle ways that the lives of species permeate, influence and even determine one another's outcomes.

Both Dubino and Ryan use the concept of 'Umwelt', a German word employed by Jakob von Uexküll to explicate the fusion of animal environment-worlds. Applying this concept, Ryan examines the interludes in *The Waves* from the perspective of a continual 'becoming', an *in*volving rather than an *e*volving of being. Arguing that Woolf emphasises an ecological, ethological, and posthumanist politics of writing, he analyses the interludes as spaces where Woolf's '*nonanthropocentric* anthropomorphism . . . recognises the primacy of nonhuman events over cultural attempts to master life through language' (149). Ryan further explicates the fusion of animal environment-worlds in Woolf's depiction of animality, drawing on Jane Bennett's *Vibrant Matter: A Political Ecology of Things*, and her argument that 'an anthropomorphic element in perception can uncover a whole world of resonances and resemblances . . . revealing similarities across categorical divides', thereby challenging human claims of privilege over nonhuman worlds (Bennett 2010: 99). In his essay, Ryan moves beyond the myopic fixation on the human to the nonanthropocentric view of life itself as an immanent heterogeneity in the structure of *The Waves*.

In the final section, **Genders, Sexualities, and Multiplicities**, three essays explore the construction and mutation of gender, sex, and identity from related but distinctively different standpoints while exploring spectrums of gender-bending and blurring as well as the social constructs that attempt to define, limit, and constrain sexual exploration. The three articles also are positioned in relation to historical and cross-cultural contexts. Dirk Schulz's *Setting The Record Queer: Rethinking Oscar Wilde's*

The Picture of Dorian Gray *and Virginia Woolf's* Mrs Dalloway (2011); Deborah Cohler's *Citizen, Invert, Queer: Lesbianism and War in Early Twentieth-Century Britain* (2010); Madelyn Detloff and Brenda Helt's recent special issue of the *Virginia Woolf Miscellany*, 'Queering Woolf' (Detloff and Helt, Fall, 2012); and Qwo-Li Driskill, Chris Finley, and Brian Joseph Gilley's *Queer Indigenous Studies: Critical Interventions in Theory, Politics, and Literature* (2011) all illustrate how grounded and relevant these arguments are in contemporary scholarship.

The first article in this section, Eileen Barrett's 'Indecency: *Jacob's Room*, Modernist Homosexuality, and the Culture of War', aligns the systemic suppression of male homoerotic relationships in the late Victorian and Edwardian eras to the rising militaristic posturing that triggered the Great War. Barrett situates her analysis of *Jacob's Room* in the context of works by John Addington Symonds, E. M. Forster, and Lytton Strachey, including his essay 'Art and Indecency'. She scrutinises several sex scandals; those focused on the Cleveland Street male brothel (during the period 1889–90), where working-class men were found to be consorting with aristocrats (including, almost certainly, the Prince of Wales), and the equally important 1906–8 German scandal in which Maximillan Harden exposed Kaiser Wilhelm's intimate relationship with Philipp, Prince of Eulenberg. Significantly, Barrett contends that this humiliating exposé influenced the rise of militaristic culture in Germany during the build-up to the Great War. Her exploration of these historical contexts adds substantially to the body of scholarship on male homosexual expression during the Edwardian and Georgian period.

In 'Multiple Anonymities: Resonances of Fielding's *The Female Husband* in *Orlando* and *A Room of One's Own*', Vara Neverow investigates how elements of a pamphlet, *The Female Husband*, anonymously published by Henry Fielding in 1746, might be evident as both subtext and intertext in *Orlando*, Woolf's faux biography of her lover, Vita Sackville-West, and in *A Room of One's Own*. In 1921, the pamphlet was identified as Fielding's work and, in 1926, two years before the publication of *Orlando*, a copy was acquired by the British Museum, thus suggesting that Woolf would have had access to the text. While Fielding is never mentioned in either *Orlando* or *A Room of One's Own*, Neverow's new research reveals how coded references to his pamphlet are integrated into Woolf's narratives in startling and revealing ways. The article builds on Neverow's earlier essay on Fielding's pamphlet, 'Bi-sexing the Unmentionable Mary Hamiltons in *A Room of One's Own*: The Truth and Consequences of Unintended Pregnancies and Calculated Cross-Dressing' (2012), expanding the analysis to include *Orlando* in the discussion of passages in Woolf's work that strongly resemble Fielding's text. In particular, these parallels include explicit references to cross-dressing and the silencing of women as well as manifest examples of Sapphic desire and the threat of public punishment of women for being involved in what was perceived as transgressive behaviour.

The final essay in this collection, Kristin Czarnecki's 'Two-Spirits and Gender Variance in Virginia Woolf's *Orlando* and Louise Erdrich's *The Last Report on the Miracles at Little No Horse*' brings a fascinating new element to Woolf studies. Very little scholarship aligning Woolf with Native American literature and culture exists. Fabienne C. Quennet, in *Where 'Indians' Fear to Tread?: A Postmodern Reading of Louise Erdrich's* North Dakota Quartet (2001), compares Erdrich's writing style to Woolf's (Quennet 2001: 55). In *Native American Literature: Towards a Spatialized Reading* (2006), Helen May Dennis acknowledges that Woolf previously explored some of the gender issues Erdrich addresses in *The Last Report* (2006: 168), but in an endnote dismissively suggests that *A Room of One's Own*, 'Virginia Woolf's polemical essay[,] lacks the dimensions of Bachelard's volume, *The Poetics of Space*' (2006: 197 n.8). Exploring new critical/theoretical territory, Czarnecki moves far beyond the existing scholarship by exploring resonances between Woolf's *Orlando* and Erdrich's *Last Report*. She reads Woolf's narrative of gender-switching in *Orlando* and aligns it with Native American traditions and the concept of 'two-spirited' individuals who are neither defined nor fixed by a single sexual identity. Her paper argues that both authors, actively seeking to undermine binary classifications of gender and sexuality, instead privilege ideas relating to multiple genders and depict gender roles and identities that evolve over a lifetime. The sex-shifting Orlando in Woolf's faux biography and gender-bending Father Damien Modeste in Erdrich's novel each experience a transformation similar to that of Native American 'two-spirited' people who are not defined by their biological bodies but by their own sense of identity. Like Orlando, who after living as man for more than a century, shifts from male physical apparatus to female during a long period of sleep, the character Agnes deWitt transitions into a new identity when, after a long sleep initiated in a massive flood, she awakes to a vision of Christ that rekindles her Catholic faith. As she wanders the devastated land, she comes upon the body of a priest, Father Damien Modeste, whom she had known. She views this discovery as a sign of God, and assumes his garments, his gender and his vocation. Czarnecki's discussion of gender evolution in Woolf's *Orlando* and Erdrich's Father Damien honours the 'two-spirited' traditions of indigenous cultures and explores new literary affiliations in Woolf studies.

What the essays in this collection amply demonstrate are the protean possibilities for reading Woolf's writing using a wide range of critical and theoretical frameworks and setting her work in a variety of social, political, historical, cultural, and geographical contexts. Scholars here take up the challenge Woolf's writing lays down. These essays encourage us to read creatively, productively, and, at times, speculatively; to engage with the rich contradictions, ambiguities, and proliferating possibilities for meanings we find in Woolf's writing; and to see resonances with the preoccupations shaping our experience of the twenty-first century to date.

Bibliography

Adams, C. J., and J. Donovan, eds (1995), *Animals and Women: Theoretical Explorations*, Durham, NC: Duke University Press.

Allen, C., and M. Bekoff (1997), *Species of Mind: The Philosophy and Biology of Cognitive Ethology*, Cambridge, MA: MIT Press.

Allen, J. (2010), *Virginia Woolf and the Politics of Language*, Edinburgh: Edinburgh University Press.

Alt, C. (2010), *Virginia Woolf and the Study of Nature*, Cambridge: Cambridge University Press.

Arnold, A. (2010), *Charleston Saved: 1979–1989*, London: Robert Hale.

Bauman, Z. [1989] (2000), *Modernity and the Holocaust*, Cambridge: Polity.

Bennett, J. (2010), *Vibrant Matter: A Political Ecology of Things*, Durham, NC: Duke University Press.

Bowlby, R. (2000), *Carried Away, the Invention of Modern Shopping*, London: Faber and Faber.

Braidotti, R. (2013) *The Posthuman*, Cambridge: Polity.

Briggs, J. (2005), *Virginia Woolf: An Inner Life*, Orlando: Harcourt.

Caughie, P. L., ed. (2000), *Virginia Woolf in the Age of Mechanical Reproduction*, New York: Garland.

Cohler, D. (2010), *Citizen, Invert, Queer: Lesbianism and War in Early Twentieth-Century Britain*, Minneapolis: University of Minnesota Press.

Collier, P. (2006), *Modernism on Fleet Street*, Burlington, VT: Ashgate.

Czarnecki, K., and V. Neverow, eds (2013), 'Virginia Woolf and Animals', special issue of *Virginia Woolf Miscellany*, 84, Fall.

Dalgarno, E. (2011), *Virginia Woolf and the Migrations of Language*, Cambridge: Cambridge University Press.

Davison, C. (2014), *Translation as Collaboration: Virginia Woolf, Katherine Mansfield and S. S. Koteliansky*, Edinburgh: Edinburgh University Press.

Dennis, H. M. (2006), *Native American Literature: Towards a Spatialized Reading*, New York and Abingdon: Routledge.

Detloff, M., and B. Helt, eds (2012), 'Queering Woolf', special issue of *Virginia Woolf Miscellany*, 82, Fall.

DiBattista, M. (2009), *Imagining Virginia Woolf: An Experiment in Critical Biography*, Princeton: Princeton University Press.

Diment, G. (2011), *A Russian Jew of Bloomsbury: The Life and Times of Samuel Koteliansky*, Montreal: McGill-Queens University Press.

Driskill, Q.-L., C. Finley, and B. J. Gilley (2011), *Queer Indigenous Studies: Critical Interventions in Theory, Politics, and Literature*, Tucson: University of Arizona Press.

Dubino, J., ed. (2010), *Virginia Woolf and the Literary Marketplace*, New York: Palgrave Macmillan.

Dubino, J. (2013), 'Virginia Woolf's Dance-Drama: Staging the Life and Death of the Moth', in 'Virginia Woolf and Animals', special issue of *Virginia Woolf Miscellany*, 84, Fall: 9–11.

Duffy, E. (2009), *The Speed Handbook: Velocity, Pleasure, Modernism*, Durham, NC: Duke University Press.

Fielding, H. [1746] (2012), *The Female Husband: Or The Surprising History of Mrs Mary, Alias Mr George Hamilton, who was Convicted of having Married a young Woman of Wells and Lived with her as her Husband. Taken from Her Own Mouth Since Her Confinement*, <http://ebooks.adelaide.edu.au/f/fielding/henry/female-husband/> (last accessed 30 December 2013).

Fordham, F. (2010), *I Do, I Undo, I Redo: The Textual Genesis of Modernist Selves*, Oxford: Oxford University Press.

Hancock, N. (2012), *Charleston and Monk's House: The Intimate House Museums of Virginia Woolf and Vanessa Bell*, Edinburgh: Edinburgh University Press.

Harris, A. (2011), *Virginia Woolf*, London: Thames & Hudson.

Hoberman, R. (2011), *Museum Trouble: Edwardian Fiction and the Emergence of Modernism*, Charlottesville: University of Virginia Press.

Humm, M., ed. (2010), *The Edinburgh Companion to Virginia Woolf and the Arts*, Edinburgh: Edinburgh University Press.

Hussey, M. (2011), *'I'd Make it Penal': The Rural Preservation Movement in Virginia Woolf's* Between the Acts, London: Cecil Woolf.

Karl, A. G. (2009), *Modernism and the Marketplace: Literary Culture and Consumer Capitalism in Rhys, Woolf, Stein and Nella Larsen*, New York and Abingdon: Routledge.

Klaus, C. H. (2010), *The Made-Up Self: Impersonation in the Personal Essay*, Iowa City: University of Iowa Press.

Koppen, R. S. (2009), *Virginia Woolf, Fashion and Literary Modernity*, Edinburgh: Edinburgh University Press.

Leick, K. (2010), 'Virginia Woolf and Gertrude Stein: Commerce, Bestsellers and the Jew', in *Virginia Woolf and the Literary Marketplace*, ed. J. Dubino, New York and London: Palgrave Macmillan, pp. 121–33.

Leonard, G. (2009), '"The famished roar of automobiles": Modernity, the Internal Combustion Engine, and Modernism', in *Disciplining Modernism*, ed. P. L. Caughie, New York: Palgrave Macmillan, pp. 221–41.

Linett, M. T. (2007), *Modernism, Feminism and Jewishness*, Cambridge: Cambridge University Press.

Lowe, G. (2012), '"Observe, Observe Perpetually", Montaigne, Virginia Woolf and the *Patron au Dedans*', in *Contradictory Woolf: Selected Papers from the Twenty-First Annual Conference on Virginia Woolf*, ed. D. Ryan and S. Bolaki, Clemson: Clemson University Digital Press, pp. 215–21.

McIntire, G. (2008), *Modernism, Memory, and Desire: T. S. Eliot and Virginia Woolf*, Cambridge: Cambridge University Press.

Neverow, V. (2012), 'Bi-sexing the Unmentionable Mary Hamiltons in *A Room of One's Own*: The Truth and Consequences of Unintended Pregnancies and Calculated Cross-Dressing', in *Contradictory Woolf: Selected Papers from the Twenty-First International Conference on Virginia Woolf*, ed. D. Ryan and S. Bolaki, Clemson: Clemson University Digital Press, pp. 134–41.

Quennet, F. C. (2001), *Where 'Indians' Fear to Tread?: A Postmodern Reading of Louise Erdrich's* North Dakota Quartet, Hamburg: LIT Verlag.

Randall, B. (2007), *Modernism, Daily Time and Everyday Life*, Cambridge: Cambridge University Press.

Randall, B., and J. Goldman, eds (2013), *Woolf in Context*, Cambridge: Cambridge University Press.

Rubenstein, R. (2009), *Virginia Woolf and the Russian Point of View*, New York: Palgrave Macmillan.

Ryan, D. (2013a), '"The reality of becoming": Deleuze, Woolf and the Territory of Cows', in 'Deleuze, Virginia Woolf, and Modernism', special issue of *Deleuze Studies*, 7(4): 537–61.

Ryan, D. (2013b), *Virginia Woolf and the Materiality of Theory, Sex, Animal, Life*, Edinburgh: Edinburgh University Press.

Ryan, D. (2015 forthcoming), *Animal Theory: A Critical Introduction*, Edinburgh: Edinburgh University Press.

Saint-Amour, P. K. (2011), *Modernism and Copyright*, Oxford: Oxford University Press.

Schulz, D. (2011), *Setting the Record Queer: Rethinking Oscar Wilde's* The Picture of Dorian Gray *and Virginia Woolf's* Mrs Dalloway, Transcript-Verlag, <http://www.transcript-verlag.de/ts1745/ts1745.php> (last accessed 1 February 2014).

Scott, B. K. (2012), *In the Hollow of the Wave: Virginia Woolf and Modernist Uses of Nature*, Charlottesville: University of Virginia Press.

Sim, L. (2010), *Virginia Woolf: The Patterns of Ordinary Experience*, Burlington, VT: Ashgate.

Simpson, K. (2008), *Gifts, Markets and Economies of Desire in Virginia Woolf*, Basingstoke and New York: Palgrave Macmillan.

Simpson, K. (2012), '"Come buy, come buy": Woolf's Contradictory Relationship to the Marketplace', in *Contradictory Woolf: Selected Papers from the Twenty-First Annual Conference on Virginia Woolf*, ed. D. Ryan and S. Bolaki, Clemson: Clemson University Digital Press, pp. 186–93.

Southworth, H., ed. (2010), *Leonard and Virginia Woolf: The Hogarth Press and the Networks of Modernism*, Edinburgh: Edinburgh University Press.

Whitworth, M. and A. Snaith, eds (2007), *Locating Woolf: The Politics of Space and Place*, New York: Palgrave Macmillan.

Woolf Studies Annual 19 (2013), Special Focus, 'Woolf and Jews', ed. M. Hussey, New York: Pace University Press, pp. 1–82.

Woolf, V. (1978), *The Diary of Virginia Woolf*, vol. 2: 1920–4, ed. A. O. Bell, New York and London: Harcourt.

Woolf, V. (2004), *A Passionate Apprentice: The Early Journals, 1897–1909*, ed. M. A. Leaska, London: Pimlico.

Woolf, V. (2005), *Hyde Park Gate News: The Stephen Family Newspaper*, ed. G. Lowe, London: Hesperus Press.

Woolf, V. and S. S. Koteliansky [1923] (2006), *Translations from the Russian*, ed. S. N. Clarke and intro. L. Marcus, Southport: Virginia Woolf Society of Great Britain.

Part One

Self and Identity

Figure 1.1   Stella, Vanessa and Virginia Stephen, c.1896 (b/w photo), English Photographer (nineteenth century) / Private Collection / The Bridgeman Art Library.

'I am fast locked up', Janus and Miss Jan: Virginia Woolf's 1897 Journal as Threshold Text

Gill Lowe

On 6 January 1897, within a week of starting to write her first personal journal, Virginia Stephen's privacy was encroached upon. She writes, 'Pauline found the key of this book so that I am fast locked up' (*PA*: 8). Virginia,[1] almost fifteen, identifies herself closely, but ambivalently, with 'this book', consistently personifying it. She locks up her journal denying it an audience, either her self or any other. Conventionally a diary is seen as a place to freely express private thoughts about self and others. Frequently young diarists use their writing to release emotions and explore ideas, but, in 1897, Virginia refuses to do this: she prefers to lock her self away. She is unwell; her mother Julia's premature death in 1895 was traumatic; during 1897 her half-sister Stella marries, becomes pregnant, suffers debilitating illness and dies. On 1 January 1898, after the grievous blow of losing Stella, Virginia reprises the act of locking, 'Here is a volume of fairly acute life (the first really *lived* year of my life) ended locked & put away' (134). The effect of combining 'ended' 'locked' with 'put away' is striking. 'Put away' implies being set aside, hidden from sight, boxed and compartmentalised. Throughout 1897 Virginia was in abeyance: 'a state of suspension, temporary non-existence or inactivity; dormant or latent condition liable to be at any time revived' (*Oxford English Dictionary* 1978: 17). This journal shows Virginia averse to creating a personal narrative; she is 'locked & put away'.

The lock is a trope described by Gaston Bachelard as 'a psychological threshold' (1994: 81). A key may turn two ways but it 'closes more often than it opens'; 'the gesture of closing is always sharper, firmer and briefer than that of opening' (73). A key often effects a negation. *A Room of One's Own* explores women's access to education; it famously dramatises a denial when Woolf is told not to trespass on the smoothly rolled turf of an Oxbridge college. For Woolf locking indicates a closing off, a limiting of self-expression, 'Lock up your libraries if you like; but there is no gate, no lock, no bolt that you can set upon the freedom of my mind' (*AROO*: 76). In the 1897 journal, Virginia uses a range of tactics to avoid reflection and to deny access to subjectivity; her mind was locked up, not free.

On 10 January 1897 she writes as if the seven-day-old journal were a delicate newborn. She wonders 'How many more weeks has it to live – At any rate it must and shall survive Nessas Collins and [As] Renshaw. It has a key, and beautiful boards, and is much superior' (*PA*: 10). It is small, 8 × 13cm, with a hard gilt-trimmed brown leather cover and a lock. The dated pages designate diurnal pauses and the journal seemed to reproach Virginia if she failed to fill each day's blank space. She laments, 'Alas Alas alas; this diary has been entirely neglected' (123). Using ideas from educational theory and applying Antonio Damasio's analysis of how consciousness develops incrementally, through *proto-*, *core-*, and *autobiographical* or *extended* selves, this essay considers the 1897 journal as a liminal text. Aged fifteen, Virginia is in stasis, tense but poised, waiting at the threshold, anticipating movement but not ready to cross into autobiographical consciousness.

This journal sits, quarantined, between two 'missing' years, 1896 and 1898.[2] It comes two years after the last edition of the Stephen children's family newspaper, *Hyde Park Gate News* (1891–5; first published 2005). With reference to the next extant journal (1899), Mitchell Leaska notes significant stylistic change, 'Her writing now became more detached, more self-conscious in style and manner' (*PA*: 135). Here 'self-conscious' suggests deliberation in the choice of devices, diction and form; implying awareness as to how the writing might be received by a reader. Leaska's use of 'self-conscious' suggests that the writer is striving hard to achieve effects, applying and testing techniques, like an apprentice. The earlier 1897 journal is also an acutely 'self-conscious' text if we interpret this expression to mean conscious of one's 'self', mentally and socially ill-at-ease.[3] Louise DeSalvo sees this as a self-conscious text in a more positive way, suggesting that Virginia is self-conscious 'about having discovered that she can think' (1987: 103). My argument is that Virginia is resisting this discovery. The voice in this journal is tentative and uncertain, even when she employs her assertive alter ego, 'Miss Jan'.

Philippe Lejeune points out that 'journal' was used as an adjective before it became a noun (2009: 57). Originally journals were a way of taking stock, literally accounting for day-to-day transactions. Writers use the form to exercise 'a modicum of power, however limited' (51) over external and internal undertakings. In the first half of the year Virginia records events, occasionally using her avatar to express opinions.⁴ DeSalvo argues that Virginia uses Miss Jan 'to help her begin the process which psychoanalysts refer to as individuation' (1987: 99); writing the diary was a way for Virginia to distance herself from her disquiet about fulfilling the expected role as compliant young woman. By July Stella is clearly unwell; Virginia's journal entries are brief, increasingly discontinuous; lacunae appear on the page. The daily exercise becomes a duty rather than a pleasure. A reader senses Virginia's unease when she does not fulfil the task of writing her journal: 'This diary has been woefully neglected lately – what with one thing & another – Improvement must be made! (hear hear)' (112). Virginia's 'reading self' appears to be cheering on the undisciplined 'writing self'. The encouraging reading voice adds 'hear hear' agreeing with the writerly voice that is instructing improvement. The discipline of recording seems important to her but there is no self-scrutiny, few articulated thoughts or feelings, nothing remotely confessional: the main narrative voice lacks a strong personality. Despite, or perhaps because of, her obvious discomfort, Virginia uses Stella's first name less often, resorting to 'she' and 'her', writing about her half-sister's illness in an irritated, resentful way. Paradoxically, when entries become shorter, in the latter part of the year, she does mention her feelings but without detail. Curt statements are often left suspended as at the end of a day's entry: 'It is all very strange' (116); 'It is hopeless & strange'; 'Most perplexing' (124); 'Very strange & unhappy' (129); 'V.S. and A.V.S. silent & miserable' (130). The subject of this text is resisting subjectivity. The teleological form of the journal with its controlling page-per-day space may be inadequate for Virginia's inchoate emergent feelings.

Autobiographical acts are frequently conceptualised spatially. The ontological aspect of life-writing is often theorised in terms of movement. The subject is in the process of becoming: negotiating a journey, in transit, finding a path, sometimes side-stepping. For much of the 1897 journal its subject is static, in an aporetic state, unable to move forward. Virginia's sister Vanessa wrote that this was a 'time of horrible suspense' (Bell 1997: 68). This journal was written at the end of the nineteenth century, at a time of incubation and evolution. Virginia is inexperienced, at a threshold, soon to move across into a new space. She is seventeen when she writes her 1899 journal and, by then, prepared to try unfamiliar modes of writing, to test out new techniques and to mimic other writers' styles.

Educationalists write about the threshold concept as 'opening up a new and previously inaccessible way of thinking', 'a transformed way of understanding, or interpreting, or viewing something without which the learner cannot progress'. The threshold concept necessitates 'a shift in learner subjectivity' (Land et al. 2005: 53). Another analysis of the process of learning accurately describes the adolescent Virginia's situation during 1897:

> Difficulty in understanding thresholds concepts may leave the learner in a state of 'liminality', a suspended state of partial understanding, or 'stuck place', in which understanding approximates to a kind of 'mimicry' or lack of authenticity. Insights gained by learners as they cross thresholds can be exhilarating but might also be unsettling, requiring an uncomfortable shift in identity, or, paradoxically a sense of loss. (Meyer et al. 2010: x)

Such affective and cognitive journeys are difficult; subjects in transition move unsteadily across thresholds. The idea of a passage to fuller understanding is analogous to the autobiographical journey. Virginia's self-consciousness restrains her, effectively keeping her stationary. She is inhibited about acknowledging an emerging subjectivity. Rather than take on the role of subject, she warily and reflexively regards her self as object.

Woolf's lifelong interest in selfhood, consciousness and creativity is seen in her early journals and anticipates twenty-first-century research in neuroscience. In *The Feeling of What Happens, Body, Emotion and the Making of Consciousness* (2000) and *Self Comes to Mind, Constructing the Conscious Brain* (2010) Antonio Damasio analyses the layered ways in which selves are created. He sets out the contingent notion of the 'self-as-object' and the 'self-as-subject'. This model is not a dichotomy but a progression. It is evolutionary, 'the self-as-knower having had its origin in the self-as-object' (2010: 8). Adhering to the idea that the self is not static but constantly changing, Damasio writes, 'There is indeed a self, but it is a process, not a thing, and the process is present at all times when we are presumed to be conscious' (8). In this journal, Virginia observes her self dispassionately as an object, refusing to accept that she has agency. She has not yet become a 'self-as-subject', 'as knower'. Damasio writes, 'The "I," is a more elusive presence, far less collected in mental or biological terms than the *me*, more dispersed, often dissolved in the stream of consciousness, at times so annoyingly subtle that it is there but almost not there' (9).

Damasio identifies three stages in the development of consciousness, stressing that it is not a 'monolith'. There is the *proto-self*; then *core consciousness* which 'provides the organism with a sense of self about one moment – now – and about one place – here. The scope of core consciousness is the here and now' (2000: 16). The core self is 'a transient entity, ceaselessly re-created for each and every object with which the brain interacts' (17). The most developed stage is *autobiographical* or *extended consciousness*, which 'provides the organism with an elaborate sense of self' and 'places that person at a point in individual historical time, richly aware of the lived past and of the anticipated future, and keenly cognizant of the world beside it' (16). The autobiographical self is the owner of what Damasio calls the 'movie-in-the-brain' (11), which is the narrative we claim and construct when relating our life stories.

Damasio chooses a theatrical metaphor to describe the 'momentous coming of the sense of self into the world of the mental' (2000: 3). He compares 'the birth of a knowing mind' (3) to a performer going through a door, stepping into the light of the stage. This is 'about the transition from innocence and ignorance to knowingness and selfness' (4). He provides a simple definition of consciousness as 'an organism's awareness of its own self and surroundings'. Consciousness 'allows us to know sorrow or know joy, to know suffering or know pleasure, to sense embarrassment or pride, to grieve for lost love or lost life' (4). Once a subject has made this transition, empathy and desire are possible because 'consciousness helps us develop a concern for other selves' as well as concern for oneself (5). '[C]onsciousness and emotion are *not* separable' so that 'when consciousness is impaired so is emotion' (16): Damasio's analysis perfectly describes Virginia's state of mind in 1897.

Virginia hides in the shade, unwilling to step forward into the light of consciousness. Damasio develops his theatrical analogy, separating the 'self-as-witness' from the self as 'protagonist' (2010: 12). Woolf seems to recognise this division in 'Sketch of the Past' when she writes, retrospectively, that there was 'a spectator in me who, even while I squirmed and obeyed, remained observant, note taking for some future revision' (*MOB*: 155). Joanne Campbell Tidwell writes: 'In her early diary, Woolf begins to see a separation between the "I" who writes and the "I" who feels and thinks. However split or contradictory this sense of self is, it nonetheless expresses developing subjectivity. The development is neither smooth nor continuous' (2008: 9). This supports Damasio's analysis of the 'self-as-object' and the 'self-as-knower' and of his recognition of the incremental but uneven process of moving from one stage of consciousness to another. He writes that 'Subjectivity is not required for mental states to exist, only for them to be privately known' (2010: 16). Virginia cannot admit the privately known autobiographical self into this journal; she effaces this self; it is elusive, 'almost not there' (9). Harriet Blodgett cites diary scholar Paul C. Rosenblatt, 'Diarists need a certain amount of egocentrism, enough to be interested in recording some aspects of the world they experience' (1989: 71). Virginia witnesses events but prefers to remain a dispassionate observer, a 'self-as-witness' rather than 'protagonist'.

'Miss Jan' is a substitute self invented by the 'real' historical referent, Virginia Stephen, so that she may present her self-as-object. She
thus presents herself as if she were other. She divides her 'consciousness into subject and object, into the observer and the thing observed'
(Klaus 2010: 8). She creates a fictional mouthpiece to objectify, and
sometimes silence, her self. Virginia probably took the name of her
alter ego from January, her birthday month. The god Janus gives his
name to the month at the 'turn' of the year. Janus sits at the gate of
the year holding a key in his right hand; double-faced he simultaneously looks in opposite directions. He is the god of doors (*ianua*),
gates, passages, bridges, transitions, of beginnings and of endings. The
Romans worshipped him at planting and harvest times; for important
transitional events in a life such as marriage or birth. The semantic link
between Janus and Miss Jan[5] seems pertinent as Virginia is pausing to
look backwards to her childhood as well as forwards, reluctantly, to
prospective adulthood.

DeSalvo writes, 'During this year, it was far easier for Virginia
Stephen to record what Miss Jan said, as Miss Jan said it, than it was for
her to deal with the feelings that she herself was having' (1987: 96). The
creation of this character allows Virginia to simultaneously perform and
observe her own bewilderment and embarrassment. 'Miss Jan' makes
her debut in a lively letter to Thoby typewritten on a windy March day
in 1896. In a farcical tableau Miss Jan is

> quite afraid of venturing out. The other day her skirt was blown over her
> head, and she trotted along in pair of red flannel drawers to the great amuse-
> ment of the Curate who happened to be coming out of Church. She swears
> that she blushed the colour of the said drawers, but that must be taken for
> granted. (*L* 1: 2)

She reappears as 'Poor Janet' in another letter to Thoby (24 February
1897) venturing out to see the Queen but, again, dramatised as comi-
cally vulnerable. Struggling to 'recross' the threshold of the street she
is 'almost crushed' by an agitated group of 'stout females from the
country' and finds herself left 'stranded' (*L* 1: 6).

Using Miss Jan is an ingenious way of simultaneously appearing
but not appearing, of being and not-being in the text. Virginia effaces
her intimate self by inventing a persona. By wearing the mask of Miss
Jan[6] she uses prosopopoeia. Leigh Gilmore cites Paul de Man's essay
'Autobiography as De-facement' where he defines prosopopoeia 'as
apostrophe, a call to the absent, dead or inanimate object'; Gilmore
writes that this 'involves giving and taking away voice' (1994: 72).
Miss Jan functions both to give and take away voice and face. Virginia

shows 'an imaginary or absent person as speaking and acting' (Smith and Watson 2010: 208). The adult Woolf reflects on the idea of a diary having a face when she re-reads hers on the 28 December 1919, 'Oh yes, I've enjoyed reading the past years diary, & shall keep it up. I'm amused to find how its grown a person, with almost a face of its own' (*D* 1: 317). She seems to be describing the successful individuation of the feeble creature she was slightly wary of when she was fifteen; by 1919 the diary is a friend with whom she may converse.

The journal form is often seen as analogous to soliloquy because its voice is considered to be unified and single. This is anathema to Virginia because it requires her to articulate subjectivity. She artfully presents what is absent by appropriating a disguise; in Damasio's terms she becomes a 'protagonist', but by proxy. Miss Jan voices opinions that Virginia prefers to leave undeclared. Ian Blyth writes that 'Miss Jan is the person to whom certain newsworthy events (more often than not those involving some form of personal embarrassment) are said to have happened'. He goes on to suggest that the Miss Janisms 'owe their existence to the habit of always using a third-person narrative voice in *Hyde Park Gate News*' (2012: 354) but the Miss Jan figure also offers a protective function. The child writer's use of the passive voice and of phrases such as 'a certain young lady', 'the two youngest females' and 'the young juveniles' was primarily to imitate a detached, anonymous journalistic style rather than to hide behind impersonation. A confident first-person-singular voice is reserved for fictional sketches, philosophical reflections, and for the narrators of invented letters in the Stephen children's newspaper. This uncertain journal, Janus-like, presents two faces, one referential and one a mask. The Miss Jan mask allows Virginia to physically defend her mind, which, looking back, she acknowledged was 'extraordinarily unprotected, unformed, unshielded, apprehensive, receptive, anticipatory' (*MOB*: 130).

Two entries in the 1897 journal suggest Miss Jan also featured as the subject of a piece of fiction. On 31 January Virginia mentions 'the History of Ms. and Js. Grand Tour'; J is Miss Jan and M stands for Miss Maria, Vanessa's surrogate. The second reference suggests that the narrative was very detailed or that Virginia was writing it very slowly, 'After tea wrote the Eternal Miss Jan, which has not passed the first day yet' (*PA*: 30). She confidently records what 'Miss Jan thought' as if she were the omniscient narrator of a traditional novel. Hiding her self behind an assertive character with an alternative perspective allows Virginia some measure control. She is constructing her self in making the text. Writing calms her so she may 'compose' her self.[7] Miss Jan also allows Virginia to present herself as a ridiculous caricature:

> Poor Miss Jan utterly lost her wits dropped her umbrella, answered at random talked nonsense, and grew as red as a turkey cock. Only rescued from this by S. proposing to go away. So we left, I with the conviction that what ever talents Miss Jan may have, she does not possess the one qualifying her to shine in good society. (*PA*: 39)

Here she is depicted as a pitiable, socially gauche, disorganised member of the group. This strategy of using a persona is not quite an act of ventriloquism. In the journal Miss Jan may be animated but she is not allowed a direct voice. The phrase 'Miss Jan says' is only used once, on 11 February. Nessa and Virginia are bicycling on muddy roads in rainy Bognor. In a detailed and, for this journal, uncharacteristically amusing and dynamic description she writes, 'we penetrated so far into the country, that footpaths ceased to exist'. They ploughed through '6 inches of sticky clay' and 'felt very desperate – The mist blew in our faces, the mud spurted all over us – and behold – here was a school of little boys marching towards us! Their remarks shall not be entered here, Miss Jan says' (*PA*: 33). Just as Virginia is beginning to create a vivid scene she halts, choosing to use her mouthpiece to censor the boys' language, disallowing repetition of what the boys said. The prim, judgemental Miss Jan has assumed an editorial role: she can gag as well as give voice to her creator.

Virginia often reports, second hand, how Miss Jan feels: 'Miss Jan rode her new bicycle, whose seat is rather uncomfortable' (*PA*: 5). Just as Virginia seems to be attending to her feelings she hands them on to her surrogate. So, on 28 April, we read:

> Stella in bed with a bad chill on her innards like she had at Christmas. They have a nurse, Dr Seton three times a day – they say she is getting better – but everyone getting miserable. Everything as dismal as it well can be. Oh dear – how is one to live in such a world, which is a Miss Janism, but very much my mind at present. To bed in my new room, which was lonely & dismal too. (*PA*: 77)

The 'Miss Janism' is almost a quotation but not quite; it is mediated, as if Virginia were reporting the words, or thoughts, of another. There is empathy and a near-alignment with the imprecise use of 'one', but Virginia is separate from Miss Jan.

Often Virginia starts to express a personal view then disowns it. This device allows her to create a distance between Miss Jan's histrionic views and Virginia's own tentative ones. On 20 April, bike-riding again, she begins by using 'I' then elides this identity to becoming Miss Jan then returns to 'I', 'If I was a poet (which Miss Jan does not claim to be) I should write something upon this way of travelling' (*PA*: 73).

The 'passing of the baton' from person to persona happens discreetly in mid-sentence. On 1 February she is angry that she will have to accompany Stella to Eastbourne:

> I have been in a dreadful temper all day long, poor creature – and lead Stella and Vanessa a life – Can not protest *too* strongly against going (though I do) or else S will have to give it up, and her poor young man would be miserable – but think of going! (*PA*: 27)

The shifting perspective is intriguing; Virginia is caught in the act of evading subjectivity. She begins with the assertive 'I' then falters, using 'poor creature' to distance her self as an object. She then omits the subject of the phrase beginning 'Can not protest', hiding the 'I do' inside parenthesis, as if reluctant to use 'I'. The 'but think of going!' may refer to her self but seems to be addressed to a second person, perhaps an invitation for a reader (her self or another) to empathise with this vexing situation. The subsequent statement, 'This is a dreadful fix –', is not defined, though it sounds like something Miss Jan might say. The dash implies that she (Virginia *or* Miss Jan) is lost for words. The final remark sounds concurrently definite *and* uncertain, 'Poor Miss Jan is bewildered'. Virginia uses Miss Jan so she may deprecate her self. On the 2 May she writes about her father's lecture, which 'was very deep rather too deep for the audience; very logical & difficult for the ignorant (i.e. Miss Jan) to follow' (79). 'Miss Jan' allows Virginia concurrently to hide and reveal her self. Her avatar features in the most detailed sections of this journal but Miss Jan disappears completely after 2 May 1897.

Virginia often eliminates the subject of a sentence so that it may be read ambiguously to refer to her selves[8] or to others. She prefers the cover of first-person plural and frequently uses 'we', 'us three' or 'us four' as protection, to convey solidarity. She uses diary shorthand eliminating 'I' or substituting it with the less definite 'one'. Woolf's ambivalence about 'I' continued into her later life; at times she wished to dodge the 'straight dark bar' seeing it as a phallic shadow on the page, a masculine mark of self-assertion, certainty and control (*AROO*: 98). Fothergill suggests that the suppression of the 'I' in diaries can be regarded as 'a gesture of self-effacement, a tacit apology for the appearance of self-preoccupation' (1995: 87). Here Virginia limits the first-person; denying the 'ego'[9] full admission.

Interestingly, when Virginia expresses her views, albeit perfunctorily, about books she seems quite comfortable about writing possessively. She writes, 'After all books are the greatest help and comfort' (*PA*: 79). To be 'Bookless' (53) is to be friendless. She writes devotedly about her companion authors, 'my beloved Lockhart – which grows more and more beautiful every day' (25); 'My dear Pepys is the only calm thing in the house –' (66); 'my cherished Macaulay' (79); 'Read Mr James to quiet me, and my beloved Macaulay' (80); 'my dearly beloved Hawthorne' (90). She personifies her stationery, seeming to code her own illness through the wellbeing of her writing materials, especially her pen, which is her agent. 'No – I shall not again desert my beloved Swan' (71). She is furious when her pen is thrown '*out* of the window', resulting in 'severe dislocation of the nibs, & general shock to the system, wh. it will probably never entirely get over.' She is bereft, 'Nothing to fill up this blank with, & therefore out of consideration to the enfeebled powers of my beloved it shall be left empty –' (106). Her pen, weakened, becomes 'terribly infirm' (119).

Virginia calls her journal 'Wonderful creature!' (*PA*: 16) but the word 'creature' is frequently chosen by her to connote an abject thing: something animate but struggling, wretched, even moribund. The demise of this journal reflects her own declining willingness to write about her life. '*Forgot what happened*. This poor diary is in a very bad way' (121); the emphasis suggests desolation. 'Again I forget – This poor diary is lingering on indeed, but death would be shorter & less painful – Never mind, we will follow the year to its end, & then fling diaries & diarising into the corner – to dust & mice & moths & all creeping crawling eating destroying creatures' (128). After a month several pages are blank. She is relieved as the pages diminish, 'I see that my pages give out – wh. is just as well' (133). She is thankful to see the year buried, 'ended locked & put away' (134). It is profoundly touching, but deeply ironic, that she should consider this to be 'the first really *lived* year' of her life (134).

The voices chosen in the 1899–1909 pieces are more able to express Damasio's 'extended consciousness'. The unease a reader perceives in the egoless 1897 journal dissipates completely. Virginia is seeking to release emergent selves, to cross the threshold into new spaces. In the 1899 'Warboys' journal 'I' is used more often and with increasing confidence, 'I must make some mark upon the paper' even if it is 'frail and somewhat disjointed' (*PA*: 135). She becomes more assertive and 'self'-determining. By signing 'AVS' after 'A Chapter on Sunsets' she is acknowledging authorship of it (155–6). There is engagement, a sense of dialogue with a potential reader. Here is the burgeoning essayistic voice, 'unmoored: explorative, open to self-doubt and prone to risky exchanges with its audience' (Saloman 2012: 3).[10] Virginia self-consciously imitates several different styles: satire, history, travel writing. There are overwritten purple passages of description. There is a tendency to use magisterial or archaic phrases such as 'methinks', 'bescrawled', 'perchance', 'dwells', 'beguile'. She uses humour and can be conversational. Authorial asides criticise the work as it is being created, '(what an awful sentence!)', 'What nonsense to write!' (*PA*: 138). 'I write this down to see if it looks any more credible in pen & ink' (162). Elizabeth Podnieks suggests that when Virginia writes that she will put on her 'dress clothes such as they are' (*PA*: 144) she is responding to the need for her writing to be more formal (2000: 15). In contrast to the earlier journal Virginia is beginning to construct an 'autobiographical self' by choosing how to 'dress' and perform as protagonist in her own narrative.

In 'The Leaning Tower' (1940), now a mature author, Woolf antici-pates twenty-first-century work on creativity and consciousness. She wonders whether a writer needs 'to become unconscious before he can create?' (*E* 6: 264). She recognises that, to be able to write autobio-graphically, the 'New Writers' had, first, to overcome Victorian avoid-ance strategies:

> By analysing themselves honestly, with help from Dr Freud, these writers have done a great deal to free us from nineteenth-century suppressions. The writers of the next generation may inherit from them a whole state of mind, a mind no longer crippled, evasive, divided. (*E* 6: 274)

She envisaged writers such as Day Lewis, Auden, Spender, Isherwood, and MacNeice seated on leaning towers, writing 'under the influence of change, under the threat of war' (267). 'There was no tranquillity in which they could recollect. The inner mind was paralysed because the surface mind was always hard at work' (273). Woolf uses a bi-layered model of consciousness: the 'upper mind' and the 'under-mind' (263). She suggests that unconsciousness is needed 'to get beneath the surface', recognising that unconsciousness is a 'gift' (274). Consciousness is paralysing. She could be recollecting her own situation, aged fifteen, when heightened self-consciousness hindered her expression and she suppressed unconsciousness to control the 'under-mind'. Lacking tran-quillity, and unable to express autobiographical consciousness, she had surrendered her voice. Woolf uses the metaphor of a veil to describe the liminal moment when the under-mind manages to outwit the censorious upper mind while it is relaxed and drowsing:

> After a hard day's work, trudging round, seeing all he can, feeling all he can, taking in the book of his mind innumerable notes, the writer becomes – if he can – unconscious. In fact, his under-mind works at top speed while his upper mind drowses. Then, after a pause the veil lifts; and there is the thing – the thing he wants to write about – simplified, composed. (*E* 6: 263)

In a section called 'The Freudian Unconscious' Damasio also writes about this process: 'very conscious creators consciously seek the unconscious as a source and, on occasion, as a method for their conscious endeavors' (2010: 178). Woolf considers the writer as one who keeps 'his eye fixed, as intently as he can, upon a certain object' (*E* 6: 259). This recalls Lily Briscoe, powerlessly suspended at a moment of creative crisis, hearing 'some voice saying she couldn't paint, saying she couldn't create' (*TTL*: 151). She fixes her eyes on the canvas and then on the hedge. She has to lose 'consciousness of outer things' before she can regain creativity; 'her mind kept throwing up from its depths, scenes, and names, and sayings, and memories and ideas, like a fountain spurting over that glaring, hideously difficult white space' (152).

Jonah Lehrer[11] demonstrates, using evidence from neuroscience, that a tranquil state is desirable for imaginative connections to be made:

> When our minds are at ease – when those alpha waves are rippling through the brain – we're more likely to direct the spotlight of attention *inward*, toward the stream of remote associations emanating from the right hemisphere. In contrast, when we are diligently focused our attention tends to be directed *outward*, toward the details of the problems we are trying to solve. (2012: 31)

Random associations are necessary for moments of insight; anxiousness does not lead to creativity: 'When we're intensely focused on something, more information is sent to the prefrontal cortex; the stage of consciousness gets even more crowded' (2012: 62). Lehrer uses 'stage' to mean a platform for a theatrical performance. He later uses a metaphor of restraint suggesting that the brain 'slips off' handcuffs (91), freeing the creative part of the mind. The 1897 journal shows Virginia in a tense, restrained state, self-consciously unwilling to move onto the stage.

When she was writing her adult diaries Woolf anticipated re-reading them in later life to create a dialogue with a younger self. By looking at these later diaries and her more direct 'open' autobiographical works we can appreciate how much suppression took place in the earlier work. 'Sketch of the Past' has some dated entries, like a journal, although it is usually regarded as an incomplete memoir, not intended for publication. At fifteen she resisted speaking personally; aged fifty-seven she consciously re-engages with the self she once was, turning back, Janus-like, to speak from the platform of the present upon which she stands (cf. *MOB*: 87, 96). She is aware that she is presenting a double perspective, 'It would be interesting to make the two people, I now, I then, come out in contrast' (87).

Woolf structures her memoir through binaries: nineteenth-century/twentieth-century; Victorian/Edwardian; London/St Ives; silence/speech; girls/boys; despair/ecstasy; private/public; dark/light. She recognises the sensitising quality of these oppositions. For instance, she contrasts the 'blaze of magnificent light' streaming through the glass dome at the end of the railway station with the shut, 'shrouded and curtained rooms' of 22 Hyde Park Gate, after her mother's death (*MOB*: 103). She describes this as a revelatory experience, 'it was partly that my mother's death unveiled and intensified; made me suddenly develop perceptions, as if a burning glass had been laid over what was shaded and dormant'. She explains how this was a 'quickening', 'surprising' 'as if something were becoming visible without any effort' (103). Analysing this passage Linda Anderson sees it as expressing 'a new intensity of perception' (1986: 70). What is noteworthy is that the visceral power of these 'moments of being' is completely missing from the journal written contemporaneously with the experience. Anderson takes a psychoanalytic approach to reading the diaries arguing that Woolf 'refused the choice of either being locked in or being locked out', concluding that she 'returns us to Freud with a renewed sense that the threshold is not hesitation' but, rather, 'its own beginning' (70).

In 'Sketch of the Past' contrasts are frequently expressed in terms of antagonistic spatial division. Victorianism is located in Old Kensington, modernism is associated with Bloomsbury; there is the upstairs/downstairs separation inside the house and between children's and adults' space. Victoria Rosner sees domestic thresholds as threatening and unsettling; they are 'sites of intersection and difference' (Rosner 2005: 65). The double doors of the sitting room set up a tension between public and private. In the 1897 journal Virginia mentions being in her 'usual position behind the folding doors' (*PA*: 82). Woolf writes retrospectively about being in 'my covert, behind the folding doors of the Hyde Park Gate drawing room. I sat there, shielded, being half insane with shyness and nervousness' (*MOB*: 114). She is like a creature hiding from the hunt. After Stella's marriage, Virginia's room is divided into sleeping and sitting sides; it is split, like her concept of the 'upper mind' and the 'under-mind'. This passage leads to a well-known metaphor which corresponds precisely to Damasio's analysis of the emerging self as evolutionary and gradual:

> But I was thinking; feeling; living; those two lives that the two halves symbolized with the intensity, the muffled intensity, which a butterfly or moth feels when with its sticky tremulous legs and antennae it pushes out of the chrysalis and emerges and sits quivering beside the broken case for a moment; its wings still creased; its eyes dazzled, incapable of flight. (*MOB*: 130)

The passage that follows describes in poignant detail the experience that Virginia preferred not to record when she was living through it.

Of her mother's death, Woolf writes 'one could not master it, envisage it, deal with it'. She is not 'fully conscious' of what it meant, 'unconsciously absorbing' her father's 'demonstrative grief' and Stella's silent grief. She writes elliptically of 'the black clothes', the suppressions', the prohibitive 'locked door of her bedroom' (130). She admits the darkness of bereavement that was missing from the day-by-day 1897 account. Then she found it 'impossible to write' (*PA*: 115) but the 1939 memoir is therapeutic. This is writing for recovery, in both senses of the word. In the later work she uses speech marks to 'quote' the words she claims she voiced to her self at the time, '"But this is impossible; things aren't, can't be, like this" – the blow, the second blow of death, struck on me; tremulous, filmy eyed as I was, with my wings still creased, sitting there on the edge of my broken chrysalis' (*MOB*: 130). This 'second blow of death' is ambiguous; it refers to another family death, Stella's, but simultaneously implies an assault on Virginia's vulnerable pubescent self. She has been inactive, encased in a hard, protective cocoon; dormant but evolving.[12] At the very moment of transition, as she unfolds her creased wings, a deliberate blow is dealt and felt. It is uncertain as to whether the chrysalis is 'broken' by the surprise attack or if the metamorphosis had already occurred. A vibrating, unsteady, emotional creature emerges. A hypothetically glorious transformation becomes associated with subterfuge and death. The new creature has managed to mutate; it is damaged but potentially free to fly into the light. This delicate, ephemeral insect stands for Virginia's fragile, exposed self. She imagines that Thoby would have seen her as a 'shell-less little creature', 'sheltered, in my room' (*MOB*: 141). In her 1930 diary she describes being ill and uses the same metaphor for being blocked creatively, 'Something happens in my mind. It refuses to go on registering impressions. It shuts itself up. It becomes chrysalis. I lie quite torpid.' Then, after stasis, comes the epiphany, 'suddenly something springs' and ideas rush into the light. Significantly, her refreshed ability to write is described as 'all the doors opening' (*D* 3: 287).

Three months after Stella's death, in continuing discomfort, Virginia longs for leathery protection, 'Life is a hard business – one needs a rhinirocerous [*sic*] skin – & that one has not got' (*PA*: 132). The small brown leather 1897 journal provided a sheltering cocoon for her thin-skinned self.[13] Her 1899 journal is physically less constrained at 13 × 21½cm and, although it has hard covers, it is not 'hide-bound'. Virginia is no longer in hiding; her writing grows more expansive and energetic. She is not defending her self from 'autobiographical consciousness'. Damasio conceptualises the coming into consciousness, as a 'passage through a threshold that separates a protected but limiting shelter from the possibility and risk of a world beyond and ahead' (2000: 3). He sees this as analogous to 'a performer who waits in semidarkness', sees the door open, 'revealing the lights, the stage, and the audience' (3) and steps into the light.

Janus-like, the door presents two possibilities, 'At times, it is closed, bolted, padlocked. At others, it is open, that is to say, wide open' (Bachelard 1994: 222). After 1897 Virginia is prepared to venture through the door; she moves across the threshold and into the light.

Notes

1. I reference Virginia (Stephen) as the writer of the works collected in *A Passionate Apprentice: The Early Journals*, 1897–1909 and Woolf as the adult author.
2. Virginia writes on 18 January that the current 'diary beats my 1896 diary' (*PA*: 16); the earlier volume has not survived.
3. In the dated entries at the end of *The Mausoleum Book* Leslie Stephen notes, on 10 April 1897: 'Virginia has been out of sorts, nervous and overgrown too' (Stephen 1977: 103).
4. Deborah Martinson suggests, without offering specific evidence, that Leslie Stephen 'read and judged all she wrote as a child and adolescent, prompting Virginia to write anything remotely personal in the diary under the pseudonym of "Miss Jan"' (2003: 13).
5. Louise DeSalvo makes the semantic link with *Jan*senism, arguing that in the early journals Virginia is exploring theological views that ran counter to her father's agnosticism. Miss Jan 'very often articulates pessimistic attitudes about the nature of the world (which she refers to as Miss Janism) that are close to, if not identical with, Jansenism' (1987: 117).
6. On 3 January 1933, Woolf wrote of the impersonality provided by a mask, 'I like masks. I like the disorientation they give my feelings' (*D* 4: 139).
7. In her diary for 28 July 1939 she wrote, 'I have composed myself, momentarily, by reading through this years diary. Thats a use for it then. It composes' (*D* 5: 227).
8. Woolf was acutely aware of the plurality of selfhood and a frequently quoted line from her 1935 diary reiterates how perplexing this was for her, 'Well of course its extremely interesting having to deal with so many different selves' (*D* 4: 329).
9. Rudolf Dekker cites Jacques Presser's definition of egodocuments as '"documents in which an ego intentionally or unintentionally discloses, or hides itself, ..."' '[t]exts in which an author writes about his or her own acts, thoughts and feelings' (2002: 7). Virginia's 1897 journal adamantly avoids introspection.
10. Randi Saloman cites Woolf's early piece 'The Decay of Essay-Writing' (1905) where she writes that essays are 'primarily an expression of personal opinion .... Almost all essays begin with a capital I – "I think", "I feel"' (*E* 1: 25).

11. The final section of Jonah Lehrer's chapter 'Virginia Woolf, the Emergent Self' in his *Proust Was a Neuroscientist* is about Lily Briscoe's artistic vision. Lehrer writes, 'Consciousness is a process, not a place. We emerge, somehow, from the moment of attention' (2007: 188).
12. See Christina Alt's *Virginia Woolf and the Study of Nature* for a detailed analysis of moths and butterflies. Alt summarises the ways in which metamorphosis has been interpreted in Woolf's work: the butterfly's association with the soul and its escape from the body; the transformation interpreted as a symbol of spiritual rebirth; as analogous with physical and sexual maturation (2010: 5–7 and *passim*). The idea of metamorphosis as a coming into the light is discussed by Bachelard: 'The word *chrysalis* alone is an unmistakable indication that here two dreams are joined together, dreams that bespeak both the repose and flight of being, evening's crystallization and wings that open to the light' (Bachelard 1994: 65).
13. For a discussion of skinlessness and 'epidermic fragility' see Hancock 2012.

Bibliography

Alt, C. (2010), *Virginia Woolf and the Study of Nature*, Cambridge: Cambridge University Press.

Anderson, L. (1986), 'At the Threshold of the Self: Women and Autobiography', in *Women's Writing: A Challenge to Theory*, ed. M. Monteith, Sussex: Harvester Press, pp. 54–71.

Bachelard, G. (1994), *The Poetics of Space*, Boston, MA: Beacon Press.

Bell, V. (1997), *Sketches in Pen and Ink*, London: Pimlico.

Blodgett, H. (1989), *Centuries of Female Days: Englishwomen's Private Diaries*, Gloucester: Sutton.

Blyth, I. (2012), 'Woolf, Letter Writing and Diary Keeping', in *Virginia Woolf in Context*, ed. B. Randall and J. Goldman, Cambridge: Cambridge University Press, pp. 353–61.

Damasio, A. (2000), *The Feeling of What Happens, Body, Emotion and the Making of Consciousness*, London: Vintage.

Damasio, A. (2010), *Self Comes to Mind, Constructing the Conscious Brain*, London: Heinemann.

Dekker, R., ed. (2002), *Egodocuments and History: Autobiographical Writing in Its Social Context since the Middle Ages*, Hilversum, Netherlands: Verloren.

DeSalvo, L. A. (1987), 'As "Miss Jan Says": Virginia Woolf's Early Journals', in *Virginia Woolf and Bloomsbury, a Centenary Celebration*, ed. J. Marcus, London: Macmillan Press, pp. 96–124.

Fothergill, R. A. (1995), 'One Day at a Time: The Diary as Lifewriting', *a/b: Auto/Biography Studies*, 10(1): 81–91.

Gilmore, L. (1994), *Autobiographics: A Feminist Theory of Women's Self-Representation*, Ithaca, NY and London: Cornell University Press.

Hancock, N. (2012), *Charleston and Monk's House: The Intimate House Museums of Virginia Woolf and Vanessa Bell*, Edinburgh: Edinburgh University Press.

Klaus, C. H. (2010), *The Made-Up Self: Impersonation in the Personal Essay*, Iowa City: University of Iowa Press.

Land, R., G. Cousin, J. H. F. Meyer, and P. Davies (2005), 'Threshold Concepts and Troublesome Knowledge', in *Improving Learning Diversity and Inclusivity*, ed. C. Rust, Oxford: Oxford Brookes University, pp. 53–64.

Lehrer, J. (2007), *Proust Was a Neuroscientist*, Boston, MA: Houghton Mifflin.

Lehrer, J. (2012), *Imagine: How Creativity Works*, Edinburgh and London: Canongate.

Lejeune, P. (2009), *On Diary*, ed. J. D. Popkin and J. Rak, trans. K. Durnin, Honolulu: University of Hawai'i Press.

Martinson, D. (2003), *In the Presence of Audience: The Self in Diaries and Fiction*, Columbus: Ohio State University Press.

Meyer, J. H. F., R. Land and C. Baillie, eds (2010), *Threshold Concepts and Transformational Learning*, Rotterdam: Sense Publishers, <https://www.sensepublishers.com/media/1177-threshold-concepts-and-transformational-learning.pdf> (last accessed 6 August 2013).

Oxford English Dictionary (1978), Oxford: Clarendon Press.

Podnieks, E. (2000), *Daily Modernism: The Literary Diaries of Virginia Woolf, Antonia White, Elizabeth Smart and Anaïs Nin*, Montreal and Kingston: McGill-Queen's University Press.

Rosner, V. (2005), *Modernism and the Architecture of Private Life*, New York: Columbia University Press.

Saloman, R. (2012), *Virginia Woolf's Essayism*, Edinburgh: Edinburgh University Press.

Smith, S. and J. Watson (2010), *Reading Autobiography: A Guide for Interpreting Life Narratives*, Minneapolis: University of Minnesota Press.

Stephen, L. (1977), *Sir Leslie Stephen's Mausoleum Book*, ed. A. Bell, Oxford: Oxford Clarendon Press.

Tidwell, J. C. (2008), *Politics and Aesthetics in the Diary of Virginia Woolf*, New York and London: Routledge.

Woolf, V. (1975), *The Letters of Virginia Woolf*, vol. 1: 1888–1912, ed. N. Nicolson and J. Trautmann, London: Chatto & Windus.

Woolf, V. (1979–85), *The Diary of Virginia Woolf*, 5 vols, ed. A. O. Bell and A. McNeillie, Harmondsworth: Penguin.

Woolf, V. (1986–2010), *The Essays of Virginia Woolf*, 6 vols, ed. A. McNeillie (vols 1–4) and S. N. Clarke (vols 5–6), London: Hogarth Press.

Woolf, V. [1927] (2000a), *To the Lighthouse*, London: Vintage.

Woolf, V. [1929] (2000b), *A Room of One's Own*, London: Penguin.

Woolf, V. (2002), *Moments of Being: Autobiographical Writings*, ed. J. Schulkind, London: Pimlico.

Woolf, V. (2004), *A Passionate Apprentice: The Early Journals, 1897–1909*, ed. M. A. Leaska, London: Pimlico.

Woolf, V. (2005), *Hyde Park Gate News: The Stephen Family Newspaper*, ed. G. Lowe, London: Hesperus Press.

Woolf, V. (2011), *The Essays of Virginia Woolf*, vol. 6: 1933–1941, ed. S. N. Clarke, London: Hogarth Press.

Chapter 2

Elusive Encounters: Seeking out Virginia Woolf in Her Commemorative House Museum

Nuala Hancock

Listless is the air in an empty room, just swelling the curtain; the flowers in the jar shift.
One fibre in the wicker armchair creaks, though no one sits there.
Virginia Woolf, *Jacob's Room*

Writers, of course, live on through their work long after their material demise. Their thoughts and ideas are kept vividly alive through the enduring medium of their words set down on the page. This phenomenon is richly represented in the case of Virginia Woolf, whose work is the subject of perpetual re-discovery and re-interpretation far beyond the chronological or geographical confines of her physical or temporally bound existence. In the twenty-first century, we dialogue with Woolf in a myriad of ways: intellectually, artistically, politically, poetically. Not only are her ideas astonishingly à propos more than seventy years after her death, her very writing style is thrilling and quickening. Reading Virginia Woolf – unfailingly – makes me *feel* more alive.

Yet however animated or animating a posthumous text, readers who enjoy or are intrigued by a writer's language or ideas are often tempted, it seems, by the possibility of an authorial encounter of a more material kind. The growing number of people undertaking literary pilgrimages, seeking a tangible link with a writer's lived past, is indicative of a desire for an exchange beyond a meeting of minds. Writers die, but the artefacts which they handled, the houses which they inhabited, the contexts in which they set their work, frequently endure. Such physical remnants of another's past offer themselves as possible sources of consolidation or illumination – of a more proximal attunement to the other's life and creative process. Visitors flock to Abbotsford, in pursuit of Scott; to Haworth, in search of the Brontës; to Hampstead and Rome, desirous of a glimpse of Keats.

But an investigation into the intimate sites and the surviving accoutrements of another's lived past is a highly charged affair. Often characterised as recreational and undertaken with a careless sense of ease, visiting a commemorative house has the capacity to enthrall, rather than to entertain; to surprise and disarray, rather than to amuse. Readers and writers customarily encounter one another through the shared forum of the published text, in an intended collaboration, in the immaterial realm of the intellect or the imagination. A visit to a writer's former inhabitation is an encounter of a very different order. Houses, rooms, and the landscapes in which they lie, are physical, tangible contexts, experienced corporeally, through movement and sensory apprehension. The boundaries between private and public are precariously ill-defined. Purpose and motive are called into question. Emotions are unexpectedly aroused. To be present in the lived spaces of another's past is to locate them in space and time, and to understand that where once, irrefutably, they were, they are – irrevocably – no longer. It is difficult to resist a pervading sense of the discordance between the former inhabitant's presence in the past, and their absence in the here and now; between the ephemeral nature of a human life, and the enduring qualities of the material world.

Virginia Woolf as Literary Tourist

Woolf's accounts of her own literary pilgrimages touch on some of the compelling yet disquieting aspects of such encounters with the material past. When she was fifteen, she was taken by her father to visit Carlyle's House in Chelsea.[1] In her journal, she lists the rooms that they visited: 'the drawing room, and dining room, and Cs sound proof room, with double walls', noting, in particular, Carlyle's 'writing table, and his pens, and scraps of his manuscripts' that she witnessed there (*PA*: 24). In 1904, she visited the Brontë Parsonage and Museum in Yorkshire, the subject of her first published article in *The Guardian* in December, 'Haworth, November 1904' (*E* 1: 5–9). In this piece, she questions the integrity of house museum visiting: 'I do not know whether pilgrimages to the shrines of famous men ought not to be condemned as sentimental journeys.' She casts doubt on her earlier experience, arguing that it 'is better to read Carlyle in your own study chair than to visit the sound-proof room and pour over the manuscripts at Chelsea' (5). The complex circumstances in which Woolf wrote this piece contribute perhaps to her ambivalence. In November 1904, she was still recovering from a breakdown following her father's death in February; the claustrophobic interiors of the family home at Hyde Park Gate had been physically dismantled; a new liberating context at 46 Gordon Square had been found (*MOB*: 45–6). But Woolf was in suspension. Judged by her doctors still to be unwell, she spent the autumn frustrated, convalescing, at first in Cambridge, and then at Giggleswick in Yorkshire with Madge and Will Vaughan (*L* 1: 159). She was impatient to recover; thus it is hardly surprising that her appetite for visiting or re-visiting the commemorative houses of 'famous men', weighty with reliquary effects, enshrined in the past and preserved for perpetuity – especially one so closely associated in her memory with her father – should be tempered.

About Haworth, too, she is deeply ambivalent, now anticipating something revelatory, now discouraged. She shares the thrill of the approach: 'Our excitement as we neared Haworth had in it an element of suspense that was really painful, as though we were to meet some long-separated friend' (*E* 1: 6). At the point in the journey where 'the interest for a Brontë lover becomes suddenly intense' the museum, 'a pallid and inanimate collection of objects' (*E*: 7), fails to sustain. If the sole justification of such pilgrimages, as Woolf argues, is to throw light on a writer's work, Haworth disappoints on that account. Certain items indicative of the Brontës as writers are 'of deep interest': 'autograph letters, pencil drawings, and other documents'. But the 'most touching case' is that which contains 'the little personal relics, the dresses and shoes of the dead woman'; '– so touching', she stresses, 'that one hardly feels reverent in one's gaze' (7). Woolf communicates here the sense of unease, the fear of voyeurism that can arise from the contemplation of the remnants of another's life. Her choice and repetition of 'touching' is interesting: it is the tangibility of materials from the past, she suggests, that gives them the power to move. In their presenting substantiality, their textural tactility, these reliquary objects put us directly in touch with the missing subject, defying chronology, dissolving the passage of time. Garments repeatedly handled and worn, once inhabited, now inert, carry a particularly bitter-sweet charge. 'Her shoes and her thin muslin dress have outlived her', Woolf reports (*E* 1: 7). The commemorative house itself leaves her cold: 'There is nothing remarkable in a mid-Victorian parsonage, though tenanted by genius' (8). It is Charlotte Brontë, the woman, who 'comes to life, and one forgets the chiefly memorable fact that she was a great writer' (7). Woolf's pursuit of Charlotte Brontë at Haworth, her essay suggests, offers understandings, despite anticipations otherwise, more personal than literary; more affecting than objective; more poignant than informative.[2]

In her much later essay from 1931, 'Great Men's Houses', published as part of 'The London Scene' for *Good Housekeeping*, Woolf is in a very different mode, celebrating the growth in London of 'great men's houses, bought for the nation and preserved entire', and arguing the case for their biographical significance ('Great Men's 2004: 37). 'We know them from their houses', she says of writers; they have a 'gift', 'a faculty for housing themselves appropriately, for making the table, the chair, the curtain, the carpet into their own image' (38). And it is the house of Thomas and Jane Carlyle which she holds up as a repository of biographical clues, 'One hour spent in 5 [*sic*] Cheyne Row will tell us more about them and their lives than we can learn from all the biographies' (38). What Woolf proposes here is a close corroboration between the harsh material conditions of this house and the mood and sensibilities of its inhabitants. The pump in the basement with its trickle of cold water, the 'cracked yellow tin bath' three floors above (38), the 'cleansing and scouring', the 'perpetual struggle' – the sheer, monstrous effort of living in this place has Carlyle groaning under his attic skylight, and Mrs Carlyle coughing in her four-poster bed (39–40). The voice of this grimly embattled house ('and all houses have voices', she proposes) is 'of pumping and scrubbing, of coughing and groaning', and its 'season' ('for every house has its season', she suggests) is always February, 'when cold and fog are in the street and torches flare' (40). At Keats's house in Hampstead, the second subject of this essay, the season, by contrast, is 'always spring' (42), and the voice of the house is 'the voice of leaves brushing in the wind; of branches stirring in the garden' (45). Here, in this resonant space, Woolf suggests, we may, if we attend, encounter Keats, although he seems to come 'silently, on the broad shafts of light, without body or footfall' (45). The presence of the absent subject here is communicated lyrically, through poetic evocation and felt adumbrations.

Shortly after visiting Carlyle's and Keats's houses in London in March 1931 by way of research for her essay, the Woolfs went on holiday to France (*D* 4: 13). Near Castillon, they visited the birthplace and home of Montaigne, venerated by Leonard Woolf as 'the first civilised modern man' (*D* 4: 21; L. Woolf 1969: 172). If Woolf is stirred by intimations of Keats at Hampstead, she is enthralled by her close encounter with Montaigne's material past in France, as evidenced by her attention to the physicality of the visit in her diary account: the stone steps to the chateau are 'narrow' and 'worn'; the door 'thick, nail studded'; the entrance into the intimate spaces of Montaigne's interior world sudden and entire: 'This is his bedroom; this is his dressing room. Here he died.' We follow Woolf as she follows Montaigne, 'down' to Chapel, 'upstairs again' to his library, rehearsing the ebb and flow of his daily rhythms and noticing, empathically, through this vicarious re-enactment, that 'he was very small'. Woolf situates Montaigne in his room, 'Here is his chair & table'; she imagines his touch and his gestures: 'He wrote those inscriptions on the beams.' Moving outside, Woolf gives voice to that sensation of temporal assimilation, that disarraying overlap of past and present time which commemorative sites engender: 'We wandered on the terrace . . . the curious musing man must have halted to look at what we saw. So lovely now; as then' (*D* 4: 21). The thrill of this embodied re-enactment of Montaigne's lived past is communicated by Woolf in three letters from the time (*L* 4: 318, 319, 321). 'My word Ethel, the very door he opened is there', she writes to Ethel Smyth (321); 'a view precisely the same he saw. Does this excite you?' she asks Vita Sackville-West (318). A few days later, they drove to Chinon to visit the castle where Jeanne d'Arc stood before the king. 'Sat on the steps to hear 2 struck by the clock wh. has rung since the 13th Century: wh. J. heard', she records. In a leap of empathic imagination, Woolf tests out the possibility of biographical disclosures – of sudden inter-subjective revelations brought on by this placial encounter with the past: 'What did she think? Was she mad?' (*D* 4: 23). The possibility of 'finding' the other through visiting the sites of their lived past is further explored in Woolf's diary when she visited Stratford in May 1934. In Shakespeare's garden, she finds him neither present nor absent but 'serenely absent-present; both at once; radiating round one' (*D* 4: 219). This subtle 'sensing' of Shakespeare pervades the site, in Woolf's account. He is vivid yet ephemeral; found, yet not found, 'yes; in the flowers, in the old hall, in the garden; but never to be pinned down' (219).

'Why does the writing make us chase the writer?' Julian Barnes asked in *Flaubert's Parrot*. 'Do we think the leavings of a life contain some ancillary truth?' (Barnes 2009: 12). 'Gazing', in Flaubert's commemorative house, at the stuffed parrot that Flaubert had on his desk while writing *Un Coeur Simple*, Barnes's character, to his surprise, 'felt ardently in touch' with the writer. This encounter between reader and writer, facilitated by the presence of this remnant from the past, allows a 'moment of contact', Barnes proposes, 'practical yet mystical – between the two of them' (Barnes 2005; Hendrix 2008: 237). It is this unexpected coupling between the historically objective and the lyrically affecting, the tangible and the visceral, that gives the physical pursuit of another's past its particular allure.

Literary Tourists in Search of Woolf

For those of us inclined to follow in the footsteps of Virginia Woolf, many richly associative terrains present themselves. From Kensington to Richmond, from St James's Park to Kew Gardens, London is impregnated with Woolf's past; the Bloomsbury Squares are sedimented with her activity. In Cornwall, Talland House and St Ives resonate with her memory. But it is in Sussex where her material past is most comprehensively preserved and curated. Monk's House, Rodmell, Virginia and Leonard Woolf's rural retreat from 1919 until her death in 1941, and Leonard Woolf's Sussex home until his death in 1969, has been open to the public as a literary house museum since 1982, under the auspices of the National Trust. Here, for over twenty years, the Woolfs lived, wrote, read, walked, received guests, shared the quotidian rhythms of life, sought tranquility and space and the outer landscape of the Downs in contrast to the pulse and tempo of London. 'But O . . . how sweet life is with L. here, in its regularity & order, & the garden & the room at night & music & my walks & writing easily' (*D* 4: 44). Here are the rooms that Woolf inhabited; here are her surviving material things.

'But let me find you among your things'[3]

Rodmell is a quiet village in the midst of the South Downs, three miles from the town of Lewes. Visitors often report having difficulty finding it; Monk's House already has a sense of the elusive about it. From a turning off the main Lewes–Newhaven road, the village is approached down a single street, whose grass verges, in spring and summer, tumble with flowers. Towards the end of the village street, quite suddenly, it seems, without preamble, here is Monk's House – a long, white, wooden-clad building, modest in its presentation, with its clicking latch gate, and low flint garden wall, barely off the road. Woolf's description of the house when she first saw it, 'Unpretending', 'long & low' ineluctably comes to mind (*D* 1: 286). There is hardly time to prepare oneself. The gate opens on to a path along the side of the house. To the right there is a formal pool garden, cool and umbrageous. The path turns towards the back of the house, from where the garden rises up in smooth ascents, towards Rodmell church spire: 'a silver extinguisher rising through the trees' (*D* 2: 138). The house itself seems to float beneath the garden. Along the length of its low facade is a glass conservatory, thick with plants. Access is achieved down a set of steep stone steps into the house – a physiologically articulated entrance into the interior. Here, in the house, hall and dining room flow into one another, without an adjoining wall. Ceilings are beamed and low; the floor dark and polished; the light soft, crepuscular; the perfume sweet, musky, of apples and damp paper. It takes a moment to adjust, sensorily, to the space and light, emotionally to this close encounter with the intimate spaces of Leonard and Virginia

Woolf's lived past. From the hall, one moves into the sitting room, whose walls are painted an idiosyncratic green – recessive, ethereal. There is something fluid about the quality of these green walls, as though the boundaries of the room were indeterminate, flowing unimpeded into the spaces of the garden. This is the room that Woolf celebrates in her diary: 'our large combined drawing eating room, with its 5 windows, its beams down the middle, & flowers & leaves nodding in all round us' (*D* 3: 89). The room is full of furniture – tables, chairs, armchairs, a desk, a green chiffonier – which connote movement and gestural positioning in the past: 'we sit and eat, play the gramophone, prop our feet up on the side of the fire, and read endless books' (*L* 4: 159). Textures are rich and various: painted wood and printed fabric, ceramics and needle point, canvas and tiles. This is a sensuous interior, expressive, communicating pleasure in material things. Surfaces are animated with the swirling motifs and visible brushstrokes created by Woolf's sister, Vanessa Bell, and her fellow artist, Duncan Grant. Through their gestural, decorative marks and painted canvases on walls, they, too, inhabit this space. There is much here that is reminiscent of Charleston, Bell's and Grant's Sussex retreat at Firle, a few miles away, across the Downs. These decorative surfaces – fresh, spontaneous, experimental even now – manifest a reciprocal linking between the houses – a shared history, a shared aesthetic, a shared approach to living. Two portraits of Virginia Woolf by Vanessa Bell hang on the dining room walls.[4, 5] The importance of her sister in Virginia Woolf's life is everywhere materially apparent.

From the dining room one moves into the kitchen, and up several steep steps into the garden. This, eccentrically, is the way to access Virginia Woolf's bedroom: 'My wide, empty room to wake in; to go to bed in crossing the garden by the pale flowers' (*D* 4: 36). Here in this room, simply furnished, a bed under the window, bookcases on the wall, garden-surrounded, is where Virginia Woolf slept, 'where the rising sun on the apples & asparagus wakes me, if I leave the curtain open' (*D* 4: 174). From her bedroom, one can make the journey across the soft organic spaces of the garden, through the orchard, and to the writing lodge. In this simple garden building, under the church yard wall, overhung by a sweet chestnut tree, Virginia Woolf wrote. The view from the French doors is, as it was, across the water meadows and towards Mount Caburn (*D* 4: 263).

To stand where she stood, to walk where she walked: what insights or understandings can be gleaned from this encounter with Woolf's material past, further to her own accounts of this place in diaries and letters, already richly informative and evocative? There is much here that is illuminating, I think, and accessible exclusively through visiting the site. It is the intimacy of Virginia Woolf's life here with Leonard that is immediately striking through this embodied encounter: the modesty of scale, the low-ceilinged rooms, the simplicity of the domestic configurations. And the mood and tenor of their existence here becomes apprehensible – its quietude, its dusky palette, its textural richness, its particular and affecting play of shifting light and shadow. If houses have atmosphere, as Woolf herself proposed, there is a tenderness at play here; an exquisite sensibility. One is reminded of Woolf's gift for making beautiful houses, despite her diffidence about her visual judgement. 'The interiors of her houses were cool and civilized', her niece remembers; 'the colours muted but various' (Garnett 1972: 85). It is clear that Virginia Woolf had a predilection for green: 'Would I be allowed some rather garish but vibrating and radiating green and red lustres on the mantelpiece?' she wrote to her sister in 1926 (*L* 3: 273). 'Oh they laughed at my taste in green paint!' she cried to her diary later that year (*D* 3: 110). Research verifies Woolf's engagement with paint colour choice, and her preference, at times eccentric, for blue-green.[6] Immersed in green in the sitting room at Monk's House, one can intimate the feeling tone, the sensate qualities of Woolf's interior world.

The topography of Monk's House is unusual, and knowable only through physical witness and enactment. There is a fluency of space – rooms flow into one another in a progressive iteration. This spatial looseness was designed and orchestrated by the Woolfs themselves: the partition wall in the sitting room was taken down in 1926: 'a perfect triumph' (*D* 3: 89); the extension from 1929 increased the linear spread of the house, making it 'longer, much longer'.[7] Negotiating these spaces reveals the porous character of this 'house of many doors' (*D* 1: 286), where living involved a constant movement in and out, a perpetual crossing of thresholds. To reach her bedroom Woolf left the house at night and stepped out into the garden; each morning, she processed towards her writing lodge, far flung, beneath the orchard wall. Ideas explored in Woolf's writing seem materially, architecturally, spatially to be performed here: liminality, porosity, inter-modal alternations, within and without, yielding boundaries loosely defined, an unimpeded flow of thought and language. To move through the spaces at Monk's House is to attune to Woolf's rhythms, as she passed through these rooms, as she walked across these floors, as she 'surged' across the lawn towards her writing lodge (*L* 4: 223), her lips 'syllabling of their own accord' perhaps (*MOB*: 93), tossing her 'brain into the air' perhaps (*D* 3: 141), composing as she walked, striding and inscribing meaning on to the surface of this place. It is to intimate her presence in felt adumbrations; to see her more keenly, in movement and gesture; it is momentarily to 'catch sight', as Hermione Lee has it, of 'a real body, a physical life' (Lee 2005: 2).

But Monk's House is a tantalisingly ambivalent instrument of biography. As potently as it suggests the presence of Virginia Woolf in the past, it reveals, with equal poignancy, her absence in the here and now. However tangible these physical enclosures, however constant these material things, Virginia Woolf is missing from this place. 'Which way did she go?' visitors ask, unaccountably anxious to clarify the route to the river that Woolf took on the day that she died. There is a dissonance played out here between what survives and what is lost; the transient and the enduring; the fragility of a human life, and the persistent continuance of the material world.

'Now is life very solid, or very shifting?'[8]

The relationship between what survives and what perishes is a question frequently raised in Woolf's work. She herself was exercised – and exhilarated – by the constant vacillations, the mutability of living. 'Now is life very solid, or very shifting?' she asks in January 1929; 'I am haunted by the two contradictions.' So fluid is the relationship between the lasting and the ephemeral – 'This has gone on forever: will last forever'; . . . [I]t is transitory, flying, diaphanous' – that she finds herself anticipating her own unexpected death or the death of others, rehearsing 'a farewell – after dining with Roger for instance; or reckoning how many more times I shall see Nessa', so 'impressed' is she by 'the transitoriness of human life' (*D* 3: 218).

Haunted by the many and untimely deaths in her own experience (her mother's, her half-sister's, her father's, her brother's), Woolf plays out the transience of life in her elegiac novels. Jacob is missing: not on the beach, late for lunch, absent from his room. We can never know him, but only follow 'hints', elusive 'glimpses', speculating, extrapolating. His room and its contents communicate his absence, quivering, vibrating in empathic lamentation for its lost occupant: 'the flowers in the jar shift. One fibre in the wicker arm-chair creaks, though no one sits there' (*JR*: 31). It is not his substance that is expressed by shifting flowers, by creaking fibres, but his insubstantiality; the lack of him. As readers we are left, suspended, contemplating Jacob's surviving material things: 'What am I to do with these . . . ?' Betty Flanders asks, as she holds out a pair of Jacob's shoes (*JR*: 155).

There is the slenderest of divisions in Woolf's work between living and dying. In *To the Lighthouse*, Mrs Ramsay slips imperceptibly from the text, her death communicated, obliquely, evasively, in parenthesis.

The house is full of her, and emptied of her. Mr Ramsay's arms are empty; the clothes that she wore indicate, in their 'emptiness', 'how once they were filled and animated'; the looking glass no longer holds a face (*TTL*: 141); 'the step where she used to sit was empty' (164); trees and flowers, 'eyeless', behold nothing (147).

Virginia Woolf is eloquent in her articulation of absence: palpable absence, creaking absence, an emptiness once filled and animated, the felt sway between absence and presence, the temporal disjuncture between then and now. Such are the vacillations played out at Monk's House. Monk's House is haunted by Woolf, as Jacob haunts her novel. Finding her missing, we must go in search of clues. Following in her footsteps we chase hints, catch glimpses, speculate, extrapolate about Virginia Woolf's past living – receiving impressions, absorbing sensations, responding to the sensory, multi-faceted encounter with the past that Monk's House engenders. At Monk's House, we go looking for Virginia Woolf, but find ourselves gathered round her absence, contemplating the promise of her and the lack of her; the memory of her and the loss of her; the nearness and the distance; where once she was, where she no longer is. Monk's House reverberates with this tension. Like the Ramsays' holiday home in *To The Lighthouse*, or Talland House and 22 Hyde Park Gate following the death of Julia Stephen, Monk's House today is both 'full' of Virginia Woolf, and emptied of her.

Museal Conundrums: This is the chair on which she did not sit

If Monk's House enacts an uneasy interplay between absence and presence, the loose and the fixed, it also raises apparent contradictions in its presentation as a commemorative house which need to be addressed. It is almost ninety years since Woolf wrote to her sister, asking if she might be 'allowed some rather garish but vibrating and radiating green' (*L* 3: 273) on the sitting room walls; it is more than eighty years since her choice of green paint was ordered from the local contractors for the walls of her new garden room. Might it be that the green paint that currently covers the sitting room walls at Monk's House has lingered materially thus? Logic suggests otherwise. And if the paint colour in the sitting room is a replacement, what else has been remade or replaced since Woolf died?

When the National Trust took on Monk's House in 1980, the principal protagonist of this commemorative site was long absent from the place. Nearly forty years had elapsed since the death of Virginia Woolf in 1941; eleven years since the death of Leonard Woolf in 1969. What material changes were carried out, during this ellipse in time, significant in a faithful commemoration of Virginia and Leonard Woolf's shared living here? From 1943 until his death, Leonard Woolf shared the house with his companion, Trekkie Parsons. In 1949, the writing lodge, 'originally built as a workroom for a writer', was converted by Leonard Woolf for Trekkie Parsons into 'a studio with the light and space required for a lithographer and artist'.[9] In this conversion, the lodge was extended outwards into the orchard and a glass front introduced into the apex, to allow more light. Thus Virginia Woolf's imaginal space, her compositional arena, was reshaped and recontextualised as the creative space of another. Virginia Woolf's paint colours, 'a sickly green, in and out', were diluted, with pink on the exterior walls. The lean-to conservatory was added to the back of the house, to 'improve the damp' in the sitting room, where during Virginia Woolf's lifetime, the relationship between house and garden was immediate and direct.[10] A fascinating documentary, *Looking Back* (1967), offers compelling glimpses of Leonard Woolf at Monk's House towards the end of this period, just two years before he died. His study is revealed, dense with books and papers, and the garden and conservatory, billowing with plants. As the camera makes its way between house and garden, it bears witness not only to the redolence and loveliness of this place and its context within the Downs, but, importantly, to the unchanging configurations of the exterior, and the enduring arrangements of the internal rooms, from that time until now.

Following Leonard Woolf's death, Trekkie Parsons, the inheritor of his estate, sold Monk's House and its contents to the University of Sussex in 1972, and donated to them the manuscripts and papers of Leonard and Virginia Woolf. During its eight-year custodianship, the University let the house to visiting scholars, who enjoyed the aesthetic and historical milieu: 'When eating in the dining room we sit on chairs backed with needle point designs by Vanessa Bell' (Ruotolo 1975: 2). Concerns began to be expressed about the University's ability to manage the deteriorating house and its fragile contents, and the extensive garden; there were fears about the implications of short leases, tenants' complaints of discomfort, and the danger of the house being modernised to secure the necessarily high rents. By late 1977, plans were announced to 'preserve the house and its contents', to install a 'living in custodian' and to open the house to the public. The National Trust was identified as a body that might 'take it on' (Bailey 1977: 2).

In the two years that separate the Trust's acquisition of Monk's House in 1980, and its opening to the public in 1982, the house was recontextualised as a literary house museum – a material re-enactment, an historic mise-en-scène, of the shared lived past of Virginia and

Leonard Woolf. A group of family members and surviving connoisseurs were brought together, to share their memories of the house, to advise on detail, to shape arrangements, to orchestrate displays. They became, in effect, the co-writers, the creative collaborators, in this material Woolfian biography. An inventory was drawn up; objects were photographed and annotated, each thing categorised and numbered, transformed into a material archive of Virginia and Leonard Woolf. Research was undertaken and interviews carried out to establish the layout and arrangement of the interiors as they were before Virginia Woolf died. A very particular, idiosyncratic green was identified by family members as the original colour of the sitting room walls. Investigations revealed a sample of green paint behind a bookcase in the upper sitting room; the Trust had it copied as closely as possible (Garnett and Miall 2007). Woolf's bedroom was equally painted, cream and green, as indicated by contemporary correspondence.[11]

As original furniture and paintings were made ready for re-installation, certain things were identified as missing from the remembered interior ensembles. Sensitive replications were sought, to help communicate more faithfully, more vividly, the spirit of the house when the Woolfs lived here. Two lamps, for example, were re-created for the sitting room by Quentin Bell and Angelica Garnett, Woolf's nephew and niece, resembling those, now lost, that they remembered having been there. The standard lamp base, in the sitting room c. 1930, was 'imported in 1984'; the pleated paper shade 'sprayed and splattered' by Angelica Garnett 'for the opening in 1982'.[12] They also sourced kelim rugs for this room of a similar size and character to those they remembered. The bed in Virginia Woolf's bedroom, a 'modern divan bed', was introduced in 1983; its 'embroidered linen bedspread' replaces an earlier disintegrating piece, introduced in 1988.[13] And what of the armchair in the sitting room that resembles, so closely, the chair in which Woolf sat for so many photographs?[14] No longer viable, it was replaced in 1982 by another chair from the 1920s,[15] and covered in a reprint of Vanessa Bell's 'Abstract' fabric, commissioned by the Trust in 1982, the original judged too fragile to be useable.

How are we to interpret these imported props? What role do they play in this historic ensemble? This introduced chair, period and style correct (historical accuracy has not been compromised here) and covered with a facsimile fabric (sensitively, professionally produced) is not the chair in those familiar photographs of Woolf. It does not bear material traces of her past, as other chairs and tables in this room do. She did not sit here. Yet meticulously chosen and presented, endorsed by familiars and connoisseurs, it acts as a highly suggestive referent to the chair that was once here. It 'recalls' its counterpart; it 'recognises' its progenitor, eliciting memories of the mood and feeling – 'the knowledge and emotions' as Ouzman has it – 'tethered' to the original (Ouzman 2006: 274). It triggers memories of images of Virginia Woolf sitting, in the upstairs room; it situates her, and others in their circle, guests, who sat in that, or a similar chair, in mind (see Humm 2006: 141). Collective participants in this performative museal ensemble, this chair, this bed, these replicated elements, take their place alongside historic artefacts, playing a mimetic role, stirring and supporting the imagination in this dramatic evocation of the Woolfs' past living here.

'So lovely now; as then'[16]

But while creative replication is included in this material biography, suggestively filling lacunae left by time, most of the contents of these interior displays are original to the house as it was inhabited and developed by the Woolfs when they lived here: tables, chairs, desks, fire screens, ceramics, decorative work on wood and tiles, paintings by Grant and Bell and Roger Fry. The integrity and the provenance of the historic collection at Monk's House are unassailable. And not only do the Woolfs' material artefacts survive, the geographical and architectural contexts that they inhabited have remained constant: the ceilings and walls that enclosed them, the tiled and wooden floors on which they walked, and the exits and entrances, the rises and descents, the fluency of movement – the topography of the place. Woolf's writing lodge may have been altered, to accommodate the creative imagination of another, but its core remains intact, and its position relative to the house, to the garden and to the Downs, is the context chosen by Virginia Woolf when it was reconstructed here in 1934. It sits, as it did, at the edge of the orchard, under the churchyard wall, overhung by the sweet chestnut tree. The view across the water meadows to Mount Caburn is as it was, 'so lovely now; as then' (D 3: 21). Her bedroom may have been inhabited by others (the bed is a substitute, the cover a replacement), yet the design of this room, its proportions, its quality of light, its position in the garden are as Woolf inhabited them. It still receives the morning sun and offers views of the night sky (D 4: 174). It remains unconnected internally to the house, such that its access is achieved, as it was, by 'crossing the garden by the pale flowers' (D 4: 36). These movements, these choreographies in space are unchanged, these spatial relations unaltered since Woolf lived and worked here. These are the very spaces that Virginia Woolf inhabited; these are indeed her surviving material things.

Notes

1. Carlyle's House, 24 Cheyne Row, Chelsea, was opened to the public in 1895, following a campaign for its purchase and memorialisation. Sir Leslie Stephen was significantly involved in this campaign. See Woolf, *Hyde Park* (2005: 183–5), and Hancock (2012: 179 n.71).
2. Woolf refers, for her visit to Haworth, to text and images in the '*Life*, by Mrs Gaskell' (*E* 1: 5), Elizabeth Gaskell's *Life of Charlotte Brontë* (1857). For fascinating discussions on the influence of Gaskell's biography on the ways in which the Brontës have been, and are, 'remembered' at Haworth, see Alexander (2008: 93–110), and Watson (2006: 106–27).
3. *L* 5: 70.
4. Vanessa Bell (c.1912), *Virginia Woolf*, oil on panel, Monk's House, Rodmell, East Sussex, National Trust Collection.
5. Vanessa Bell (c.1933–4), *Virginia Woolf at 52 Tavistock Square, London*, watercolour and pencil on paper, Monk's House, Rodmell, East Sussex, National Trust Collection.
6. It was Virginia Woolf who selected the colours for the rooms created by the extension in 1929. Two pounds of green paint were ordered for the new garden room that became her bedroom, and two pounds for the sitting room upstairs. See correspondence between Leonard Woolf and Philcox Bros (L. Woolf 1929–48: 18 October 1929).
7. Leonard Woolf in conversation with Malcolm Muggeridge (*Looking Back* 1967).
8. *D* 3: 218.
9. Letter from Leonard Woolf to the surveyor, Chailey Rural District Council (1929–48: 6 November 1948). Courtesy of the Society of Authors.
10. Interview with Mrs Ian Parsons, 27 February 1980 (Monk's House: D).
11. The decorator's list for this room when it was first painted includes '2½ lbs white paint/ 2lbs green paint' (L. Woolf, Leonard Woolf Papers: 18 October 1929).
12. NT/Monks/F11, Monk's House Inventory (2007), National Trust Archive, Scotney Castle, Kent.
13. NT/Monks/F39, T7.
14. See Humm 2006: 138.
15. NT/Monks/F18.
16. *D* 3: 21.

Bibliography

Alexander, C. (2008), 'Myth and Memory: Reading the Brontë Parsonage', in *Writers' Houses and the Making of Memory*, ed. H. Hendrix, New York and London: Routledge, pp. 93–110.

Bailey, R. E. (1977), 'Monk's House, Rodmell', *Virginia Woolf Miscellany*, 9, Winter: 2.

Barnes, J. (2005), 'When Flaubert Took Wing', *The Guardian*, 5 March, <http://www.theguardian.com/books/2005/mar/05/fiction.julianbarnes> (last accessed 23 September 2013).

Barnes, J. [1984] (2009), *Flaubert's Parrot*, London: Vintage.

Garnett, A. (1972), 'Angelica Garnett', in *Recollections of Virginia Woolf by her Contemporaries*, ed. J. R. Noble, New York: Morrow, pp. 83–8.

Garnett, A., and P. Miall (2007), Interviews with the author, May and November.

Hancock, N. (2012), *Charleston and Monk's House: The Intimate House Museums of Virginia Woolf and Vanessa Bell*, Edinburgh: Edinburgh University Press.

Hendrix, H., ed. (2008), *Writers' Houses and the Making of Memory*, New York and London: Routledge.

Humm, M. (2006), *Snapshots of Bloomsbury*, New Brunswick, NJ: Rutgers University Press.

Lee, H. (2005), *Virginia Woolf's Nose: Essays on Biography*, Princeton and Woodstock: Princeton University Press.

Looking Back (1967), film, dir. S. Peet, UK: BBC.

Monk's House Reference and Archival material (2007), Folder D and Inventory, National Trust Archive, Scotney Castle, Kent.

Ouzman, S. (2006), 'The Beauty of Letting Go', in *Sensible Objects*, ed. E. Edwards, C. Gosden, and R. Phillips, Oxford and New York: Berg, pp. 269–94.

Ruotolo, L. P. (1975), 'Living in Monk's House', *Virginia Woolf Miscellany*, 4, Fall: 1–2.

Watson, N. J. (2006), *The Literary Tourist*, Basingstoke and New York: Palgrave Macmillan.

Woolf, L. (1929–48), Leonard Woolf Papers, Part 11, Sussex Property 3e, University of Sussex Special Collections.

Woolf, L. [1969] (1975), *The Journey Not The Arrival Matters*, New York and London: Harcourt Brace Jovanovich.

Woolf, V. (1974–84), *The Diary of Virginia Woolf,* 5 vols, ed. A. O. Bell, New York and London: Harcourt Brace Jovanovich.

Woolf, V. (1975–80), *The Letters of Virginia Woolf,* 6 vols, ed. N. Nicolson and J. Trautmann, New York and London: Harcourt Brace Jovanovich.

Woolf, V. (1986), *The Essays of Virginia Woolf,* vol. 1, 1904–1912, ed. A. McNeillie, London: Hogarth Press.

Woolf, V. [1922] (1992), *Jacob's Room*, London: Penguin.

Woolf, V. [1927] (2000), *To the Lighthouse*, London: Penguin.

Woolf, V. (2002), *Moments of Being: Autobiographical Writings,* ed. J. Schulkind, London: Pimlico.

Woolf, V. (2004a), *A Passionate Apprentice: The Early Journals,* 1897–1909, ed. M. A. Leaska, London: Pimlico.

Woolf, V. [1931] (2004b), 'Great Men's Houses', in *The London Scene*, London: Snowbooks Ltd, pp. 37–47.

Woolf, V. (2005), *Hyde Park Gate News: The Stephen Family Newspaper*, ed. G. Lowe, London: Hesperus Press.

Part Two

Language and Translation

Chapter 3

'Can I Help You?':
Virginia Woolf, Viola Tree,
and the Hogarth Press[1]

Diane F. Gillespie

In the turbulent mid-1960s, John Lennon and Paul McCartney wrote a personal cry for 'Help!', the title song for both movie and soundtrack album. Suddenly famous, the Beatles confronted lives transformed in a variety of ways. Had they written a line like 'Help me if you can' during the 1930s, an advice column called 'Can I Help You?' in London's *Sunday Dispatch* might have echoed reassuringly. For eight years, actress and writer Viola Tree (1884–1938) answered letters from 'hundreds and thousands' (Tree 1937: 14) of people. Lacking self-confidence and facing unfamiliar social situations, they asked for advice on how to behave.

In the spring of 1937, Viola Tree 'thrust' upon Leonard and Virginia Woolf a manuscript with the same title (*L* 6: 111). In it, Tree drew upon material from her etiquette column as well as from her personal experience of various kinds of social occasions. Virginia, although continuing to read some submissions, was by then less involved with everyday work at the Hogarth Press. When their manager died suddenly (Marder 1989: 224; Willis 1992: 294), however, both Woolfs worked closely with Tree's *Can I Help You?* until its publication in the fall of that year. Tree's personal treatment of manners parallels some of Virginia Woolf's own experiences in society, echoes those of characters she had created in her fiction, and anticipates concerns in her future writing. During a time of escalating totalitarian sentiment on the continent following her nephew Julian Bell's death in Spain in July of 1937, Woolf was researching and drafting her own version of a *Can I Help You?* book, one with national and international implications. *Three Guineas*, a blend of interconnected letters and replies that appeared in 1938, is about 'how we can help you to prevent war' (*TG*: 11).

Woolf's largely business relationship with Tree supports recent research, like Helen Southworth's essay collection (2010), that emphasises the Hogarth Press's increasing involvement in a variety of modernist cultural controversies and discussions. *Can I Help You?* reflects the personal experiences of many living in a period of great social change and class fluidity. Like Woolf's, Tree's view of conventional social behaviour was an evolving mixture of qualified respect and spirited resistance. Tree was the eldest of three daughters of famous actor-manager Sir Herbert Beerbohm Tree (1853–1917) and actress Helen Maud Tree (1858–1937) as well as the niece of essayist and caricaturist Max Beerbohm (1872–1966).[2] Educated at the Academy of Dramatic Art and the Royal College of Music, Tree for a time pursued an operatic career. Her *Castles in the Air: A Story of My Singing Days* (1926), published earlier by the Hogarth Press, includes a photo of her costumed for the role of Salome in Richard Strauss's notorious opera.[3] She was known, however, primarily as a stage actress. Her famous father, knighted in 1909 for his contributions to the British Theatre, wrote in 1913 that he lived in a time when 'the barbed wire fences' separating 'classes are being relegated to the limbo of the human scrap-heap' (H. B. Tree 1913: 4). Herbert Beerbohm Tree, as his daughter confided to Woolf, would 'have loved a duke for a son in law!' (*D* 3: 86). Woolf might well have confided, in return, George Duckworth's determination to launch his half-sisters, Virginia and Vanessa, into society. Their father, Leslie Stephen, was, after all, a prominent, educated man of letters who had been knighted already in 1902 for his intellectual contributions. As daughters of men whose prominence bridged some class boundaries, both Viola and Virginia contemplated possibilities and problems inherent in a traditional feminine social role along with their inclinations towards modern and democratic impulses in society.

Several scholars have treated Woolf's mixed reactions to social hierarchies and rituals, as well as to aristocrats and their houses,[4] but closest to my topic is a thoughtful 2008 article by David Dwan. He discusses manners, especially in Woolf's *To the Lighthouse* (1927), in the context of philosophical scepticism. In the face of meaningless flux and incoherent identities, he concludes, social rituals are useful, even necessary – so long as we recognise them as fiction and do not let them harden into dogma (Dwan 2008: 261, 263). 'Manners', Dwan writes, may be 'structures without foundations', but they 'stand fast nonetheless' as 'a consoling presence in an otherwise uncertain world' (250). Viola Tree's *Can I Help You?* offers a context for Woolf's simultaneous challenges to, and selective acceptance of, certain conventional social roles and rites. Tree's book humorously affirms pleasing behaviour, however evolving, as an art form helpful, at best, in fostering harmonious human relationships in lives well lived.

'Her vulgarity is *not* vulgar'

The Hogarth Press not only participated in modernist cultural discussions but also, as Elizabeth Willson Gordon notes, 'performed an impressive balancing act, oscillating between the poles of commercial and noncommercial, democratic and elitist' (2009: vii).[5] That the Woolfs should offer a self-help book on manners by a stage celebrity has not escaped criticism. It is an easy genre to mock,[6] and there are some, then and now, who judge a publication entirely by its appearance or author. Did the Hogarth Press imprint on such a book violate both professional and personal standards, as some have implied? It is true that in 1924, as J. H. Willis notes (1992: 379), Virginia Woolf had penned a satirical review of the Nonesuch Press's *Weekend Book*, a small, 'prettily printed' collection of poetry and 'games and songs and recipes and quips and cranks', suitable, she says, 'to hand to one's hostess in return for a candlestick' (*E* 3: 414). Yet, as Willis also notes, the Hogarth Press went ahead and published, 'presumably without blushing or laughing' (379), what seems to be its own pretty little book, elegantly illustrated by Tree's daughter Virginia Parsons,[7] and subtitled *Your Manners—Menus—Amusements—Friends—Charades—Make-Ups—Travel—Calling—Children—Love Affairs* (Fig. 3.1).[8] Willis attributes this implied publishing faux pas to Tree's being an 'old friend' whose memoir the Woolfs had published a decade earlier (1992: 369). On that occasion, Vita Sackville-West, a relatively new Hogarth author herself,[9] had reprimanded Woolf in a letter: 'And oh, dear, idolized Virginia that you are, how *could* you publish Viola? it makes me vomit. I don't like you to sell your soul' (Sackville-West 1985: 126).[10]

Whether Sackville-West was jealous, teasing, or genuinely dyspeptic, Woolf fired back a defence of author and book, one that also helps to explain the later publication of Tree's *Can I Help You?* 'You are utterly wrong about Viola', Woolf wrote. After pointing out that memoirs should not be read 'as if they were poems', she added, 'Don't you see her vulgarity is *not* vulgar, her irreticence is *not* unashamed: an aroma – she aims at that: life: fact: not the thing we go for', she added tactfully, 'but I cant make you understand: try reading as if you were catching a swarm of bees; not hunting down one dart like dragon fly' (*L* 3: 268).

Although some grammarians frown on double negatives, speakers and writers employ them, as Woolf does, for both emphasis and nuance. 'Not unashamed' suggests that Tree is aware and somewhat critical of her volubility and frankness. Simultaneously, the double negative allows Woolf not only to voice her own reservations, but also to defend Tree, and to suggest the coexistence of double or multiple interpretations

CAN I HELP YOU?

Your Manners—Menus—Amusements—
Friends—Charades—Make-Ups—Travel—
Calling—Children—Love Affairs

By VIOLA TREE

Illustrated by VIRGINIA PARSONS

PUBLISHED BY LEONARD AND VIRGINIA WOOLF AT THE
HOGARTH PRESS, 52 TAVISTOCK SQUARE, LONDON, W.C.
1937

Figure 3.1   *Can I Help You?* Frontispiece ('Hyacinths and Cyclamen') and title page drawings by Virginia Parsons. Courtesy of Manuscripts, Archives and Special Collections, Washington State University; permission of Georgia Tennant, Josie Tennant, and Silvy McQuiston.

of her behaviour. Woolf, embracing verbal ambiguity, concluded in 'Craftsmanship' (1937) that 'the nature of words to mean many things' overrides the 'few trifling rules of grammar and spelling . . . we can put on them' (*E* 6: 94, 96). She was also increasingly suspicious of systems in general – grammatical, philosophical, theological, or cultural – that reduced people and aspects of human existence to over-simplified dualities or rankings. Woolf found ways to let positive and negative reactions to Tree remain in tension, accumulate variations around them, and suggest multiple perspectives.

Woolf's seemingly contradictory statement that Tree's 'vulgarity is *not* vulgar' implies different interpretations of her behaviour. Woolf assumed that the aristocratic Sackville-West, however unconventional herself, was attacking Tree personally. Although Sackville-West had not used the word 'vulgar', it was a common criticism of women who displayed themselves publicly on stage. In *Castles in the Air* Tree shows that she is well aware of the word[11] when she lists instances of 'great vulgarity' among her own expressions and those of her time (1926: 44). Then, in *Can I Help You?*, she remembers a dressing-room visit from Sackville-West herself, with Harold Nicolson, after a dramatic performance. '"We don't know what makes you so good"', Sackville-West said on that occasion, '"– your pauses – or your knees"'. If Tree suspects a charge of vulgarity, she archly makes the best of it. 'That was lovely, puzzling praise', she writes (1937: 166). Remembering how, in her youth, 'a stage career was thought a deterrent to marriage' for the socially ambitious (11), Tree quotes the society hostess who criticised her more openly: '"You can't float about on a wire as Ariel with no petticoats and appear at a ball half an hour later in white satin"' (22).[12]

According to social historians, 'vulgar' was the criticism most feared by the rising middle class (e.g. Wildeblood and Brinson 1965: 39), hence multiple editions of hefty etiquette bibles by authorities like Emily Post in America and Lady Troubridge in England.[13] Vulgarity, to people who considered themselves more cultured or refined, was not just common or coarse speech and behaviour; it was also inappropriate flaunting of wealth, fashionable dress, or social connections. Although Tree appeared on stage and may have been pretentious on occasion, she was too complex and self-aware for 'either-or' judgements. In her person and in her writing, she reflected longstanding ideals, if not always of modesty, at least of honest self-criticism and, perhaps more difficult, of '"consideration for others"' (Wildeblood and Brinson 1965: 40). She also had wit; common-sense intelligence; sensitivity and kindness; and the ability to live intensely, learn from, and describe her experiences.

Some of Viola Tree's rich 'aroma' (*L* 3: 268) emerges in a sketch Woolf wrote in 1926 after Tree visited to consult about her *Castles in the Air* memoir.[14] Again, Woolf's description is full of contradictions and qualifications: 'She is a flamboyant creature – much of an actress – much abused by the Waleys & Marjories;[15] but rather taking to me.' 'She has', Woolf continues, 'the great egotism, the magnification of self, which any bodily display, I think, produces.' Woolf tries to get down snatches of her conversation. She

[e]asily reverts to the topic of her own charms: how she shd. have married the D[uke]. of Rutland. "Lord — (his uncle) told me I was the woman John really loved. The duchess said to me . . . ". So she runs on, in the best of clothes, easy & familiar, but, reserved too; with the wiles & warinesses of a woman of the world, half sordid half splendid, not quite at her ease with us, yet glad of a room where she can tell her stories, of listeners to whom she is new & strange.

Even though she 'will run on by the hour', Woolf notes, Tree 'is very watchful not to bore'. Finally, her 'charm' disguises the fact that she is 'a good business woman' of 'considerable acuteness' (*D* 3: 86). Are there hints of Viola Tree in Woolf's description of Mrs Manresa's complex impact in *Between the Acts* (1941)? 'Vulgar she was ... But what a desirable, at least valuable, quality' since her 'quite genuine' lack of inhibitions enabled everyone else to 'take advantage of the breach of decorum, of the fresh air that blew in' (*BTA:* 41).

The General Strike of 1926 slowed sales of Tree's memoir, yet one reviewer called it 'delightful', with the 'occasional gift of tart epigram' (Birrell 1926: 212). The major reservation concerned quotations from candid letters she had written to her fiancé Alan Parsons.[16] Most reviewers concluded, however, that if she does not care about people reading the letters (Review 1926b), and if Parsons does not mind either, then 'why should anybody else'? (Review 1926c). The *Times Literary Supplement* reviewer thought the book may be indiscreet, but it 'is honourably exempt from any of the faults of a section of the public who, rightly or wrongly, think their intimate affairs of acute interest to everyone else' (Review 1926a). In other words, Tree's voluble lack of reserve was disarming because, as Woolf said, it is '*not* unashamed' (*L* 3: 268). As Tree herself explains, 'If I have a good quality, it is not being ashamed of making a fool of myself, and there is ample evidence of it in this story, and the fact that I have not eliminated its follies in order to make myself appear wise' (1926: 12–13).

'Am I a Snob?'

A decade later, in early December 1936, Virginia read her neither entirely vulgar nor unashamed essay 'Am I a Snob?' to the Memoir Club (*D* 5: 26 n.1). Here she focuses, not on her youthful 'tea-table training' or the social failures that frustrated her conventional half-brother George Duckworth (*MOB:* 150, 154–7), but, in a self-critical tone not unlike Viola Tree's, on her adult forays into society. Unlike Desmond MacCarthy and Maynard Keynes, men secure from the beginning in their fine educations and positions in society, Woolf is insecure about her 'own standing'. She must always impress her worth upon herself and others by 'flourishing ... in other people's faces' an invitation containing 'a title or an honour' (*MOB:* 206). She is not, she hopes, like George Duckworth, whose 'snobbery was of so gross and palpable a texture that' she 'could smell it and taste it from afar' (207). She admits, however, that she is 'intrigued and delighted' by aristocratic 'indifference' to what other people think (207–8), and that she is 'a coronet snob' (preferably 'old coronets'), 'a lit up drawing room snob', and a 'social festivity snob' (210).[17] Never mind that aristocratic hostesses invite her to their parties because she is a well-known writer. This

notice feeds her vanity, but it does not cure her 'dress complex' (210).
She remains anxious about how she will appear and comport herself in
society, not as a writer, but 'as a woman' (208, 211–12).[18] If Woolf is
a snob, then the definition must balance her uncertain social position
in relation to masculine hierarchies with her own earned reputation as
a writer; it must balance her persistent worries about dress and acceptable behaviour with her admiration for aristocratic self-confidence and
love of festive gatherings.

Virginia Woolf's self-mocking analysis of her own pretensions,
and candour about her insecurities, certainly prepared her to appreciate Viola Tree's *Can I Help You?* when she and Leonard read the
manuscript in March 1937. In the course of considerable business-like
correspondence between Tree and the Hogarth Press (Hogarth Press
Archive), both Woolfs indicated their agreement on a list of cuts. At the
same time, they encouraged Tree to retain her irreticence, the entertaining stories and unabashed personal comments that would enliven the
book.[19] They also accepted her suggestion of an arguably pretentious
but effective marketing strategy. Tree's uninhibited name-dropping
became an index of well-known people – from actors and aristocrats
to poets, painters, and politicians – and the draft order form included a
boxed excerpt (Tree 1927–38: 29 August 1927).[20]

Tree begins *Can I Help You?* by defending herself against two potential criticisms: first that she is guilty of 'snobbery' (1937: 12) and second
that she is no authority on manners. Her defence, as Woolf might say,
is not uncritical. Tree describes her coming out in society as a young,
marriageable woman being appraised by parents of marriageable men.
She wonders if it 'would have been better' had she '*not* dipped into
social life, dinner parties, time-wasting luncheons, extravagant clothes,
opera boxes' since, she writes, all the 'young men's mothers looked
down their noses at me . . .; and that made me a little dissatisfied with
the . . . cloistered devotion to duty' of the stage. 'It also made me', she
adds, 'what unworldly people have often called "snobbish"' (11–12).
Like Woolf, Tree wants to qualify her acceptance of the label 'snob'. It
means, in her case, 'a love of Lords and Ladies', not 'for their titles', but
for 'what they have to give' and 'for their beautiful manners and beautiful manors' that reflect 'generations of tradition . . . that everybody . . .
seeks unconsciously or consciously to imitate' (12). Unconsciously or
consciously Woolf imitated Tree's verbal echo. It reappears when, in
Between the Acts, La Trobe's megaphone includes '*the amiable condescension of the lady of the manor – the upper class manner*' (BTA:
187–8) reflecting centuries 'of customary behaviour' at which young
people earlier in the novel have 'laughed; but respected' (27).[21]

In her own democratic way, Tree suggests that pleasing behaviour, whether more or less conventional, can benefit all social classes, increase beauty in life, and foster confidence, fair play, and kindness both on social occasions and in the home. She admits that sometimes she leaves society dinners wondering, '"What does it mean? What did we gain or achieve?"' Yet she thinks it 'right that there should be clever, beautiful and elegant people dining' for, 'in a crisis they will don mackintoshes, eat at canteens, serve others, drive lorries, as untiringly or more untiringly than the rest'. After such historic upheavals, however, 'down they sit again in their tiaras, with four glasses, eight knives and forks, festoons of orchids, fences of cigars, laughter, rapture' (1937: 59). Tree casts herself as 'an onlooker, an entertainer', which on occasion she was invited to be,[22] 'or a critic' at such events (59).

Still, Tree admits to loving compliments on her own best manners (1937: 14) and, in her chapter on 'Deportment and Dancing', on her posture in contrast to that of the modern girl who is 'backed like a camel, or indeed like a whale' (185). In this chapter she has her own version of Woolf's British Museum scene in *A Room of One's Own*. Here Tree tries and fails to find out how good posture was, and still might be, taught effectively. Although she sees no angry 'Professor von X' stabbing his paper with his pen (*AROO*: 31), Tree does observe with mild irony professors 'to my right and left, intent on perhaps more important tasks' than her own which is merely 'to help and educate' young women (Tree 1937: 186).

Excellent posture notwithstanding, Tree's pride is, as Woolf might say, not unhumble. If Tree admits to snobbishness in her youth (1937: 14), at least according to her own definition, elsewhere in the book she identifies with, and provides advice for 'humblish people' (86). She admits that her family considers her 'rude, tactless, even farouche' (15). This 'decline in manners' she attributes first to a busy stage career that gave her '*no leisure, no method and a terrifying optimism*', and then to marriage, motherhood, and limited finances (15, 23–4). She quotes a 'wit' who had recently told her, '"You haven't manners now, you have manner"' (14). Still, she insists she can give advice on etiquette because her parents 'were born hosts' (16–17, 21–2); because, for five decades, she has 'mixed with all worlds, and loved them all' (18, 24–5); and because, for eight years, she has penned her advice column for the *Sunday Dispatch* (25).

Viola Tree has produced not just an etiquette book, but another memoir, a buzz of personal observations on social mores from before and after her singing career. She confides in her reader, italicises for emphasis,[23] and expresses opinions on everything from the general awfulness of bridesmaid's dresses in her 'Weddings' chapter (1937: 129) to, in her chapter on 'Hostesses', the common sense of eating hot food when served rather than waiting for a whole table to begin (34–5). Yet, in spite of Tree's twelve chapter headings and numerous subheadings, the book seems loosely constructed because, as she explains, 'digression is the apple of mine eye' (28, 25). When 'the curtain rises' on an imaginary dinner party, for example, she admits to a digression about who should go to the door to greet guests, drops a couple of names (the Duchess of Rutland and Bernard Shaw), and concludes that it is 'rightly more democratic' to go to the door oneself. '*There is no shame in this*', she insists (36).

Although Tree quotes instances from her *Sunday Dispatch* columns, advice in her *Can I Help You?* book often takes the form of amusing inventions of ineffective and effective letters, invitations, announcements, and speeches, as well as humorous, present-tense scenes complete with asides and stage directions. For her descriptions and dramatisations of dinners, from small to grand, she mixes with real people's names those of invented dinner guests with Restoration comedy-of-manners names like 'Mrs Halibut-Cod' (first name 'Zero'), 'La Belle Helene', 'Lord Copse', 'Miss Dot Dash', and 'Commander Spithead' (31–2, 52).[24] Tree's chapters often end with gentle lists of 'Avoids'. After a subsection on a 'Small Dinner', for example, she reminds a hostess to 'Avoid bickering or an open row with your husband. The marriage bell must ring all the time' (47).

Tree's theatrical experience enables her to describe how to play the social drama's usual and unusual parts. Among the roles included in her chapters are hostess, guest, public speaker, bride and groom, and traveller. Two chapters, more unconventional, exemplify the tone of her advice in *Can I Help You?* 'Manners to Children' emphasises the parental role, not (as one might expect) that of a well-behaved child. Virginia Parsons created a pretty but somewhat lifeless illustration, 'Children at Ease with Dog', to reinforce her mother's point that children should have pets, but the drawing does not communicate the lively humour of Tree's advice or honesty about her own parental performance (Fig. 3.2). Tree covers a variety of possible and impossible children's pets, from old ponies to armadillos, and advises parents to 'Bear with' children's animal 'crazes' (1937: 93). She has a whole list of 'instances of bad manners to children', among them 'Sending them alone to dentists' and 'Punishing, correcting and reproving them before their friends or relatives' (97). Above all, she says, childhood should be remembered as a happy time (99–100). 'My children are neither prodigies nor dandies,' she confides, 'but they enjoy things . . . I have heard my daughter continually say that she is happy – a confession rarely heard from girls of my

Figure 3.2   *Can I Help You?* 'Children at Ease with Dog' by Virginia Parsons. Courtesy of Manuscripts, Archives and Special Collections, Washington State University; permission of Georgia Tennant, Josie Tennant, and Silvy McQuiston.

own youth' (99). Tree even includes a sub-section called 'Some Instances of Bad Manners to Dogs' (101). Sensitivity to both children and animals might have benefited Woolf's Bart Oliver, who embodies Tree's 'Avoids' by terrorising his dog and frightening little George to tears in *Between the Acts* (12–13).

In the final chapter, 'A Lover's Good-Bye', Tree says that both women and men must have the courage and good manners necessary to make clean breaks with ill-suited people (1937: 247–8). No '"Let us meet once more"', no 'lingering look or press of finger-tips', just a firm departure, preferably in a symbolic month like November and in 'an impersonal place' like an art gallery, she says (247–8). Although Tree advises lovers not to 'feel the difference in class' since 'barriers are breaking every day' (252), she creates a story about 'the two people in the picture', a travelling salesman and a rich, spoiled schoolgirl (Fig. 3.3). 'Obviously too many miles apart' and knowing it, they drag out the relationship in ways painful for them both (248). Tree's conclusion to this chapter applies to the whole book: 'good manners or fine behaviour' are meant to avoid 'giving pain to others' (252).

'She could transmit something into words'

Tree includes several verbal nods to Bloomsbury and Virginia Woolf in *Can I Help You?* An example of a dinner invitation imagines a hostess using 'a new Duncan Grant picture' to lure a potential guest (1937: 28). In response to requests for games suitable for social occasions, Tree creates a dramatic chapter on 'Charades' with one character brightly costumed 'as a Bloomsbury, with red skirt, green boots, and white shirt' (147). Virginia Woolf herself had mocked, even more graphically, her sister Vanessa's clothing designs that 'almost wrenched my eyes from the sockets – a skirt barred with reds and yellows of the vilest kind, and a pea green blouse on top, with a gaudy handkerchief on her head, supposed to be the very boldest taste' (*L* 2: 111). In her 'Travel' chapter, Tree recommends packing Woolf's *The Voyage Out* (1915) because, she writes, 'Whenever I read Mrs Virginia Woolf's prose, I am transported, and so I hope will the traveller be' (1937: 173). More obliquely, in a chapter on 'Country Calling', Tree recreates the beginning of a disastrous visit during which guest's and hostess's dogs fight. 'Only a very great writer', Tree adds, 'could begin conversation intelligently after such a scramble'. She can do so, a note explains, because 'her social technique is only stylized, and . . . she herself is more interested in the conversation and the psychology of the moment' than in 'small local happenings' (226).

Figure 3.3   *Can I Help You?* 'A Lover's Good-Bye' by Virginia Parsons. Courtesy of Manuscripts, Archives and Special Collections, Washington State University; permission of Georgia Tennant, Josie Tennant, and Silvy McQuiston.

Is Virginia Woolf this 'very great writer' and was this perhaps an actual incident? Between the stories Tree liked to tell the Woolfs when she visited, perhaps Virginia added anecdotes of her own.[25]

Viola Tree 'put on the body' Shakespeare's sister 'has so often laid down' (*AROO*: 118), both with her stage career and, through her etiquette book, with her desire to use her experience to 'help and educate' others (1937: 186). In November of 1938, a year following the publication of *Can I Help You?*, however, Tree died suddenly of pleurisy. Noting in her diary sketch that Viola was '2 years younger' than herself, Woolf recalls:

> the quality of her skin: like an apricot; a few amber coloured hairs. Eyes blistered with paint underneath. A huge Goddess woman, who was also an old drudge; a big boned striding figure; much got up, of late. Last time I saw her . . . she was in her abundant expansive mood. I never reached any other; yet always liked her. Met her perhaps once a year, about her books. (*D* 5: 187)

Tree had dined with the Woolfs when her first book appeared, and Woolf now recalls 'tea in Woburn Sq.' with her:

> the butter was wrapped in a newspaper. And there was an Italian double bed in the drawing room. She was instinctive; & had the charm of good actress manners; & their Bohemianism, & sentimentality. But I think was a sterling spontaneous mother & daughter; not ambitious; a great hand at life; I suppose harassed for money; & extravagant; & very bold; & courageous – a maker of picturesque surroundings. So strong & large, that she shd. have lived to be 80. (*D* 5: 187)[26]

Tree, Woolf adds, 'could transmit something into words' (*D* 5: 187). If a great writer's 'social technique is only stylized', according to Tree (1937: 226), and Tree, according to Woolf, 'had the charm of good actress manners' (*D* 5: 187), then the social behaviour of both women was an acquired veneer, a role each might assume with varying degrees of confidence and success. Although liking each other, neither penetrated much beneath surfaces. Each admired the other's writing, but both Tree's claim to be 'transported' by Woolf's (1937: 173) and Woolf's acknowledgement of Tree's ability to 'transmit something into words' are complimentary generalities (*D* 5: 187). Woolf's comment that Tree was 'not ambitious' (187) suggests that she, unlike Sackville-West perhaps, had few pretensions, at least as a writer, and thus deserved appreciation for her spontaneous, personal anecdotes of daily life and relationships.

We can imagine Woolf reading *Can I Help You?* and relating it not only to her own public and private experiences, but also to her already published fiction. Woolf must have enjoyed, for example, Tree's attempt to imagine herself as an insecure dinner guest subjected, like Lily Briscoe at Mrs Ramsay's table in *To the Lighthouse*, to 'the searchlight that the hostess is wont to play upon her guests' (1937: 55; cf. *TTL* 92). Just as Tree reminds herself that society's elegant dinner parties are abandoned when crises demand aristocratic help, so Lily, balking but acquiescing in a less formal setting, has to remind herself that a man's duty 'to help us, suppose the Tube were to burst into flames' balances the conversational openings she must try to give socially inept Charles Tansley. What would happen, she wonders, 'if neither of us did either of these things?' (*TTL*: 91–2). One of Tree's footnotes also would have amused the author of *To the Lighthouse*. Although 'second helpings' are not really 'the highest good manners', Tree admits that she herself is 'most guilty' (1937: 210 n.1). She would have forgiven Mr Carmichael, silently condemned by Mr Ramsay for requesting more soup (*TTL*: 95). Social etiquette, however changing and sometimes onerous, demands tolerance and embodies interconnected responsibilities of one person or group to another.

Can we help you?

As she was helping with the publication of *Can I Help You?* Woolf was researching and writing her own version of an advice book. Published by the Hogarth Press in the year Tree died, *Three Guineas* (1938) is about private and public behaviour, about not giving pain to others, on domestic, national, and international scales. Woolf's narrator creates responses to – and notes relationships among – three letters asking for help and advice. One is from a man who, unusually, asks a woman for help to prevent war. Related are two from women, one requesting help to rebuild a women's college, and one wishing to help women enter the professions. The answers question obvious ways of assisting: 'to sign a letter to the newspapers; . . . to join a certain society; . . . to subscribe to its funds' (*TG*: 11). Instead, the advice rings variations on Viola Tree's operant word 'help'. Educated men's daughters can 'help . . . to prevent war' (11) only by describing the world as they see and experience it (e.g. 58). Woolf does accept the need to help support 'colleges for the daughters of educated men' and to help them 'earn their livings in the professions' (36–7) but only if women then take into the public world what they have learned in the private one. They must earn only enough money 'for the full development of body and mind', refuse to 'sell . . . [their] brain[s] for the sake of money', prefer 'ridicule, obscurity and censure' to 'fame and praise', and rid themselves of 'pride' and 'unreal loyalties' (80). In these ways, newly-educated and professional women will neither practise nor communicate the values that lead to war.

Without making exaggerated claims for Tree's *Can I Help You?* I think it appealed to Woolf for several reasons. She saw parallels to her own experiences in society and to ways she had reflected social life in her fiction. She also valued candid glimpses of women's lives, and Tree's was a fascinating one. Moreover, as Woolf had insisted in *A Room of One's Own*, fashions, shopping, and 'the feelings of women in a drawing-room' are just as important as masculine preoccupations with war and sports (*AROO*: 77). To these reasons I would add that Tree's book anticipates 'the sort of education' Woolf says in *Three Guineas* 'is needed' to teach everyday ways of peace to a competitive society sliding again towards war (*TG*: 33).

If Tree realised that some of her flights of fancy may cause 'the elect' to 'laugh in their sleeves' (1937: 12), Woolf realised that, in *Three Guineas*, she risked not only laughter but derision (e.g. *L* 6: 229, 239). Vita Sackville-West, Woolf reports in letters, charged her with 'misleading arguments' (*L* 6: 243). Worse, Q. D. Leavis accused her of '"dangerous assumptions, ... preposterous claims and ... nasty attitudes"'. 'I thought I should raise their hackles – poor old strumpets', Woolf wrote of the Cambridge ladies' intellectual snobbery (*L* 6: 271 and n.1).

The flight of fancy probably most irritating to the Cambridge ladies was Woolf's 'experimental college', 'new college' and 'poor college'. It would help prevent war by including 'arts that can be taught cheaply and practised by poor people' (*TG*: 33–4) and by using books and paintings that are 'new and always changing' (34). Instead of the 'arts of dominating ... of ruling, of killing, of acquiring land and capital', its teaching would include the everyday 'arts of human intercourse; the art of understanding other people's lives and minds, and the little arts of talk, of dress, of cookery that are allied with them' (34). These are some of the arts of everyday life that Tree describes in *Can I Help You?* Because she demystifies and undermines hierarchical values and traditional social protocol with a personal, humorous touch, we can imagine that Tree's book would appeal to the 'good livers' and 'good thinkers' Woolf sought to teach in her imaginary college (*TG*: 33–4). When the Hogarth Press's draft order form quotes reviewers who call Tree helpful, wise, witty, kind, and amusing, it too emphasises personal qualities helpful in maintaining a peaceful, civilised society.[27]

In her memoir, 'A Sketch of the Past', begun in April 1939, Woolf once more contemplates manners learned in her youth. She calls them a 'game' of 'upper middle class Victorian society' (*MOB*: 150). On the one hand, the rules constituted a ruthless 'social machine' unquestioningly polished and driven by people like George Duckworth (152). On the other, if she could verbalise images and experiences she had absorbed in society (155–6), Woolf could make the manners game 'useful. It has its beauty', she adds, 'for it is founded upon restraint, sympathy, unselfishness – all civilized qualities. It is helpful in making something seemly out of raw odds and ends' (150). Like manners, words helped Woolf not only to deprive the shock of 'some real thing behind appearances' of 'its power to hurt' but also 'to put . . . severed parts together' and to envision 'the whole world [. . . as] a work of art' (72).

As Woolf and Tree challenged and negotiated rules of the manners game, each combined words in her own way to suggest basic human values – among them beauty, tolerance, kindness, and responsibility – worth affirming amidst confusions of traditional versus modern motives and behaviour. Both women articulated insights and strategies to help mitigate their own degrees of uncertainty and discomfort along with those of other people. Can we help you to understand, their books ask, how to prevent hurting others on scales both small and large in this rapidly changing world? Harold Nicolson, quoted on the Hogarth Press draft order form for *Can I Help You?*, detected larger implications of Tree's self-help book. Basically, he says, it is more about life than about manners.[28] Help with social etiquette and war prevention may seem unrelated as subjects. Sometimes Tree's and Woolf's advice or goals may seem fanciful. Nevertheless, both *Can I Help You?* and *Three Guineas* reflect their authors' convictions about how to live effectively. They write 'to help and educate' each reader (Tree 1937: 185–6) to live sincerely and fully, to become, in the face of contradictions and complexities, what Virginia Woolf called Viola Tree, 'a great hand at life' (*D* 5: 187).

Notes

1. My thanks to David Higham Associates, Jean Rose of the Random House Group, and Nancy Fulford for access to the Hogarth Press papers in Special Collections at the University of Reading Library; and to Trevor Bond of Manuscripts, Archives and Special Collections (MASC) at the Washington State University (WSU) Libraries where Leonard and Virginia Woolf's personal library is housed (Library). I especially wish to thank Georgia Tennant, Jo Tennant, and Silvy McQuiston for permission to reproduce their mother Virginia Parsons's illustrations for Viola Tree's book. A short version of this essay appears in Gillespie (2012) and a treatment of Tree's Chapter V 'Weddings' appears in Gillespie (2013).
2. In 1920, Viola, along with her mother and sister Iris (1897–1968), the other well-known Tree daughter, contributed to Max Beerbohm's edition of Sir Herbert Beerbohm Tree's memoirs. Viola also managed theatres,

directed and wrote plays, and published on various topics in newspapers and for *Vogue*. She had several minor film roles in the 1920s and 1930s.

3. Strauss's opera, the libretto based on the German translation of the French play by Oscar Wilde, was a demanding role for a soprano. It was produced in 1896 in Paris but, largely because of its dance of the seven veils, was banned in Vienna until 1918 and not produced in London until 1931.

4. See, among others, Zwerdling (1986: 87–119), Rosenfeld (2001), Adolph (2005), Johnston (1997), and Fernald (1994) on class distinctions; Schröder (2006) and Rudikoff (1999) on country or aristocratic houses and their occupants; and Simpson (2008) and Minow-Pinkney (2010) on social rituals.

5. Other books in the advice genre include *Adventures in Investing* by 'Securitas' (1936) and *Diet and High Blood Pressure* by Dr I. Harris (1937) (Porter 2004: 7). The Hogarth Press's two detective novels by C. H. B. Kitchin (1929, 1934) initially seemed a similar anomaly (Gillespie 2003: 36), as did the Press's 'Religion' category in catalogues of the 1920s and 1930s (Gillespie 2010: 75–7).

6. Ada Leverson (1862–1933), who wrote novels and journalism, did parodies of advice columnists (Blain, Clements, and Grundy 1990: 654) including Tree's 'Can I Help You?' series in the *Sunday Dispatch* (Blain, Clements, and Grundy 1990: 1094).

7. Parsons did seven illustrations: 'The Right Way to Hold Your Knife and Fork', 'Hyacinths and Cyclamen', 'The Right Nightgown', 'Children at Ease with Dog', 'Sea Food', 'Fox Crowned with Oak', and 'A Lover's Good-Bye'. Leonard Woolf liked the drawings (L. Woolf 1925–37: 7 June 1937).

8. The copy remaining in the Woolf's library (Library) has 'Travellers copy' pencilled in on the peach-coloured cover above the title and no page numbers for the illustrations. The blurb in the inside flap lists Tree's qualifications as an author of a book on manners.

9. Tree's 1926 memoir is among the Woolfs' library in MASC at WSU, as are Sackville-West's *Seducers in Ecuador* (1924) and *Passenger to Teheran* (1926) (Library).

10. Yet Sackville-West states matter-of-factly to Harold that she and Woolf were joined by Tree for coffee at the Eiffel Tower restaurant in June of 1926 (Sackville-West 1992: 147). Sackville-West also offers to help Woolf by doing the index for Tree's *Castles in the Air* (122–3). Woolf does not always defend Tree either. She assures Molly MacCarthy, for example, that she need not feel inferior to 'those pert misses', Tree among them, 'who have shaved themselves to resemble nothing so much as tubes of piping' (*L* 3: 143).

11. Tree hopes, for instance, that the Woolfs will not consider vulgar her plan to give a party to celebrate publication of *Can I Help You?* (Tree 1927–38: 26 January 1938).

12. Tree, whose stage debut had been in Edinburgh as Viola in *Twelfth Night* was playing, in 1904, Ariel in Shakespeare's *The Tempest*.

13. In 1937, Post's nearly 900-page *Etiquette* appeared in a revised edition after twenty-five reprintings of the 1922 edition by Funk and Wagnalls. Tree

herself directs readers to Troubridge's *Book of Etiquette: The Complete Standard Work of Reference on Social Usage,* also much reprinted after its initial 1913 publication (1937: 34 n.1; 52 n.1; and 222 n.1).

14. In the Press correspondence about Tree's memoir, *Castles in the Air,* Leonard writes the letters but consistently summarises and defers to Virginia's advice (L. Woolf 1925–37: 14 and 30 October 1925).

15. Arthur Waley (1889–1966) published translations of Japanese and Chinese texts. Marjorie Thomson or Joad (c.1900–1931) worked for the Hogarth Press from 1923 to 1925 (Library).

16. In 1912 Viola Tree had married drama critic Alan Parsons (1889–1933) who died young (age 44). One of their two sons, David Tree (1915–2009), followed in the family theatrical tradition. Their daughter, Virginia (1917–2003), who studied at the Slade and illustrated *Can I Help You?,* married into the nobility.

17. Beerbohm Tree offers a whole list of 'kinds of snobbery': 'the snobbery of riches; . . . of power, of aristocracy . . . . of Socialism, . . . of dogma, . . . of culture – the snobbery of what Americans call the "high-brows" – perhaps the most fearsome snobbery of all . . . There is nothing meaner than the contempt of the greatly endowed for those less favoured than themselves' (1913: 20).

18. Minow-Pinkney provides a recent discussion of Woolf's ambivalence about 'the famous social hostesses of the day' (2010: 233, 236).

19. According to Leonard's letter, both he and Virginia were responsible for editing *Can I Help You?* (L. Woolf 1925–37). Virginia also worked, not without complaint, on index and proofs (*L* 3: 251, 245). Leonard and Press manager Dorothy Lang, however, made formatting decisions (L. Woolf 1925–37: 8 June 1937).

20. Among the names in the box are playwright and novelist Clemence Dane (Winifred Ashton) (1888–1965), actress Edith Evans (1998–1976), dancer Isadora Duncan (1877–1927), and British Minister of War, the seventeenth Early of Derby (1865–1948) (Tree 1927–38: 29 August 1927).

21. La Trobe, however, subjects ladies and manors to a humbling, levelling principle: *'we're all the same',* all merely *'orts, scraps and fragments'* trying to build *'the great wall'* of *'civilization'* (*BTA*: 187–8).

22. In 1927, Woolf attended a gathering at Lady Colefax's at which Tree 'acted' as part of the entertainment (*L* 3: 318).

23. Tree gave the Press, via its manager, permission to take out the italics if the printers did not want to do them. The italicised comments remained (Tree 1927–38: 2 August 1937).

24. Woolf displays a comparable kind of wit later in *Between the Acts* when La Trobe's parodic Restoration drama includes 'Lady Harpy Harraden', 'Sir Spaniel Lilyliver', and 'Sir Smirking Peace-be-with-you-all, a clergyman' (125–6).

25. Both the young and the adult Virginia were known for social infelicities. There was, for instance, Lady Strachey's visit to Virginia Stephen at Fitzroy Square during which Hans the dog 'made a mess on the hearthrug' and neither woman mentioned it (Grant 1995: 136). There was both Woolfs' embarrassed late entrance in their printing clothes for a formal dinner party Rose Macaulay gave in 1926 (Bell 2: 120–1; *L* 3: 251).

26. Woolf wonders if Tree 'undermined that castle, with late hours; drink?' but admits she does not know (*D* 5: 187).
27. Paraphrased from draft order form (Hogarth)
28. Paraphrased from draft order form (Hogarth).

Bibliography

Adolph, A. (2005), 'Luncheon at "The Leaning Tower": Consumption and Class in Virginia Woolf's *Between the Acts*', *Women's Studies*, 34: 439–59.

Bell, Q. (1973), *Virginia Woolf: A Biography*, 2 vols, London: Hogarth Press.

Birrell, F. (1926), Review of Viola Tree's *Castles in the Air*, *Nation and Athenaeum*, 39, 29 May: 212.

Blain, V., P. Clements, and I. Grundy (1990), *The Feminist Companion to Literature in English: Women Writers from the Middle Ages to the Present*, New Haven, CT: Yale University Press.

Dwan, D. (2008), 'Woolf, Scepticism and Manners', *Textual Practice*, 22(2): 249–68.

Fernald, A. E. (1994), 'Class Distinctions', *Virginia Woolf Miscellany*, 42, Spring: 3.

Gillespie, D. F. (2003), 'Virginia Woolf, the Hogarth Press, and the Detective Novel', *The South Carolina Review*, 35(2): 36–48.

Gillespie, D. F. (2010), '"Woolfs" in Sheep's Clothing: The Hogarth Press and "Religion"', in *Leonard and Virginia Woolf: The Hogarth Press and the Networks of Modernism*, ed. H. Southworth, Edinburgh: Edinburgh University Press, pp. 74–99.

Gillespie, D. F. (2012), '"Please Help Me!": Virginia Woolf, Viola Tree, and the Hogarth Press', in *Contradictory Woolf: Selected Papers from the Twenty-First Annual International Conference on Virginia Woolf,* ed. D. Ryan and S. Bolaki, Clemson: Clemson University Digital Press, pp. 173–80.

Gillespie, D. F. (2013), 'Wedding Rituals: Julia Strachey, Virginia Woolf, and Viola Tree', *Woolf Studies Annual*, 19: 171–93.

Gordon, E. W. (2009), *Woolfs'-head Publishing: The Highlights and New Lights of the Hogarth Press*, Edmonton: University of Alberta Libraries.

Grant, D. (1995), 'Virginia Stephen', in *Virginia Woolf: Interviews and Recollections,* ed. J. Stape, Iowa City: University of Iowa Press, pp. 135–9.

Hogarth Press Archive, Reading: University of Reading, Special Collections Service.

Johnston, G. (1997), 'Class Performance in *Between the Acts:* Audiences for Miss La Trobe and Mrs Manresa', *Woolf Studies Annual*, 3: 61–75.

Library of Leonard and Virginia Woolf, Pullman: Washington State University, Manuscripts, Archives and Special Collections.

Marder, H. (1989), *The Measure of Life: Virginia Woolf's Last Years*, Ithaca, NY: Cornell University Press.

Minow-Pinkney, M. (2010), 'Virginia Woolf and Entertaining', in *The Edinburgh Companion to Virginia Woolf and the Arts*, ed. M. Humm, Edinburgh: Edinburgh University Press, pp. 227–44.

Porter, D. (2004), *Virginia Woolf and the Hogarth Press: Riding a Great Horse*, London: Cecil Woolf.

Review of Viola Tree's *Castles in the Air* (1926a), *Times Literary Supplement*, 29 April: 314.

Review of Viola Tree's *Castles in the Air* (1926b), *New Statesman*, 27, 29 May: 171.

Review of Viola Tree's *Castles in the Air* (1926c), *Saturday Review of Literature*, 3, 2 October: 159.

Rosenfeld, N. (2001), 'Links into Fences: The Subtext of Class Division in *Mrs Dalloway*', *Literature Interpretation Theory*, 9: 139–60.

Rudikoff, S. (1999), *Ancestral Houses: Virginia Woolf and the Aristocracy*, Palo Alto: Society for the Promotion of Science and Scholarship.

Sackville-West, V. (1985), *The Letters of Vita Sackville-West to Virginia Woolf*, ed. L. DeSalvo and M. A. Leaska, New York: William Morrow.

Sackville-West, V. (1992), *Vita and Harold: The Letters of Vita Sackville-West and Harold Nicolson*, ed. N. Nicolson, New York: G. P. Putnam's Sons.

Schröder, L. K. (2006), '"The Lovely Wreckage of the Past": Virginia Woolf and the English Country House', *English*, 55: 255–80.

Simpson, K. (2008), *Gifts, Markets and Economies of Desire in Virginia Woolf*, Basingstoke: Palgrave Macmillan.

Southworth, H., ed. (2010), *Leonard and Virginia Woolf: The Hogarth Press and the Networks of Modernism*, Edinburgh: Edinburgh University Press.

Tree, H. B. (1913), 'Our Betters: A Medley of Considered Indiscretions', in *Thoughts and After-Thoughts,* London: Cassell, pp. 3–35.

Tree, V. (1926), *Castles in the Air: A Story of My Singing Days*, London: Hogarth Press; New York: George H. Doran.

Tree, V. (1927–38), Letters, Hogarth Press Archive, Reading: University of Reading, Special Collections Service.

Tree, V. (1937), *Can I Help You? Your Manners—Menus—Amusements—Friends—Charades—Make-Ups—Travel—Calling—Children—Love Affairs*, London: Hogarth Press.

Wildeblood, J. and P. Brinson (1965), *The Polite World: A Guide to English Manners and Deportment from the Thirteenth to the Nineteenth Century*, London: Oxford University Press.

Willis, J. H. (1992), *Leonard and Virginia Woolf as Publishers: The Hogarth Press 1917–41*, Charlottesville: University of Virginia Press.

Woolf, L. (1925–37), Letters, Hogarth Press Archive, Reading: University of Reading, Special Collections Service.

Woolf, V. [1929] (1957), *A Room of One's Own,* New York: Harcourt Brace Jovanovich.

Woolf, V. [1938] (1966), *Three Guineas,* New York: Harcourt Brace Jovanovich.

Woolf, V. [1941] (1969), *Between the Acts,* San Diego: Harcourt Brace Jovanovich.

Woolf, V. (1974–84), *The Diary of Virginia Woolf,* 5 vols, ed. A. O. Bell and A. McNeillie, New York and London: Harcourt Brace Jovanovich.

Woolf, V. (1975–80), *The Letters of Virginia Woolf,* 6 vols, ed. N. Nicolson and J. Trautmann, New York and London: Harcourt Brace Jovanovich.

Woolf, V. (1985), *Moments of Being: Unpublished Autobiographical Writings*, 2nd edn, ed. J. Schulkind, San Diego, New York, and London: Harcourt Brace Jovanovich.

Woolf, V. (1986–2010), *The Essays of Virginia Woolf*, 6 vols, ed. A. McNeillie (vols 1–4) and S. N. Clarke (vols 5–6), London: Hogarth Press.

Woolf, V. [1927] (1989), *To the Lighthouse*, San Diego: Harvest/Harcourt Brace Jovanovich.

Zwerdling, A. (1986), *Virginia Woolf and the Real World*, Berkeley: University of California Press.

Chapter 4

Bilinguals and Bioptics: Virginia Woolf and the Outlandishness of Translation[1]

Claire Davison

Richard Dalloway is aboard the *Euphrosyne*, a cargo boat carrying 'dry goods to the Amazons' (*VO*: 38), when he adds an intriguing insert to a letter his wife is writing:

> R. D. *loquitur*: Clarice has omitted to tell you that she looked exceedingly pretty at dinner, and made a conquest by which she has bound herself to learn the Greek alphabet. I will take this occasion of adding that we are both enjoying ourselves in these outlandish parts, and only wish for the presence of our friends (yourself and John, to wit) to make the trip perfectly enjoyable. (*VO*: 52)

It is not rare to find Woolf's texts gesturing to the 'outlandish', but while the early-twentieth-century idiom tended merely to denote anything strange, uncivilised or exotically foreign, Woolf's usage always points to something more misleading or paradoxical. What and where are 'these outlandish parts' that Dalloway refers to? Does he very literally mean that to be at sea is 'outlandish'? Should we understand that anywhere outside of England is outlandish to the proper Tory traveller, inspiring sententious national complacency? Or is he merely extending his wife's imagery to confirm that outlandishness is the key feature of the whole bunch of eccentric countrymen playing out their roles on board ship? The entire, very perplexing chapter points to all these connotations, as well as many others. Whatever the case, Dalloway's marginalia themselves perform outlandishness by playing with foreign allusions and coded languages – French, Latin, Greek, deflected euphemisms of seduction and gallant niceties of the *beau monde* – within the epistolary conventions of a letter that may well never reach its destination. Etymology hardly helps to elucidate his meaning. The *Shorter Oxford English Dictionary* notes that the adjective derives from 'outland', a noun now limited to archaic or regional usage, formerly a common word of good English stock designating either outlying lands on feudal domains left for tenants to work, or alien peoples and unknown tongues. Its signifying potential lingers on today in the adjective 'outlandish', but its geographical anchorage is all but effaced.[2]

This archaic outland, however, has immense poetic and political potential, conjuring up unknown regions off familiar maps of nations and dominions, where the boundaries dividing domestic from alien are highly tenuous, which is certainly apt for the whole narrative project of *The Voyage Out* and beyond. The outland evokes a sense of freedom by releasing the mind from conventions and frontiers, while also hinting at lurking danger or transgression. Since its roots are in the land, it conjures up images of tilled soil and harvests harking back to times immemorial before territory was taken over by geopolitics. Its linguistic ramifications suggest insights into the dynamics of land and language that problematise the relations between mother tongue and fatherland, nation and nativity. It proves particularly operative as a means to explore Woolf's reading of literatures in translation, and in particular what, for the reading public of the turn of the century, was the quintessentially outlandish literature of Russia.

What I aim to explore here are Woolf's experiments in thinking 'outlandishly' across borders, languages, and translations, all of which prove startlingly timely within contemporary philosophical approaches to translation's transformative, performative potential, and with an affective spatiality of its own. A number of recent critics have faulted the ethnocentric impulse behind her readings of foreign literatures,[3] explored foreign literary influences in her works, or traced new foreign dynamics inspired by her reception abroad, which in each case work within what are essentially national spaces and identities. By contrast, I would like to look at how she reads foreign literatures encountered outside their native literary and linguistic territory. Whether engaging in translation conceptually, metaphorically or literally, we find Woolf working from a sense of *dislocation*[4] – an outland[5] or landscape gradually revealed to the mind that is neither homely and familiar, nor closed, alien, and unknowable. It is somewhere in between, where boundaries, identities, and mindsets can be creatively refigured, as the *Euphrosyne*'s passengers sense as they sail in uncharted waters: 'They all dreamt of each other that night, as was natural, considering how thin the partitions were between them, and how strangely they had been lifted off the earth to sit next to each other in mid-ocean' (*VO*: 53).

An overwhelming sense of contradictoriness appealing for resolution is what first strikes the reader engaging with Woolf's understanding and practice of translation. At first glance, she appears more convinced by its shortcomings than its creative potential. An entry from her 1918 diary notes 'the immeasurable difference between the text & the translation' (*D* 1: 184). In 'The Perfect Language' she willingly acknowledges that 'we have owned so much indebtedness to translators' but affirms that 'some knowledge of the language is a possession not to be done without' (*E* 2: 118) so as to counteract 'the necessarily coarse medium of a translation' ('Tchekov's Questions', E 2: 247). Meanwhile, a surfeit of readings in translation prompts a desire for the more familiar comforts of home, or at least homespun outlandishness:

> After all, our long and forced diet upon Russian fiction skinned in translation of its style and thus made negative and neutral should not lead us to forget that the English character is often eccentric and the English language often exuberant. ('The Novels of George Meredith', E 4: 533)

Nor are such ambivalent assessments limited to translations from Russian. In 'Phases of Fiction', the weariness attributed to reading Dostoevsky prompts her to abandon not more Russians but the French satirists, in favour of native English authors (*E* 5: 72). And French too would appear fully accessible neither within nor outside translation:

> One scarcely dare say it but it is true – nobody knows French but the French themselves. Every second Englishman reads French, and many speak it, and some may write it, and there are a few who claim – and who shall deny them? – that it is the language of their dreams. But to know a language one must have forgotten it, and that is a stage that one cannot reach without having absorbed words unconsciously as a child. ('On Not Knowing French', E 5: 3)

'The Russian Point of View' is the essay most commonly taken to encapsulate Woolf's conception of translation, working from the arresting image of 'mutilation' like a Babelian curse condemning translation to approximation and distortion:

> What we are saying amounts to this, then, that we have judged a whole literature stripped of its style . . . Thus treated, the great Russian writers are like men deprived . . . of all their clothes . . . but it is difficult to feel sure, in view of these *mutilations,* how far we can trust ourselves not to impute, to distort, to read into them an emphasis which is false. (E 4: 182; my italics)

No matter how violent and eminently quotable the 'stripped and mutilated' metaphor may be, however, it is surely a mistake to take it as Woolf's last word. Not only does it come at the beginning of the essay, where Woolf's wilfully misleading assertions tend to cluster, but the essay was written specifically for *The Common Reader,* the formal method of which relies on a 'surface manner' not to be taken at face value.[6] As the closing essay artfully remarks, 'it is just when opinions universally prevail and we have added lip service to their authority that we become sometimes most keenly conscious that we do not believe a word that we are saying' (*E* 4: 237). On closer scrutiny, 'The Russian Point of View' turns out to be a minefield masquerading as refined table talk. As I have argued elsewhere,[7] there is little that is not recycled cliché or conventionalism before the final two paragraphs: the conventional tea-table tone (complete with garrulous but entirely unreliable 'we'); the cameo portraits of the Russians and Russian literature drawing on all the stereotypes in circulation since the late 1890s; and the form–content binary left over from classical rhetoric. Even the supposed entropic effect of translation was a commonplace, bolstering the general presumption that native languages and domestic literatures were inevitably richer, purer, than foreign imports.

Woolf's essay, however, deftly sidesteps such 'niceties', even while paying lip service to them, changing viewpoint to reveal a finer understanding of each author which confirms that translation *works*: 'Even in a translation we feel that we have been set on a mountain-top and had a telescope put into our hands. Everything is astonishingly clear and absolutely sharp' (*E* 4: 188). The telescope itself is another conventionalism and the trope was popularised by the French critic Melchior de Vogüé when explaining Tolstoy's narrative art in terms of the cultural differences between East and West:[8]

> Imagine the Latin and the Slav before a telescope; the former uses the instrument to home in, meaning that he deliberately reduces his field of vision to see things smaller and more clearly; the latter deploys the full power of the lenses, broadens the horizon and sees things blurred, but further off. (1987: 295)[9]

Woolf's usage is rather different. While de Vogüé looks through Tolstoy's telescope to see Russian landscapes, Woolf has Tolstoy turn the telescope on us, so that we 'wish to escape from the gaze Tolstoy fixes on us' (*E* 4: 189). The difference is huge. De Vogüé upholds the tradition of taking the literary text and its translation as a transparent lens to be seen through, reading literature for its ethnographic value; Woolf creates a transformative, bioptical effect. Her Russian point of view through Tolstoy's telescope is entirely reflexive: it looks at what 'we' see of a literature recently brought to the attention of an enthusiastic British public, but also wonders what the Russians see, and what they see of us. We are left with a dazzling reciprocal gaze of two subjects catching each other in the act of looking, and seeing through each other's eyes, no longer knowing who is the foreigner and who the native. It is hardly surprising that the bewildered mind finally concludes that home ('the place of its birth') might be a safer source of truth.

The subtle reversal doubtless comes too late in the essay for it to be entirely convincing, and we have to turn to an earlier essay, Woolf's

'The Perfect Language' (1917), even if its immediate concern is Greek rather than Russian, to find more explicit insights into her lifelong interest in languages in translation, explicitly transcending the meretricious 'us–them' binaries that overshadow the originality of 'The Russian Point of View'. The ideal method for engaging in foreign texts, she affirms here, is to encounter the foreign script side by side with a crib, so that in the space between the two, a 'spirited version', comes into being that dances off the foreign words and sends off new sparks of understanding and unexpected perspectives ('The Perfect Language' *E* 2: 115). This intuitive sense of a dynamic interface between languages is timely in aesthetic terms, but positively avant-garde as a concept, conjuring up a creative 'space' that is neither written into the original text as some form of essential truth, nor necessarily inscribed or even inscribable in the printed translated text. It comes from words being caught in flight, in flashes of understanding, literally in translation. Woolf's figure of the reader-translator as acrobat, 'flying through space from bar to bar' (115), is not just bridging two worlds separated by language, space, or time, but actually experiencing the thrill of letting go (of the trapeze, of certitudes, of native mastery), being held in the air, experiencing 'a queer feeling that the solid ground upon which we expected to make a safe landing has been twitched from under us, and there we hang asking questions in mid air' ('Tchekov's Questions', *E* 2: 245). The figure is an astonishing harbinger of much new-millennial third-space thinking. More specifically, it evokes French philosopher Heinz Wismann's 'Luftmensch' – 'a walker in the air, weightless, rootless, a magnificent Yiddish term that's hard to translate', held 'in the in-between of languages' (Wismann 2012: 45, 89). As Wismann explains:

> Reflexivity is the place where movement is realised . . . I am at a certain distance, like the 'Luftmensch' suspended somewhere in the air, and who above all is not afraid of falling. This is what I call confidence. Being modern and ancient at the same time, being both at home and not at home, being both reassured and anxious . . . I've tried to express it, but the words are hard to find. It's an in-between which is nothing like indecision; it's simply the way to refuse to be assimilated by one side or to be totally enthralled by it. (2012: 45)

This is the creative in-betweenness, the literal and metaphorical 'outlandishness', that 'The Russian Point of View' only hints at tantalisingly, and that 'On Not Knowing Greek' also intuits:

> It is necessary to take that dangerous leap through the air without the support of words which Shakespeare also asks of us . . . Connecting them in a rapid flight of the mind we know instantly and instinctively what they mean, but could not decant that meaning afresh into any other words. (*E* 4: 44)

Clearly, the thrill inspired by the acrobatic feat does not depend on reading unknown literatures from 'outlandish parts', such as Russian, Ancient Greek, or Shakespearean English. Contemporary French fiction inspires the same feeling:

> But the word poetry reminds us of our precarious foothold in these parts. Just as one is secretly persuaded that no Frenchman, Russian, German, has the instinct for English poetry in him – he can acquire everything but that – so confidence fails us when we try our wings in this particular form of flight. ('On Not Knowing French', *E* 5: 6)

An awareness of what happens in between languages, in translating, rather than just in the translated text as a final product, constantly works its way into Woolf's thinking, whether readers are translating for them-selves, or engaged in reading others' translations. 'Phases of Fiction', for example, makes play of 'that little fillip which we get from reading a language whose edges have not been smoothed for us by daily use', while native language becomes hackneyed by over-use: 'As for English, alas, it is *our* language – shop-worn, not so desirable, perhaps' (*E* 5: 45). Again, Woolf is conceptualising translation reflexively, not just focusing on what foreign literatures lose when translated, but also on what English lacks if approached monolingually: 'Habit has made English – the ordi-nary daily English of which most books are made – as colourless, as tasteless as water' ('On Not Knowing French', *E* 5: 4). The same reflexive movement, troubling the boundaries of native dominion and foreign otherness, allows her to envisage a space for feeling foreignness from the inside, and reading 'foreignly': 'And if it is a delight to have a change of scene, it is also a delight to have a change of tongue.' Further,

> a curious word, unknown and therefore uncoloured by habit, emerges, so that we can feel it and see it apart from the text, and wonder for a moment what sort of meaning we shall fill it with when we have looked it up in the dictionary. (*E* 5: 4)

She willingly concedes that such an 'outlanded' reader may hear echoes in the text that a native reader would dismiss or deny, but still affirms the aesthetic validity of such a reading, even implying that the native reader might learn from it (taking a stab in passing at the presump-tuousness of those English intellectuals who claimed to read French like natives). The space she stakes out for reading as an impure bilin-gual, or between text and crib, is of course perfectly consonant with the overall project of *The Common Reader,* defending the outsider's, non-specialist's, daring but modest approach over a specialist's over-confident mastery, and championing the specific literary and poetic resources available to non-natives when the senses and not the mind are most fully alert:

> the words give out their scent and distil their flavour, and then, if at last we grasp the meaning, it is all the richer for having come to us sensually first, by way of the palate and the nostrils, like some queer odour. Foreigners, to whom the tongue is strange, have us at a disadvantage. The Chinese must know the sound of Antony and Cleopatra better than we do. ('On Being Ill', *E* 5: 202)

A sense of feeling one's way or looking anew through the prism of translation is a recurrent motif in Woolf's essays, notebooks, letters and reviews (and of course her fiction) showing her thinking via translation, double language codes and forms of imperfect bilingualism rather than merely writing about translation.[10] It is never a transparent window but a transformative lens, with a contextual anchoring too. The most salient example is her reading of the Russians. After all, it was not the discovery of Russian fiction per se that fuelled the 'Russian fever' that took hold of the Georgian generation, but a rediscovery of Russian in English. The late Victorians, Edwardians, and most of Woolf's generation first discovered Russian literature in French (a more familiar foreign language) or in English versions retranslated from French. The shock of rediscovering the Russians rendered directly into English was certain. Here were familiar narratives, but slightly off-key, where the accent could fall differently, as Woolf so often remarks. *Crime et châtiment* translated by Dérely, for example, reads very differently from Constance Garnett's *Crime and Punishment*, creating a new voice that was reminiscent of, but not identical to, French; nor was it wholly consonant with English (contributing to the sense of strange familiarity that Woolf constantly alights on). This again creates what I am calling an outlanded voice, belonging to no national tradition, despite having clear family resemblances with French naturalism and the Victorian novel (which Dostoevsky had read in French). Garnett's translations also revealed passages that the French translators, for reasons of stylistic embellishment, formal elegance or publishers' pragmatism, had deleted. The second epilogue to *War and Peace,* for example, was omitted from the first French translation, on the grounds that it shattered the formal balance and introduced a new, essayist's voice that jarred with the harmonious family narrative. De Vogüé had his word to say on this matter too: 'The appendices were not translated into French, and so much the better; no reader could have put up with their wearisome pointlessness' (1987: 315).

More percipient for my present purposes, the new English translations could uncover a different sense of the Russian language that had been hidden from view in French. They literally removed the veil of elegant style that was a prerequisite of the French '*belles infidèles*' tradition still very much in vogue in the late nineteenth century, which used the translated text to celebrate the grace and splendours (and the civilising mission) of French. A second feature that is unveiled in the English, but which was inevitably occluded in French, was all that had been written in French in the original. For most nineteenth-century Russian writers, French was an 'outlanded' language spoken by the alienated upper classes: not a native, mother tongue but an adopted one, spoken alongside, and often in preference to, native Russian, partly as euphemism, partly as conceit, and partly because they mastered it better. This outlanded tongue and the double-level code-switching had disappeared in French translation, but it resurfaces in English translation. The difference can be seen instantly from a single example from *The Possessed*:

> Il n'est pas fou, mais c'est un homme à idées courtes, – répondit-il avec une sorte d'ennui. Ces gens-là supposent la nature et la société humaine autres que Dieu ne les a faites, et qu'elles ne sont réellement. On coquette avec eux, mais du moins ce n'est pas Stépan Trophimovitch. Je les ai vus dans le temps à Pétersbourg, avec cette chère amie (oh! combien je l'ai offensée alors!), et je n'ai pas peur ni de leurs injures, ni même de leurs éloges. Je ne les crains pas davantage maintenant, mais parlons d'autre chose. (Dostoïevski 1886: 120)
>
> 'He's not mad, but one of those shallow-minded people,' he mumbled listlessly. *Ces gens-là supposent la nature et la société humaine autres que Dieu ne les a faites et qu'elles ne sont réellement.* People try to make up to them, but Stepan Verhovensky does not, anyway. I saw them that time in Petersburg *avec cette chère amie* (oh, how I used to wound her then), and I wasn't afraid of their abuse or even their praise. I'm not afraid now either. *Mais parlons d'autre chose.* (Dostoevsky 1913: 121)

The imperfectly bilingual code-switching is as much a sociopolitical marker as a source of grotesque and near-slapstick comic effects. They are an intrinsic part of Stepan Trofomovitch's preposterous snobbery, for example, or what Woolf's reading notes describe as his 'mystical rant' (Rubenstein 2009: 168) in *The Possessed*, or the pathos of the landed gentry's cultural and affective alienation in Turgenev, further details that Woolf picks up on in her reading notes: '"how the French ridicule R[ussian]n French. T[urgenev]'s sensitiveness: a man always living abroad – uneasy"' (Rubenstein 2009: 218).[11]

Woolf and her generation, in other words, were often *rereading* the Russians, seeing them anew, as if through new optical devices, or hearing them through new sound filters. Neither the French nor the English translation was the *right version*, and neither could claim to be the perfect equivalent of the Russian, but they were echoes,[12] best heard alternately, or in alternative visions, best seen side by side, rather like the bifocals and colour-filters that Tolstoy recommends the writer to wear in *Talks with Tolstoy*, a text Woolf aptly discovered through co-translation:

> One has to behave like Pokhitonov who has spectacles with double glasses divided in two (looking at the distance and at his work), to look now through these and now through those, and to put on now the bright and now the dark glasses. (Woolf and Koteliansky 2006: 267)

It is more than likely, but impossible to affirm, that such bioptical reread-ings of the Russians sensitised the modernist generation to the determin-ing role played by the translator and the transformative potential of translations. It invites a different reading, at any rate, of some of Woolf's more double-edged observations on translation. Reading Proust, for example, when Woolf abandoned the French version in favour of the Moncrieff translation, she observes in her reading notes that 'If you want to see what style is, it is best to read a translation' (Dalgarno 2011: 107–8). Whatever the case, Woolf's heightened sense of a translator's impact on the text being translated confirms that translation was not a transparent window to be looked through, but a complex picture to be looked at with an expressive power of its own. This is surely one of the reasons that drew Woolf and so many of her compeers to engage in co-translations with Koteliansky in the early 1920s. Referring to a dinner party exchange with Charles Sanger, her diary notes:

> Charlie not very encouraging about Russian – at least he says the literature is scarcely worth the trouble. Nothing but the great novels, & these adequately translated. But I doubt whether any English pupil can judge of this. A person with my taste shut up in a library might unearth treasures. Anyhow this is provision for old age. Also we talk of Russia next year – also language helps one to understand writers atmosphere, like seeing their country. (*D* 2: 99)

Co-translation was very literally a case, not of playing the foreign and the domestic off against each other as binary opposites, but 'thinking between foreignnesses' in a cross-boundary leap where both make sense together. The inevitable 'self-disidentification' that this entails (con-tinuing to speak in the first person, but speaking in part for or through another source speaker, willingly giving up native ease to sense how it feels to be partially outside a language) is exactly where Wismann sees binary thought giving way to co-produced, reflexive thinking:

> If you are in a single cultural or linguistic environment, and rely only on that, the relation you have with other worlds – whose interest, wealth and appeal you may acknowledge – is inevitably of a different nature altogether. It is merely alterity confronted with something that is the self or the same.

Whereas as soon as you move 'between', there are two alterities, since the origin becomes other too. (2012: 39)

However short-lived her co-translating experience was (and rare diary entries and archived letters certainly suggest that Woolf soon tired of the fastidious demands her co-translator made of her),[13] her Russian engagements meant touching on the material strangeness and changing familiarity of language: its touch, feel, sound, and unexpected echoes. Although for a long time, critics sidelined the co-translations when assessing Woolf's work on the grounds that she knew little or no Russian herself (a choice that has fortunately changed radically over the past decade), it is clear that 'not knowing Russian' (Rubenstein 2009: 10) was not a handicap but a strength. It meant the co-translating partner had to liaise with another reader and listen, explore, negotiate meaning, and witness the minor miracles that occur when unknown patterns of sound and an all but hermetic script suddenly converge to reveal half-familiar flashes of understanding. It could work as a bridge to one of the essential, contrapuntal forms of modernity, playing, writing, speaking, both alongside and via the intermediary of other voices, in a creative space, part personal, part impersonal, that could only be attained by means of a fellow partner's coevally imperfect mastery. A comparison of Woolf's co-translations and various others signed or co-signed by Koteliansky reveals a network of rich and tangible signs that bear her imprint, suggesting a genetic permeability or reflexive interface where the minute, stylistic craftsmanship required of the co-translators/co-editors could be fuelled with creative literary energies, while also feeding back into the writer's own experimental poetics.[14] Again, it is the creative space conceptualised by Wismann: 'The space that you see emerging between languages is not essentially a line of transmission where traditions communicate, but a strange space, where the confrontation of two languages engenders another, irreducible third one: a rec-reative space' (2012: 103).

Recent critics have pointed to thematic overlaps that can been discerned by reading Woolf's co-translations alongside her own works: Furman (2009) traces a path from 'Stavrogin's Confession' (Dostoevsky) to *Mrs Dalloway*; and Reinhold (2005) points to passages retained for the Hogarth translation of Goldenveizer's diary (*Vblizi Tol'stovo*, literally *Close to Tolstoy*) that suggest Woolf's personal preferences, such as Tolstoy's thoughts on university education, brain work, madness, the art of music, the moment, and the significance of artistic form. Other rich interfaces can be identified in the same source texts by focusing less on specific thematic appeals, however, and more on what was happening stylistically or co-editorially for example. To start with the Tolstoy memoirs, Woolf and Koteliansky's co-translation is half the length of Goldenveizer's 350-page diary (January 1896–December 1909), which meant their selection criteria had to be quite ruthless. In Beasley's words, 'Kotelianskii and Woolf retain most of Gol'denveizer's quotations from Tolstoi, and they excise almost everything else, including Gol'denveizer's own reflections on his relationship with Tolstoi, and descriptions of Tolstoi's family and acquaintances' (2013: 17). Reinhold observes more succinctly that the condensed English translation 'leaves the reader under the impression that Woolf thought it very important to get straight from the horse's mouth what Tolstoy thought about arts, and modern art in particular' (2005: 240). But reading their translation side by side with Goldenveizer's Russian text also reveals a specific image of Tolstoy that the co-translators are crafting, as they scale down the original text and pick out a representative selection of extracts.

Certainly, their method involves writing out much of Goldenveizer's own life, as well as omitting the historical background of both Tolstoy's youth and the years when Goldenveizer was writing. At the same time, there is no apparent effort to favour only artistic or intellectual pursuits. Passages on Voltaire, Thoreau, Coleridge, the philosophy of music, the meaning of happiness, and contemporary governments disappear, but we find out how Tolstoy prefers taking his breakfast, how he mistakenly ate worms rather than fishing with them, and how his wife woke him up by sneezing (Woolf and Koteliansky 2006: 195, 248, 249). Nor is there any apparent will to direct the diary towards what is culturally appealing: English, American, German, and French cultural or political references with which an Anglophone readership would easily feel at home often disappear, as do materials liable to pander to quaint, contrived, anglicised visions of Russia. The reader will not find Goldenveizer's depictions of 'the moon and the group round the samovar, the voices and the flowers and the warmth of the garden' (*E* 3: 316) of which there are many, or his soulful, twilit performances of Chopin nocturnes, or the endless chess games (700, according to the 1959 Soviet edition [Gol'denveizer 1959]), or an encounter with a wolf, all of which would have found an easy audience eager to engage with Russian clichés.[15] This abbreviated translation reduces the diary's scope as a historical or ethnographical document, and dissolves its thematic unity and linear development, but it accentuates the timeless, aphoristic quality, making it far more modern in the sense defined in 'How it Strikes a Contemporary': random, fragmented, 'snatched from life but not transmuted into literature' (*E* 4: 238). Goldenveizer, for instance, is increasingly concerned by the failing health of his mentor, and apprehends the moment of his death, making detailed notes on Tolstoy's own concerns for his weakness, his recurrent bouts of memory loss, and his regrets for the books he will never write. Woolf and Koteliansky's diary records only one moment of illness, and it focuses instead on Tolstoy's vigour and his seemingly unquenchable thirst for knowledge. To quote but one example: 1909, the last year of their diary, consists of just two entries taking up thirty lines. The first records Tolstoy's sudden recollection of an old nurse, followed by reflections about how he works best (after playing patience, not listening to music); the second, the closing note of the volume, is a brief note from 24 May, aphoristically capturing Tolstoy's thoughts on Goethe:

> It is amazing! So far back as 1824 Goethe wrote that sincerity was become almost impossible in art because of the multitude of newspapers, journals and reviews. The artist reads them, involuntarily pays attention to them and cannot be perfectly sincere. What would he say if he lived now! (Woolf and Koteliansky 2006: 290)

Their volume thus concludes on a sparkling note of literary reflection between writers. Goldenveizer's is rather different. His record of the year 1909 is the longest section in the diary – more than sixty pages. It is also the most lengthily narrativised, the most elaborate in terms of Tolstoy's religious and philosophical teaching and his most recent writing. It gives detailed coverage of Tolstoy's growing friendship with Chertkov and Mechnikov (267–90; 319–24); his thoughts on spiritual and moral life and the quest for happiness (294–8); the evils of modern times and the meaning of scientific knowledge, the planets and the universe (280–8; 307–9); and his preoccupation with age and death (298–301; 306). It documents the immense fame Tolstoy had by then acquired, with frequent references to visiting journalists, photographers and even French filmmakers (268–9; 295–6; 317–19). Between such heightened moments of grandeur, and the increasingly tender farewells, which Tolstoy acknowledges might be their last (314; 319–24), the volume inspires a growing feeling of pathos, and a sense of a great destiny (Gol'denveizer 1959).

By contrast, Woolf and Koteliansky's Tolstoy remains human-dimensioned, ageless, quirky and accessible, suggesting a deliberate intention not to do honour to the great man, or to carve a monument, but merely to capture a vibrant sense of a life being lived. They offer us a Tolstoy in keeping with their times, appealing to

> those senses which are stimulated so briskly by the moderns; the senses of sight, of sound, of touch – above all, the sense of the human being, his depth and the variety of his perceptions, his complexity, his confusion, his self, in short. ('How It Strikes a Contemporary', *E* 4: 239)

However linguistically precise each chosen extract is, the English diary is a translation of an 'outlandish' sort – the translations are creative recastings taking Tolstoy out of his Russian culture and context, but not to the extent of making either an exotic foreigner or an honorary Englishman of him. This perhaps explains the vivid impact that the diary could still have on Woolf eighteen years later, resuming her Russian readings for an essay on Tolstoy (that would never be written):

> Always the same reality – like touching an exposed electric wire. Even so imperfectly conveyed – his rugged short-cut mind – to me the most, not sympathetic, but inspiring, rousing; genius in the raw. Thus more disturbing, more 'shocking', more of a thunderclap, even on art, even on lit.re than any other writer. I remember that was my feeling about W&P. (*D* 5: 273)

Again, we find translation cutting through protective outer layers, and galvanising the senses: yet another eloquent proof of its performative potential.

Woolf's co-translation of Dostoevsky's 'Stavrogin's Confession' can illustrate different forms of 'thinking through languages', showing how her earlier 'Russian fever' could be transformed into something 'inestimably decisive, transformative and enduring' (Rubenstein 2009: 162). The censored chapters from *The Possessed* form the crux of the novel, staging the moral-philosophical founding of the plot and revealing Dostoevsky's 'true genius' for sounding out human psychology, 'when he turns to explore aberrant extremes, and intuits the deep human significance of what looks like madness' (Frank 2009: 216). This direct contact with Dostoevsky's consummate art of psychology via co-translation then re-emerges in later essays, notably: 'The Narrow Bridge of Art': 'With all the suppleness of a tool which is in constant use, [prose] can follow the windings and record the changes which are typical of the modern mind. To this, with Proust and Dostoevsky behind us, we must agree' (*E* 4: 436). This in turn paves the way to 'Phases of Fiction':

> But when we have arranged our perspective a little, it is clear that we are still in the same world – that it is the mind which entices us and the adventures of the mind that concern us . . . There is a simplicity in violence which we find nowhere in Proust, but violence also lays bare regions deep down in the mind where contradiction prevails. (*E* 4: 68)

Nowhere in the novel, other than in the censored chapters, are the dramas of Stavrogin's inner mind played out. Woolf's insights as an essayist are therefore drawing directly on her experience of having been 'in translation', in the dialogic labyrinths of Dostoevsky's prose, speaking as and speaking on behalf of the tormented mind that had been silenced for fifty years.

But there is more to it than this. As naturally as 'Phases of Fiction' may appear to alight on James, Proust and Dostoevsky to illustrate 'The Psychologists', their association is in fact thoroughly unexpected in the idiom of the times. The poised, finely crafted aestheticism of Proust and James was a very far cry from the popular image of Dostoevsky novels as 'seething whirlpools', their complex artistry hardly being noted by Anglophone critics before the 1970s. Woolf's originality here lies in the way she does not so much read a foreign literature in parallel with English fiction (in a more domesticating or familiarising dynamic) but observes two foreign literatures – French and Russian – through bifocals which constantly lead her away from, and then back to England. Rather than marking a linear evolution from an ultimate dissatisfaction with Russian literature to more intuitively 'felt' meanderings of Proust (see Dalgarno 2011: 95), this bioptical gaze opens up very comparative readings of literatures in and across translations. Looking through a French–Russian–English optic avoids the foreign–domestic, or self–other binaries that two-way comparisons tend to fall into, and also shows up literary resonances and affiliations that would escape a uniquely national or monolingual approach.[16]

How does this work in practice? Woolf began reading Proust in 1922, after lengthy Russian readings, but the border-crossing, interlingual, and transcultural resonances echo on until 'Anon', passing via *Orlando*, for example, which in so many ways thinks playfully through Tolstoy and Proust.[17] Orlando and Sasha's love affair depends on them both speaking outlanded, outlandish French: 'For heaven be praised, he spoke the tongue as his own; his mother's maid had taught him' (O: 23). The encounter with the Russian princess also teaches Orlando that language, irrevocably forged by time and land, whether mastered, imperfectly known or native, must wander, travel, and elude its users. Their boundary-crossing escapades may be sources of delight, but land and language prove unable to contain them: 'Ransack the language as he might, words failed him. He wanted another landscape, and another tongue' (O: 35). 'Phases of Fiction' works similarly, as Woolf's reading notes on *The Possessed* show: 'They threw themselves into each other's arms – wept – a gap between the emotions – not so closely knit as P[roust]'s'; 'The scene is absurd: violates the commonsense; more than Proust . . . and to spend his time playing preference – unlike Marcel' (Rubenstein 2009: 166, 169).

In fact, nearly all Woolf's comparative essays include curious couplings of French and Russian authors, like deliberate excursions into unexpected spaces: Chekhov and Maupassant; Turgenev and Flaubert; Dostoevsky and Proust; Tolstoy and Balzac, Tolstoy and Flaubert, Tolstoy and Proust. Even the unlikely association of 'Tchekov on

Pope'[18] is compounded by French literature constantly working itself into the sidelines. Seeking new angles of approach to the classics, Woolf toys with reading Pope 'by the light of Tchekhov. It may be Proust; it may be Wells, it may be Tchekhov' (Rubenstein 2009: 176). She sees the insularity of English literature being lit up not 'by the bright star of France but by the cloudy Russian harvest moon' (177), and pinpoints the limits of earlier literary criticism in the days when 'Matthew Arnold had not read Tchekhov he had not read Bernard Shaw he had not read Proust' (188).

Anachronistic, oblique, *outlandish* readings like these, across literary traditions, dislocating the boundaries and sites of foreignness, are metaphorised spatially through changes in focus: 'Under the Russian magnifying glass, . . . its circumference vast, its boundaries fluid, its horizon a welter of the wind and waves' (Rubenstein 2009: 188). And this in turn conjures up a revitalised sense of the land: 'Just as our English fields lose all their hedges and turn to lakes of mist on an autumn morning, so the heart expands under the Russian influence, the features spread, the boundaries disappear' (177). These ramblings across borders meld and so displace England, Russia, and France: 'The French words, in their lucidity, in their intelligence, seem to break through our island mists and to lie before us serene in sunshine' ('On Not Knowing French', *E* 5: 6).

These out-of-place readings show Woolf listening to the voice or playing the part of the foreigner within, but this foreigner is never a threat, an uncanny double, or an exoticised Other, but a figure of belonging in movement, in phases. Likewise, they are not forays into utopic world citizenships, or privileged republics of letters: 'Cosmopolitanism is twaddle', she notes when reading Turgenev's *Rudin*, quoting Lezhnyov (Rubenstein 2009: 210).[19] Her 'outlanded' excursions include a homeward journey, since remaining 'at sea' or up in the air annuls the mutable in-betweenness of being more than one. These returns, however, have the advantage of finding home itself transformed, 'like a house which is miraculously habitable without the help of walls, staircases or partitions' ('Phases of Fiction', *E* 5: 75). They can create a bridge between wanting no country, in its national, patriotic acceptation, yet acknowledging a deep-seated, sensually alert awareness of having been nurtured by the land. In Wismann's words:

> Between languages doesn't mean living in none. To the contrary, possessing one language of origin means you can respond to what it evokes, spontaneously, without even reflecting. And the inadequacies which appear when that language is being used sometimes – as a means to control and therefore to instrumentalise – prompt the desire to recast the language to let it fulfil its promises. (2012: 99)

Woolf's image of moving through languages is more poetical; it starts with more optical devices, and a sense of losing the land:

> A further instinct will lead us to pass over such famous satirists as Voltaire and Anatole France in favour of someone writing in our own tongue, writing English. For without any disrespect to the translator, we have grown intolerably weary in reading Dostoevski, as if we were reading with the wrong spectacles or as if a mist had formed between us and the page. ('Phases of Fiction', *E* 5: 72)

And it is preserved through a sensual alertness that can be found at home, but also in translation. In 'The Cherry Orchard' she writes:

> I do not know how better to describe the sensation at the end of *The Cherry Orchard,* than by saying that it sends one into the street feeling like a piano played upon at last, not in the middle only but all over the keyboard and with the lid left open so that the sound goes on. (*E* 3: 248)

Woolf's 'outlandish' literary voyages remained essential nodes in her poetic and critical thinking, and they point to very tangible ways in which her Russian readings were being transmuted into more lasting creative forms. But they are political engagements too. With national boundaries rising ever more ominously and more defiantly in the 1910s and 1920s, Woolf's outland could resist territorial exclusivity and nationalist hierarchies with its permeable boundaries across which networks and byways between lands and literatures could be drawn. This might explain why, when asked by Sandra Wentworth Williams 'whether he read Greek and whether . . . if he had to sacrifice one it would be the French Literature or the Russian' (*JR*: 199), Jacob decides to read Chekhov, but offers no reply.

Notes

1. This article contains materials taken from my 2014 publication *Translation as Collaboration: Virginia Woolf, Katherine Mansfield and S. S. Koteliansky,* in both condensed and expanded forms. I would like to thank the publishers for permission to re-use these sections.
2. Definitions include:
   '1.   Outlying land: *spec.* (*hist.*) the outer part of an estate, feudal manor, etc., assigned to tenants. OE.
   2.   A foreign land. Arch
   3.   A foreigner, a stranger. *Obsolete* exc. Scot. ME
        (Outlandish, noun) now obsolete, A foreign language'. E17–M18.
        (*Shorter Oxford* 2002: 2037)
3. See Aiello (2003: 665), Kaye (1999: 32), Dalgarno (2011: 7).

4. See, for example, her remarks about the 1920 production of *The Cherry Orchard*: 'the English person who finds himself at dawn in the nursery of Mme Ranevskaia feels out of place'. The review uses the same figure of a 'leap through the air' that will be explored here, a feat which produces 'a sense of dangerous dislocation'. Language too plays out the disquieting sense of space, heard in 'the strange, dislocated sentence' (*E* 2: 246, 247, 248).

5. My thanks to fellow Woolfian, Anne-Marie Smith-Di Biasio, with whom I began exploring this concept. See Smith-Di Biasio (2013).

6. This is Woolf's retrospective assessment (*MOB*: 129). Woolf's 'turn-and-turn-about' technique is splendidly analysed by Melba Cuddy-Keane (2003: 142).

7. See Davison-Pégon 2007; Davison 2012.

8. De Vogüé's *Le roman russe* (1886) was decisive on both sides of the Channel in shaping the reception of the Russian novel and it likewise privileges the mountain-top view: 'he who has not climbed to the top will never know the exact lay-out of the province ... Likewise the foreigner who has not read Tolstoy indulges in self-flattery when he purports to know nineteenth-century Russia' (1987: 294).

9. This and subsequent quotations have been translated from French by the author.

10. Dalgarno's *Virginia Woolf and the Migrations of Language* (2011) explores similar territory, although her 'migrating languages' are more often metaphorical, or already translated.

11. Notes on *The Possessed* are from Reading Notebook 14, Holograph RN1.14. Notes on Turgenev's *Fathers and Children* from Reading Notebook 1, Holograph RN1.1 (Berg Collection; referenced in Rubenstein 2009). These notebooks were first transcribed, annotated, and published in Rubenstein 2009, with notes linking Woolf's comments directly to the Russian source texts. The Turgenev quotation that inspired her comment on the comic snobbery reads: '"that Great Russo-French jargon which the French ridicule so"' (Rubenstein 2009: 218).

12. An extremely unstable image in Benjamin's famous essay, the echo amplifies the original ring rather than palely reproducing it. See his 'The Task of the Translator' (1997: 77).

13. See Beasley (2013), Reinhold (2003; 2005).

14. See Davison (2014).

15. See, for example: the evening spent with the Molokans, 25 January 1898 (Gol'denveizer 1959: 46–7); the reception with friends, 24 February 1901 (82–3); the moonlit evening, 16 September 1901 (98); and the encounter with a wolf, 12 July 1900 (74).

16. Consonant with Wismann's 'thinking in-between' (Wismann 2012: 39–45), a French–Russian–English optic also recalls Benjamin's sense of translation as literature's necessary afterlife but without Benjamin's mystical echoes (Benjamin 1997: 72–3).

17. Although beyond the scope of the present essay, multilingual and cross-dressing games are used by both Tolstoy and Proust to explore transgressive dimensions of love. See, for example, the Mummers' scene in *War and Peace* (Tolstoy 2007: 520–9), and Swann's perception of Odette as a work

of art, where grammatically constructed gender as well as the figure in the painting blur all clear gender binaries (Proust I: 229–31). The same holds for perceptions of the nominally ambiguous loved ones, such as Albertine or Gilberte (Proust II: 122–5; V: 70–3).

18. As unlikely as the coupling may appear, Woolf was not alone in bringing Pope into resonance with Chekhov. See Clutton-Brock's review (1921) of Leonard Woolf and S. S. Koteliansky's translation of Chekhov's notebooks.

19. Turgenev was of course the 'honorary Frenchman' among the Russian authors, as Woolf's reading notes, essays and reference books underline. He was also very much at home in England (Garnett 1991: 95–6).

Bibliography

Aiello, L. (2003), 'Fedor Dostoievskii in Britain: The Tale of an Untalented Genius', *Modern Languages Review*, 98(3): 659–77.

Beasley, R. (2013), 'On Not Knowing Russian: The Translations of Virginia Woolf and S. S. Kotelianskii', *Modern Language Review*, 108(1): 1–29.

Benjamin, W. [1923] (1997), 'The Task of the Translator', trans. H. Zohn, London: Fontana Press.

Clutton-Brock, A. (1921), 'In the Kitchen', *Times Literary Supplement*, 21 April: 257.

Cuddy-Keane, M. (2003), *Virginia Woolf, the Intellectual, and the Public Sphere*, Cambridge: Cambridge University Press.

Dalgarno, E. (2011), *Virginia Woolf and the Migrations of Language*, Cambridge: Cambridge University Press.

Davison, C. (2012), 'Virginia Woolf and the Russian Oxymoron', in *Contradictory Woolf: Selected Papers from the Twenty-First International Conference on Virginia Woolf*, ed. D. Ryan and S. Bolaki, Clemson: Clemson University Press, pp. 229–42.

Davison, C. (2014), *Translation as Collaboration: Virginia Woolf, Katherine Mansfield and S. S. Koteliansky*, Edinburgh: Edinburgh University Press.

Davison-Pégon, C. (2007), 'Tangents in a telescope: Virginia Woolf's Georgian Tolstoy', *Etudes britanniques contemporaines*, 33: 17–32.

De Vogüé, M. [1886] (1987), *Le roman russe*, Paris: Plon.

Dostoïevski, F. [1871] (1886), *Les Possédés*, trans. V. Dérély, Paris: Plon.

Dostoievsky, F. [1871] (1913), *The Possessed*, trans. C. Garnett, London: Heinemann.

Frank J. (2009), *Dostoevsky, A Writer in His Time*, Princeton: Princeton University Press.

Furman, Y. (2009), 'Translating Dostoievskii, Writing a Novel of One's Own: The Place of "Stavrogin's Confession" in the Creation of *Mrs Dalloway*', *Modern Languages Review*, 104: 1081–97.

Garnett, R. (1991), *Constance Garnett: A Heroic Life*, London: Sinclair-Stevenson.

Gol'denveizer, A. B. [1922] (1959), *Vblizi Tolstovo*, Moscow: Gostudarstvenno izdatel'stvo khudoj'estvenoy' literaturii.

Kaye, P. (1999), *Dostoevsky and English Modernism 1900–1930,* Cambridge: Cambridge University Press.

Proust, M. [1913–1927] (2007), *A la recherche du temps perdu,* 7 vols, Paris: Gallimard.

Reinhold, N. (2003), 'Virginia Woolf's Russian Voyage Out', *Woolf Studies Annual,* 9: 1–27.

Reinhold, N. (2005), 'A Railway Accident: Virginia Woolf translates Tolstoy', *Woolf Across Cultures,* New York: Pace University Press, pp. 237–48.

Rubenstein, R. (2009), *Virginia Woolf and the Russian Point of View,* New York: Palgrave.

Shorter Oxford English Dictionary (2002), 5th edn, Oxford: Oxford University Press.

Smith-Di Biasio, A.-M. (2013), 'Minoan Woolf: "The Pale Borderland of No-Man's Language"', in *Contemporary Woolf/Woolf Contemporaine,* ed. C. Davison-Pégon and A.-M. Smith-Di Biasio, Montpellier: Presses universitaires de la Méditerranée, pp. 167–78.

Tolstoy, L. N., [1869] (2007), *War and Peace,* trans. R. Pevear and L. Volokhonsky, London: Vintage.

Wismann, H. (2012), *Penser entre les langues,* Paris: Albin Michel.

Woolf, V. (1977–1985), *The Diary of Virginia Woolf,* 5 vols, ed. A. O. Bell and A. McNeillie, New York and London: Harcourt Brace Jovanovich.

Woolf V. (1986–2011), *The Essays of Virginia Woolf,* ed. A. McNeillie (vols 1–4), and S. N. Clarke (vols 5–6), New York and London: Harcourt Brace.

Woolf V. [1922] (2000), *Jacob's Room,* Oxford: Oxford World's Classics.

Woolf, V. (2002), *Moments of Being: Autobiographical Writings,* ed. J. Schulkind, London: Pimlico.

Woolf V. [1928] (2008), *Orlando,* Oxford: Oxford World's Classics.

Woolf V. [1915] (2009), *The Voyage Out,* Oxford: Oxford World's Classics.

Woolf, V., and S. S. Koteliansky (2006), *Translations from the Russian,* ed. S. N. Clarke and intro. L. Marcus, Southport: Virginia Woolf Society of Great Britain.

Part Three

Culture and Commodification

Chapter 5

'Unity – Dispersity':
Virginia Woolf and the Contradictory Motif of the Motor-Car[1]

Ann Martin

The motor-car has become an emblem of the disruptive forces of the 'new' in early-twentieth-century culture. As a 'symbol of modernity' (Sachs 1992: 32), it collides with bicycles and caravans, introduces bodies to the pains and pleasures of speed, and alters perspectives on time, space, and social place. However, the tension between tradition and modernity was also mediated by the automobile, particularly through luxury *marques* such as Lanchester, Daimler, and Rolls-Royce. The aura of class privilege surrounding these bespoke vehicles signalled the continuity of carriage and car, which advertising strategies of the day were careful to maintain, especially as middle-class consumers entered the automobile market. In an era of technological and socioeconomic change, motor-cars may speak to innovation and transformation, but they play a significant role in the reiteration of existing social structures too.[2] These seemingly contradictory meanings and the motor-car's place in understanding modern British identity are what Virginia Woolf explores, both as an author and as an owner of three automobiles.

Woolf's representations of motor-cars speak to their varied significance in early-twentieth-century Britain and to her recognition that cars are a form of fashion. Like fashion in 'its dual nature as system and event' (Koppen 2009: 26), there is a slippage between the 'system, idea or aesthetic' and the 'particular practices' of individuals who use the car in distinct ways (Entwhistle 2000: 3). For example, while certain *marques* may reinforce established social status, as Lady Lasswade's 'magnificent car' does in *The Years* (132), they may also enable individuals to perform identities that are not necessarily theirs by birth or marriage. Thus, in *Between the Acts*, Ralph Manresa's 'great silver-plated car' is positioned as a prop that is linked to his attempt 'to look the very spit and image of the landed gentry' (42, 37). The different registers of meaning with which the automobile can be associated – conservative or self-consciously modern; rooted in landed identity or marking social ascension – are manifest in its different roles, whether the car arrives at the Opera House, is driven from the city to Pointz Hall, or is parked in the Woolfs' shed at Monk's House.

The performative or public dimension of car ownership is prominent in Woolf's personal writings, where she notes the social connotations of specific *marques*. After purchasing two Singers – affordable cars that connected the Woolfs to drivers within their circle as well as to a broader British motoring community – she and Leonard advanced to a 1933 Lanchester 18, a luxury car that would have cost at least twice as much as either Singer. In her diary and letters, Woolf writes about the Lanchester with excitement and pride. Using phrases taken directly from Lanchester advertisements, she deliberately draws attention to that marketing at a number of points and, in doing so, parodies the image that is associated with the car; even so, the language still works to situate Woolf in an exclusive community of Lanchester owners. Her allusions are reminders of the car's cultural status and its reflection of her own financial success.

The car is, in fact, a site at which Woolf's unease about social position intersects with her self-conscious relationship to consumerism: her 'participation in, yet distance from, the market' (Simpson 2008: 9). Both attitudes are implicit in Woolf's ambivalence towards the notion of community, as the reality of her class consciousness often 'sits uneasily alongside' a view of social connectedness (Light 2008: xvii). While the Singer enabled the Woolfs to enter into a newly emerging car culture, and to learn from and compare experiences with friends and acquaintances, the Lanchester represents the 'individualistic' dimension of motoring that separates the motorist from the masses (Minow-Pinkney 2000: 162). As Woolf herself notes, the 18 is a first-class experience (*D* 4: 141); though much less expensive than its more powerful contemporary, the Rolls-Royce 20/25, it is a work of art. Thus, even when motor-car ownership connects Woolf publicly to a community of owner-drivers, and enables her to point ironically to the incongruity of her own performance of class, the car seems to move her conceptually beyond the common motorist, the common consumer, and common experience.

In her fiction too, Woolf uses the motif of the motor-car as it is linked to both community and its divides, particularly in instances of shared experience that are followed by dissolution. However, the very provisionality of the individual's relationship to the group may be a desirable quality in Woolf's social vision. The car's association with apparently oppositional impulses – modern and traditional; democratic and hierarchical; private and public – signals its cultural mobility, which can and does lead to connections across apparent social divisions, even though these connections may disperse as quickly as they arise. In other words, Woolf uses the motor-car to figure moments of temporary social unity which involve diversity and difference.

Instances of such community are distinguished from a homogeneous, authoritative nationalism in 'The Cheapening of Motor-cars', a short essay published in the *Nation and Athenaeum* in 1924, where Woolf condemns the car's threat to the vitality of the English countryside and prefigures her ambivalent depiction of the automobile and urban social relations in *Mrs Dalloway*. After 1927, though, when she became an owner-driver herself, another view of motor-cars appears. For Kitty Lasswade and Mrs Manresa, as for Orlando, the automobile is a tool through which individuals can assert their independence, even within a class structure, and come to relate authentically with others. The car's mediation of the private and the interpersonal, the modern and the traditional is emphasised in *Between the Acts*, when it is placed in stark contrast to the divisive effect of the fighter planes that interrupt the Reverend Streatfield's speech. The motor-car is a riposte to uniformity, as members of the audience, once unified, disperse in separate automobiles with different responses to Miss La Trobe's version of 'Britain', and model a local community that, in its ability to come together momentarily, provides an alternative to the unreflective patriotism of the Second World War.

Modernism and its conflicts find an obvious correlative in the motor-car. If speed is 'the single new pleasure invented by modernity', as Enda Duffy puts it, the car is the representative vehicle of a '*new* physical sensation' (2009: 3, 8). That sensation underwrites 'modern shock modes of perception', where new kinds of art display their 'heady engagement with technology's speed, danger, [and] immediacy' (Laity 2004: 426). Indeed, Garry Leonard uses the car's motor as a metaphor for avant-garde representations of modernity: 'both generate energy from irreconcilable dynamics (explosion and conversion)' (2009: 226). Shock is also central to Makiko Minow-Pinkney's readings of the motor-car in Woolf's work, where motoring, like other experiences of technology, 'necessitates new modes of thought and aesthetic representations adjusted to it' (2000: 163). As Melba Cuddy-Keane et al. note, motor-cars affect 'the subjective perception of time and distance' (1996: 74). For Andrew Thacker, such experiences produce 'a kaleidoscopic sense of the modern self that [Woolf] embraced for its potential to unsettle fixed structures of power' (2003: 184), where the challenge to conventional understandings of subjectivity suggests motoring's larger social effect.

Indeed, as a sign of shifting times, the car 'offered a new pleasure to the masses' (Duffy 2009: 6) as well as another conduit for self-fashioning. Given the cost of buying and maintaining an automobile, car ownership was a mark of socioeconomic privilege well into the twentieth century, representing one of the 'dominant symbols of prestige' in modernity (Sachs 1992: 11). Such connotations led to its use by 'the rising, moneyed urban bourgeoisie' to claim social power (12), and what is most striking about debates concerning the automobile in Britain is how often the status of the driver becomes the focus. Initially, it was the real and perceived irresponsibility of 'flying millionaires' that generated both contempt and restrictive legislation for motorists (Montagu and McComb 1977: 18). William Plowden notes that automobiles were also implicated in the perceived divide between city and country: 'cars, often registered in urban districts, passed through rural areas on roads to whose upkeep their owners made no contribution, pounding them to pieces and spreading dust over crops, houses and passers-by' (1973: 16). When motor-cars became more affordable, such urban/rural tensions became more pronounced. By the 1920s, cars had become 'a prime marker of the newly affluent lower-middle class' (Thacker 2003: 156) who bought automobiles expressly 'to go out and explore the countryside' (Morrison and Minnis 2012: 277). Private car ownership rose throughout the interwar period from an estimated 110,000 vehicles to 2.3 million, and it played no small role in the founding of the Campaign for the Preservation of Rural England (CPRE) in 1926 (Kohl 2006: 193–4).

The goal of the CPRE was not only to protect natural landscapes from the effects of motor-cars, but, more broadly, to establish planning that would lead to harmony between the traditional and the new, where '*town* and *country* were opposite but complementary' (Hussey 2011: 9). However, the wider conservation movement resulted in the popularisation of an 'ideal version of the countryside' that, in some interpretations, was nostalgically grounded in a feudal social order (Berberich 2006: 209). This image of England failed, of course, to reflect the lived experiences of 'those who depended on the rural economy for their livelihood' (O'Connell 1998: 153), and, ironically, was also being invoked in automotive magazines, motoring guides, and films to promote the pastoral beauties of Britain as viewed from the car (Hankins 2012: 252). Garages and petrol stations opened up to meet the needs of tourists, as did pubs, camp sites, and shops; wealthier members of the middle class moved to the country, building new estates in order 'to emulate upper-class and aristocratic landowners' (Berberich 2006: 209). As Sean O'Connell points out, 'the consumption of an almost imaginary traditional rural world' led to the increased and not always desirable presence of modernity in that very space (1998: 154).

The Roads Act of 1920 sought to address increased automobile traffic by establishing 'a centralised road system' (Richardson and O'Gallagher 1977: 173), and Woolf criticises this very initiative in her column 'The Cheapening of Motor-cars'. The road, she argues, is 'losing its old character' (*E* 3: 440) as it is being widened, levelled, and resurfaced; that is, being rebuilt for motor-cars. The speed of the traffic has increased because of such modifications, and 'the procession of vehicles is irregular and chaotic' (440). Woolf links the middle-class motorists' domination of the countryside to the actual incursion of 'military operations': it is 'the approach of a military car' that causes walkers to move to the verge and 'cyclists either to dismount and stand still or risk some perfectly wanton onslaught on the part of the military upon the common amenities of the King's highway' (440). Where the country road is associated with life – dogs, children, pedestrians, cyclists, 'untidy hedges', different colours of stone – that natural diversity is disrupted by noisy, speeding vehicles driven by individuals whose 'consideration and humanity' are put into question (440). New roads and new drivers from the city are interrupting an historical sense of rural community, for it is not only the road's regional distinctiveness that is under threat; the 'irregular charm' of the road, dating back to an older England and connecting King to commoner, is being replaced by an anonymous series of machines that are as unnatural and alienating as the artificially straightened motorways (440).

Three years later, Woolf's tone regarding motor-cars has shifted when she experiences for herself the 'physical and social liberation' of driving (Minow-Pinkney 2000: 162). She also finds an unanticipated sense of community that links her to fellow owner-drivers. As Woolf states in a diary entry for 11 July 1927, four days before her Singer arrives, 'We talk of nothing but cars' (*D* 3: 146). The 'we' refers to the Woolfs, but it encompasses others, including Vanessa Bell, who was a contributing factor in Woolf's almost giddy sense of anticipation:

> This is a great opening up in our lives. One may go to Bodiam, to Arundel, explore the Chichester downs, expand that curious thing, the map of the world in ones mind. It will I think demolish loneliness, & may of course imperil complete privacy. The Keynes' have one too – a cheap one. Nessa thinks it will break down at once. (147)

The Woolfs had bought a second-hand and 'somewhat decrepit' Singer – which they called 'The Old Umbrella' – for a reasonable £275 (Spater and Parsons 1977: 174). Colin Borley of the Singers Owners' Club UK has suggested that, given the price they paid, it was probably a 1926 Singer 14/34, which would have retailed new for about £350 (2012).[3]

The Singer made travel between London and Rodmell much easier, but it opened up other avenues for the Woolfs too, as they entered enthusiastically into British car culture. They took lessons, had accidents, and dealt with the mechanics of the car, including problems with gears and ignition failures. Indeed, their first outing in the Singer was a rather frustrating experience, as conveyed to Vita Sackville-West:

> the bloody thing wouldn't start. The accelerator died like a duck – starter jammed. All the village came to watch – Leonard almost sobbed with rage. At last we had to bicycle in and fetch a man from Lewes. He said it was the magnetos – would you have known that? Should we have known? Another attempt today, we are bitter and sullen and determined. We think of nothing else. Leonard will shoot himself if it dont start again. (*L* 3: 407)

Their library expanded to include George Morland's *Motoring without Trouble: The Owner-Driver's A.B.C.* and John Prioleau's *Car & Country: Week-End Signposts to the Open Road* (King and Miletic-Vejzovic 2003). They bonded in new ways with their motoring friends: Vita Sackville-West, of course, but also T. S. Eliot. 'I'm glad to think that we now have another subject in common – motor cars', Woolf writes to him on 24 August 1927, and continues:

> Did Leonard tell you how our entire life is spent driving, cleaning, dodging in and out of a shed, measuring miles on maps, planning driving expeditions, going expeditions, being beaten back by the rain, eating sandwiches on high roads, cursing cows, sheep, bicyclists, and when we are at rest talking of nothing but cars and petrol? Ours is a Singer. (*L* 3: 413)

Motoring introduces Woolf to a different kind of community, and one which leads to a different kind of connection to the English landscape that was, after all, complementary to a pedestrian experience. And while Woolf seems to replicate the behaviour of motorists she has earlier condemned for treating the road as 'a mere racing-track', there is a distinction: those drivers are a segment of 'a population seemingly in perpetual and frantic haste not to be late for dinner', whereas the Woolfs do not have to drive back to the city nor home from work, their workplace being located in their country home, the Woolfs owning their own means of production (*E* 3: 440).

Given Woolf's 'pleasure in her earning power' (Simpson 2008: 14), it is significant that they bought the Singer with advance sales from *To the Lighthouse*, and in 1929, when the Woolfs' annual income rose to over £3,100, they were able to buy a new car (Alexander 1992: 156). This was their Singer Sunshine Saloon, a convertible with a chain-driven retractable roof (Borley 2012). As described in a motoring column, '[i]ts main feature consists in the ability to roll back the roof by winding a small lever, so that the car can be transformed into an open car, and vice versa, in a few moments' ('1928 Singer' 1928: 4). Of course, another selling feature was that Sunshine Saloons sold new for about £270, representing 'fine examples of a low-priced car with a high-class performance' (4).

The marketing of this mainstream car – Singer was in the same rank as Morris and Austin – emphasises the automobile's connection to social status, or rather to a feeling associated with an imagined social status. And this is what Woolf experiences in 1932 when she and Leonard bought a Lanchester. Unlike Singer, however, Lanchester was a luxury *marque*, and though the 18 was available in four different models, the prices were above the reach of the average consumer. As the Motoring Correspondent for *The Times* writes of the two models on display at the 1932 Olympia Motor Show,

> one is a four-seated saloon with sliding roof at £595, and the other is a Continental saloon at £660. The 6-cylinder, 17.96-h.p. chassis costs £450. These cars, like the Tens, have the Daimler fluid flywheel self-changing transmission, with four quiet-speeds, which make them additionally interesting and attractive to drive. ('Olympia' 1932: 9)

It would appear that the Woolfs saw these very vehicles. In a letter to Ethel Smyth on 21 October 1932, Woolf apologises for missing the opera: 'It was my fault for going to the motor show before a dinner party. I've been drowsy all day' (*L* 5: 112). On 10 November, Woolf notes: 'we've bought a Lanchester: to be delivered on Dec. 10th. Grey & green. I dont think we've ever been so happy, what with one thing & another. And so intimate, & so completely entire, I mean L. & I' (*D* 4: 130). The pleasure that comes from drafting *The Pargiters* and visiting Lady Ottoline Morrell is only accentuated by the purchase of a car that represented approximately three times the annual income of a working-class family (Mowat 1955: 490).

Her pleasure would, however, be deferred when the Woolfs were lent a courtesy car on 30 December 1932. While she mentions repeatedly in her diary that 'it is still only a substitute', Woolf nevertheless notes that driving the 18 'is like travelling first instead of third' (*D* 4: 141). Then their very own car arrives:

> And I was forgetting to say that The Deluge [*Lanchester car*] came yesterday. It was expected at 1.15. At 3 Julian & Angelica arrived. at 4 as A. & J. were going to the shop to buy sweets L. pruning, cried out its come. And it had gone. It swept up the village past us, but returned. In colour & shape it is beyond the wildest dreams – I mean it is elegant green silver beautifully

compact modelled first & not too rich – not a money car. We drove it to Lewes, & shall now take it to London; & so, I say, write letters. A cloudy, goose wing day with silver shields. (143)

Her expansive, excited, exultant tone seems entirely justified: it is a beautiful car, and Leonard drove it for the next 22 years (Spater and Parsons 1977: 174).[4]

Woolf's intention to 'write letters' signals the primary medium through which she explored her new identity as a Lanchester owner. In so doing, she uses language taken from Lanchester advertising, and especially prominent are references to 'the Daimler fluid flywheel'. This phrase denotes the distinctive and patented feature named for the Daimler Motor Company of Coventry, which had taken over Lanchester in 1930, and which was the official automobile manufacturer for the Royal Family. It was a tagline used repeatedly in advertisements and had a logo with its own slogan, 'Smooth as Flight' (Lanchester 1934: v), which emphasised the smoothness for which the transmission was known. The phrase became central in marketing Lanchesters, 'The Easiest Cars in the World to Control' (Lanchester 1933: iii). The fluid flywheel also had a prominent place in owner's manuals, sales brochures, and notices from independent car firms selling Lanchesters and comparable *marques* (Stratton-Instone 1932: 2).

Perhaps not surprisingly, Woolf refers to the fluid flywheel in almost all of her letters about the Lanchester. She wrote to Ethel Smyth on 6 January 1933, 'we have bought a brand new and very expensive car . . . It is on the fluid flywheel system. It will cruise – how I love technical words – at 50 miles an hour' (*L* 5: 146). On 15 January, she wrote to Eliot, 'we have bought a new Lanchester – with a fluid fly wheel. It came after two months delay, last night' (*L* 5: 150). On 15 April, she informed Hugh Walpole that 'Leonard has bought a new car, with a fluid fly wheel, so we must run it over the Alps' (177), and when they were in Italy in May, she provided updates on the transmission to Vanessa: 'So far we have had no accidents, but some moments of agony when the fluid wheel has stuck, or the gear gone wrong' (185).

Woolf was enjoying this new language, lifted directly from Lanchester adverts and brochures; and however self-aware or ironic she might have been about that fact – as she certainly was in a letter to Vita Sackville-West on 14 February 1933 – the prestige of the commodity was on her mind:

I was going to say our car has come – silver and green, fluid fly wheel, Tickford hood – Lanchester 18 – well what more could you want? It glides with the smoothness of eel, with the speed of a swift, and the – isn't this a good blurb? – the power of a tigress when that tigress has just been reft of her young in and out up and down Piccadilly, Bond Street. The worst of it is we cant live up to it. I've had to buy a new coat. But whats the good? Theres my hat. Thats all wrong – thats a Singer saloon hat. (*L* 5: 157)

In an earlier letter to 'dame Ethel', she has discussed this very coat and the effect of the car on her sense of self:

I feel ever so rich, conservative, patriotic, religious and humbuggish when I drive in it, and I enjoy this new Virginia immensely. She's one of the nicest people I know, and would love a party at Lady Roseberys above everything. (*L* 5: 154)

Woolf is recognising, parodically, the ways in which her identity can be and is being fashioned and received through the medium of the car.

While the ironic performance of voice is a given in these (and so many other) letters, it is less clear what identity is being performed. Her appreciation of the elegance of the vehicle is complicated by her awareness of and unease with the position it signifies: the Lanchester *was* a money car, as she very well knew. Indeed, when the Woolfs take the Lanchester 18 to Italy in 1933, she invokes that knowledge in two significant moments of class awareness. First, when speculating in her diary about the future of one of the hotel maids, she notes the woman's appreciation of the car: 'will [she] marry? Will [she] become one of those stout black women who sit in the door knitting? No: I foretell for her some tragedy; because she had enough mind to envy us the Lanchester' (*D* 4: 154). If the Italian woman's desire for social status is implied here, it is a fascinating echo of Woolf's allusion to Lady Rosebery in relation to herself. But Woolf knows it is a com- modity to envy: when she takes a photograph of what she identifies as a Singer in Lerici on the same trip (see Humm 2006: 142), it might be a nostalgic gesture back to the good old days of third-class travel, but the vehicle stands in clear contrast to her new first-class automo- bile. In these instances, she is distinguishing herself from the maid and Singer drivers – as she distinguished herself from the Keynes with their 'cheap' car – even as she undermines such pretension in the reference to Victorian social ambitions.

The crux is, however, that Woolf's success as a writer and publisher had led to a kind of class ascension, and as much fun as she had with the Lanchester as a vehicle, she was also enjoying a traditional form of privilege: landed gentry owned expensive cars. In a letter to Vita Sackville-West from 2 September 1927, for example, Woolf compares herself to a privileged retainer when Dorothy Wellesley's sponsorship of the Hogarth Living Poets series has been secured, writing 'I'm her's for life. I have the use of the Rolls Royce and wine to taste' (*L* 3: 415). At other times, she takes a more serious and reflective stance, as in a diary entry from 31 May 1929: 'We voted at Rodmell. I saw a white gloved lady helping an old farm couple out of her Daimler' (*D* 3: 231). Where this instance of *noblesse oblige* is a gesture that links individuals, the car also makes social divisions overt: 'A Rolls Royce means £5000 a year', Woolf writes in June 1932, having stopped the Sunshine Saloon in Hyde Park and 'watched a people on the verge of ruin' (*D* 4: 108). Financial privilege in the midst of financial instability draws out her wariness of 'very powerful cars . . . with luxurious owners' (108). Indeed, it is a topic she has already examined in *Mrs Dalloway*, and to which she returns in *The Years* and *Between the Acts* through an extended consideration of how class and community are signified through the motor-car.

In *Mrs Dalloway*, the shocking noise that disrupts the order of fashionable Bond Street comes from 'a motor car which had drawn to the side of the pavement precisely opposite Mulberry's shop window' (15). In that startling moment – 'oh! a pistol shot in the street outside!' – and in the car's subsequent progress to Buckingham Palace, Woolf associates the automobile with social differences (14). The car links the spectators on the city streets through a common focal point, but the scene ends with uncertainty about its passenger's identity and inconclusive interpretations of the sky-writing before the crowd disperses. The status of community is thus debatable: 'interconnectedness' is evident on the level of the narration, as thoughts and actions stream together (Boone 1998: 181), but the hollow spectacles of car and airplane seem to 'underline the citizens' alienation from each other' (Duffy 2009: 144). Moreover, the car is overtly associated with 'royalty, the upper class, and Empire', traits represented by Sir William Bradshaw's car, a symbol of 'the patriarchal power game and establishment ideology' (Minow-Pinkney 2000: 161). The discourse of patriotism seems a false unifier at best, as temporary as Big Ben's 'leaden circles' (*MD*: 4) and as vulnerable as the 'thin thread' that links Hugh Whitbread and Richard Dalloway to Lady Bruton following their luncheon together (123).

The vulnerability of such connections may speak, however, to agency, where the integrity of the social structure is contingent upon its recognition by the individuals it affects. It is the spectators' 'emotional' reaction to the car as signifier of the state that, according to Ban Wang, 'establishes a common identity' (1992: 180). Given that the crowd's responses to the car and its occupants vary, Woolf creates in this scene 'a heterogeneous play of meanings and mental associations', which suggests 'the arbitrary relation of the state symbol to its authoritative meaning' (182–3). In other words, while the car calls for 'veneration', that call is met with different reactions and, despite or because of the number of perspectives in play, privilege is shrouded in uncertainty as much as authority (*MD*: 17). The passenger of the car – 'Queen, Prince, Prime Minister' – is hidden behind both the window blind and a vague sense of 'greatness' (17), a quality not readily demonstrated by the Prime Minister at Clarissa's party: at least one attendee notes: 'He tried to look somebody. It was amusing to watch' (189). The actions of the chauffeur, described from Rezia's perspective, are equally unclear: 'opening something, turning something, shutting something' (16). On the one hand, the uncertainty works to sustain an aura of separation and the car is thus representative of the class divides of the exploitative social system. On the other hand, the spectators' differing interpretations are able to emerge because of the absence of an authoritative version of the car and its occupants. Such 'greatness' is illusory and elusive, recognisable as it is created by the spectacle and its reception.

Interestingly, the lack of specificity in the scene has led to misreadings of the noise the car makes. The 'violent explosion' is often read as indicating a car engine is backfiring, but Miss Pym's response signals that the noise is actually an exploding tyre. She smiles 'apologetically with her hands full of sweet peas, as if those motor cars, those tyres of motor cars, were all *her* fault' (*MD*: 14). Given the narrowness of wheels at the time, the use of natural rubber, and the number of horseshoe nails on the roads, punctures were a common occurrence and time-consuming to repair. On the evening of 8 August 1921, for example, Queen Alexandra's car was stopped at Holborn Circus for almost an hour because of a flat tyre. *The Times* reported that 'a considerable crowd collected' as cab drivers and passers-by helped out with what was a difficult task: two jacks were broken in the process, and a third had to be borrowed from a nearby newspaper office ('Queen' 1921: 5).

Unlike the scene on Bond Street, where a 'male hand' draws down the blind to shield the passenger and maintain 'an air of inscrutable reserve' (*MD*: 15, 17), passers-by 'soon recognized' the widowed Queen, and apparently for that hour, she and Princess Victoria accepted flowers and bowed in response to the crowd's 'greetings' ('Queen' 1921: 5). When 'some ragged little girls' danced for the Queen, 'she stood up and clapped her hands in acknowledgement' ('Late' 1926: 5), and once the car was fixed, 'Cheers were raised, and the Queen said, "Thank you very much", with a smile' ('Queen' 1921: 5). The similarities between the fictional and the historical flat tyre are extremely suggestive;

however, where Queen Alexandra's public interactions with the people are of a piece with her annual Rose Day drives through the city in an open carriage, the motor-car in *Mrs Dalloway* speaks to a privilege that maintains the passenger's privacy to the exclusion of a lived experience of community.

Significantly, *Mrs Dalloway* was written and published before Woolf owned an automobile, and the novel's presentation of the motor-car differs from the dizzying drive that ends *Orlando* and the social navigations that Kitty Lasswade achieves through her cars in *The Years*. In these texts, the automobile is experienced from the inside, not just viewed from the outside, and Woolf figures the individual's relationship to different communities through the car's place in their navigation of private and public selves. For example, just as Lady Lasswade feels privately that her evening dress is 'ridiculous' when she attends a committee meeting in the 1910 section, so she feels that her car causes Martin to 'sneer' at her public persona (*TY*: 131, 132). Her awkwardness is replaced by 'a sense of relief', however, once the car has delivered her to the Opera House, where she finds spectators 'dressed exactly as she was' (133). A similar dynamic emerges in the 1914 section when, after a dinner, Kitty feels awkward among the other women and Martin, again, emphasises her social place: '"A very brilliant party, Lady Lasswade", he said with his usual tiresome irony' (191). Once the guests are gone and she has changed her clothes, the automobile takes her to the train, at which point 'the tension went out of her body' and she relaxes into the first-class railway car (197). Disconnected from the social role she plays, even as that role disconnects her from others, Lady Lasswade uses the chauffeur-driven automobile to escape class trouble.

When Kitty arrives in the country and is met at the station by Cole, her experience of the class structure shifts and seems to have less to do with publicly performed privilege and more to do with reciprocal duties that join people together. After lifting back the hood of the new automobile, 'a birthday present from her husband' (*TY*: 199), Cole drives her to the family estate. Beeping the horn at dogs, avoiding horse-drawn farm wagons, and 'driving too fast', Kitty thinks appreciatively, her chauffeur coaxes the motor up Crabbs hill, 'show[ing] off his engine' with a quiet pride (199, 200). The trip connects the two, not only because Cole has 'none of the servile ways of the London flunkey' (200), but also because they can connect through the car: Kitty values the power of the vehicle and the skill of her driver, which will be mentioned when she tells 'his Lordship' how well both performed (201). The two individuals are still divided by class, but unified through roles made meaningful by the car as it operates in this cultural space.

While Woolf's rather idealistic vision here of the countryside and its sense of community is consistent with 'The Cheapening of Motor-cars', the focus on the individual's experience of motoring marks a difference. In the 'Present Day' section of *The Years*, for instance, North navigates London almost two decades after the scene between Kitty and Cole, and his motoring is linked less to class privilege or social structures as the city opens up to the independent owner-driver. North has 'not mastered the art of driving in London' and is tremendously disoriented in 'his little sports car' (225). Still, his jerky movement through green lights and between vans, among hooting horns and horse-drawn coal carts to Sara's rooms on Milton Street displaces traditional associations between motor-cars and the landed gentry: he has sold his farm in Africa and is exploring a diverse urban scene. North's experience of motoring also stands in contrast to the story Sara tells of the couple in a Rolls-Royce and the cruelty of the woman who 'took advantage of the pause under the lamplight to raise her hand ... and polish that spade, her mouth' (236). Cars as symbols of privilege and inequity divide individuals, leading to exclusion and alienation, exemplified by Sara's story. But automobiles also enable autonomous movement, leading to connections that offer another vision of community. North's interaction with the city is determined not just by its street signs and traffic lights, or by the value of his automobile, but also by his family's lived experiences of London and his own negotiations of its streets.

Woolf continues to explore the private uses and public connotations of motor-cars in *Between the Acts*, where they become connected to a sense of community that, in keeping with Miss La Trobe's pageant, does not necessarily correspond to official patriarchal or patriotic norms. There are significant intersections between Woolf's final novel and *Mrs Dalloway* in this regard: just as the car is a passing focal point, so the pageant draws people together only for an afternoon, and reactions to Miss La Trobe's history of England are as varied and uncertain as the crowd's readings of the automobile as it passes them by. Further, the *marques* named by Woolf share the status that is symbolised by the car on Bond Street: 'I shouldn't have expected either so many Hispano-Suizas ... That's a Rolls ... That's a Bentley' (180). Such prestige is acknowledged through Giles's display of veneration for the Manresas' chauffeur-driven vehicle. The design on the door 'with the initials R. M. twisted so as to look at a distance like a coronet', has a powerful effect: it 'touched his training. He must change', he feels (*BTA*: 42). Like the citizens in London, he has been hailed by the connotations of the luxury motor-car, and his response both reflects and reinforces the commodity's cultural significance.

However, the crest on the Manresas' car door merely looks '*like* a coronet' and even then, only 'from a distance' (*BTA*: 42; my emphasis). The less stable social status of the car's passengers also signals a difference between this automobile and the vehicle of the authority figure who arrives at Buckingham Palace. Isabella identifies William as a 'gentleman; witness socks and trousers' (35), but the fact that she relies on his dress for his designation is telling: his clothes are only 'scraps and fragments' of an apparent identity (36), and from Giles's perspective, William Dodge is not a 'downright plain man of his senses', but rather 'a teaser and twitcher; a fingerer of sensations; picking and choosing; dillying and dallying' (55). Though Mrs Manresa may be respectable and monied enough, she is 'over-sexed, over-dressed' (37), and makes up her past with the same skill that she uses to powder her face, redden her lips, and deploy the commodity of the car. Arriving '[u]ninvited, unexpected, lured off the high road' with the intention 'to be with her kind' (34, 35), the spectacle of Mrs Manresa and her motor-car arises from her awareness of and tactical engagement with class distinctions.

While she may embody the figure whom Woolf parodies in her letters about the Lanchester, Mrs Manresa's performance of a public identity speaks to only one of the levels according to which the car has meaning. Her automobile enables a display of wealth, just as the pageant enables a display of English patriotism, but motor-cars in *Between the Acts* are also vehicles through which individuals come to Pointz Hall and re-form community on a local and interpersonal level. The event 'brings people together' (143) in a physical and experiential sense, but unlike '[t]he motor bike, the motor bus, and the movies' that are blamed for their absences from church (69), the cars that convey audience members become part of the pageant. The delays and interruptions that 'torture' Miss La Trobe (73) include the late arrival of 'Mr and Mrs Rupert Haines, detained by a breakdown on the road' (74). The role that nature plays in the form of wind, cows, and rain is echoed by '[t]he horns of cars on the high road' that are heard during the 'Present time. Ourselves' section (159, 158). The varied fragments of conversation that follow the pageant – questions, observations, interpretations – arise as audience members move 'across lawns, down paths, past the house to the gravel-strewn crescent, where cars, push bikes and cycles were crowded together' (177). Though they may leave in their separate vehicles, Fords as well as Hispano-Suizas that are driven by owners as well as by chauffeurs (181), they are mingling still and moving in common ways: 'Can't we give you a lift?'(180). In the search for different vehicles, distinctions seem to be dissolved – 'Bless my soul, what a dither! Nobody seems to know one car from another!'

(180) – and this collective experience suggests a suspension of a divisive social order through the act of gathering and the interactive nature of the performance.

The 'common effort' (137) called for by the pageant does not result in an authoritative answer, however, as illustrated by the Reverend Streatfield's explanation or 'summing up', which ends with an unanswered question: 'Surely, we should unite?' (173). Even his appeal for contributions to a common cause is fragmented, divided by the spectacle of military nationalism that shadows the novel as a whole. Twelve planes 'in perfect formation' interrupt his speech (174), and they symbolise a technology with much less 'static' than the ticking, gurgling gramophone (Pridmore-Brown: 408) and under much more control than the individually dispersing vehicles: 'Some drove; others cycled. A gate swung open. A car swept up the drive to the red villa in the cornfields' (*BTA*: 192). The jumbled departure of the villagers, the uneven reception of Miss La Trobe's visions of Englishness, and the crowd's lack of unanimity regarding the afternoon's experience stand in stark contrast to the ostensibly coherent national identity represented by the airplanes and the patriotic direction in which they all fly. Given the impulse towards dictatorial uniformity in 1939, however, '*Dispersed are we*' suggests not only a lament for division, but also the triumph of momentary connection (178). The gramophone's warbling of '*Unity – Dispersity*' (181) points to the constantly shifting balance between the community and the individual, between social markers of position and local uses of class narratives.

In *Between the Acts*, Woolf uses the motor-car to depict the local experiences that create a provisional sense of community and that are made meaningful through that communal interaction, however temporary and contingent. It is a dynamic that speaks to Michele Pridmore-Brown's reading of 'a pluralist politics' in Woolf's work, and one 'that affirms internal difference and that consists in a perpetual formation, expansion, and linking of subject positions', thus representing an alternative to 'domination' (1998: 417, 418). This community does not stand as one thing only, but rather involves shifting perceptions of self in relation to other. Given its associations with both modernity and tradition in Woolf's *oeuvre*, the automobile's place in such configurations is emblematic of the subject's potential to interact with the possibilities of national and cultural narratives in identity performance and in political practice. However, its layered meanings suggest too the ambivalence with which Woolf regarded the social systems represented by and negotiated through the contradictory motif of the motor-car.

Notes

1. My thanks to Maggie Humm; to the editors; and to Suzanne Bellamy for their support, suggestions, and contributions. This is for James.
2. Along with the works cited in the text, *Coventry Motor Companies* (2010) and Perkin (1976) also provided much important background information.
3. See plate 124 in Humm 2006: 119.
4. See plate 171 in Humm 2006: 159.

Bibliography

'The 1928 Singer: Newest Models on View', *The Singapore Free Press and Mercantile Advertiser*, 28 April 1928, <http://newspapers.nl.sg/Digitised/Article/singfreepressb19280428-1.2.14.aspx> (last accessed 19 August 2013).

Alexander, P. F. (1992), *Leonard and Virginia Woolf: A Literary Partnership*, New York: Harvester.

Berberich, C. (2006), 'This Green and Pleasant Land: Cultural Constructions of Englishness', in *Landscape and Englishness*, ed. R. Burden and S. Kohl, New York: Rodopi, pp. 207–24.

Boone, J. A. (1998), *Libidinal Currents: Sexuality and the Shaping of Modernism*, Chicago: University of Chicago Press.

Borley, C. (2012), email, 29 August.

Coventry Motor Companies (2010), Memphis: Books LLC.

Cuddy-Keane, M., N. Aleksiuk, K. Li, M. Love, C. Rose, and A. Williams (1996), 'The Heteroglossia of History', in *Virginia Woolf: Texts and Contexts*, ed. B. Rigel Daugherty and E. Barrett, New York: Pace University Press, pp. 71–80.

Duffy, E. (2009), *The Speed Handbook: Velocity, Pleasure, Modernism*, Durham, NC and London: Duke University Press.

Entwhistle, J. (2000), *The Fashioned Body: Fashion, Dress, and Modern Social Theory*, Cambridge: Polity.

Hankins, L. K. (2012), '"As I spin along the roads I remodel my life": Travel Films "projected into the shape of Orlando"', in *Contradictory Woolf: Selected Papers from the Twenty-First International Conference on Virginia Woolf*, ed. D. Ryan and S. Bolaki, Clemson: Clemson University Digital Press, pp. 250–8.

Humm, M. (2006), *Snapshots of Bloomsbury: The Private Lives of Virginia Woolf and Vanessa Bell*, London: Tate.

Hussey, M. (2011), *'I'd Make It Penal', the Rural Preservation Movement in Virginia Woolf's Between the Acts*, London: Cecil Woolf.

King, J., and L. Miletic-Vejzovic (2003), *The Library of Leonard and Virginia Woolf: A Short-title Catalog*, Pullman: Washington State University Press, <http://ntserver1.wsulibs.wsu.edu/masc/onlinebooks/woolflibrary/woolflibraryonline.htm> (last accessed 19 August 2013).

Kohl, S. (2006), 'Rural England: An Invention of the Motor Industries?', in *Landscape and Englishness*, ed. R. Burden and S. Kohl, New York: Rodopi, pp. 185–205.

Koppen, R. S. (2009), *Virginia Woolf, Fashion and Literary Modernity*, Edinburgh: Edinburgh University Press.

Laity, C. (2004), 'T. S. Eliot and A. C. Swinburne: Decadent Bodies, Modern Visualities, and Changing Modes of Perception', *Modernism/modernity* 11(3): 425–48.

Lanchester (1933), 'Lanchester', *Punch, or the London Charivari*, 31 May: iii, <http://www.ebay.com/itm/1933-Lanchester-18-Saloon-Ad-London-News-Chronicle-wj4874-IKZ6JA-/350733848466> (last accessed 19 August 2013).

Lanchester (1934), 'Daimler Engineers', *Punch, or the London Charivari*, 26 September, <http://www.ebay.com/itm/Rare-Original-1934-LANCHESTER-18-Auto-Print-AD-Vintage-Car-ADVERT-/190626419574> (last accessed 19 August 2013).

'The Late Queen Alexandra: A Tribute' (1926), *The Queenslander*, 9 January: 5, <http://trove.nla.gov.au/ndp/del/article/22750467> (last accessed 19 August 2013).

Leonard, G. (2009), '"The Famished Roar of Automobiles": Modernity, the Internal Combustion Engine, and Modernism', in *Disciplining Modernism*, ed. P. L. Caughie, New York: Palgrave Macmillan, pp. 221–41.

Light, A. (2008), *Mrs Woolf and the Servants: The Hidden Heart of Domestic Service*, London: Penguin.

Minow-Pinkney, M. (2000), 'Virginia Woolf and the Age of Motor Cars', in *Virginia Woolf in the Age of Mechanical Reproduction*, ed. P. L. Caughie, New York: Garland, pp. 159–82.

Montagu, Lord of Beaulieu, and F. W. McComb (1977), *Behind the Wheel: The Magic and Manners of Early Motoring*, New York: Paddington.

Morrison, K., and J. Minnis (2012), *Carscapes: The Motor Car, Architecture and Landscape in England*, New Haven, CT: Yale University Press.

Mowat, C. L. (1955), *Britain Between the Wars: 1918–1940*, Chicago: University of Chicago Press.

O'Connell, S. (1998), *The Car in British Society: Class, Gender and Motoring 1896–1939*, Manchester: Manchester University Press.

'The Olympia Show' (1932), *The Times*, 19 October: 9, <http://find.galegroup.com/ttda/infomark.do?&source=gale&prodId=TTDA&userGroupName=usaskmain&tabID=T003&docPage=article&searchType=BasicSearchForm&docId=CS151201619&type=multipage&contentSet=LTO&version=1.0> (last accessed 19 August 2013).

Perkin, H. (1976), *The Age of the Automobile*, London: Quartet.

Plowden, W. [1971] (1973), *The Motor Car and Politics in Britain*, Harmondsworth: Pelican.

Pridmore-Brown, M. (1998), 'Of Virginia Woolf, Gramophones, and Fascism', *PMLA: Publications of the Modern Language Association*, 113(3): 408–21.

'Queen Alexandra in The City' (1921), *The Times*, 9 August: 5, <http://find.galegroup.com/ttda/infomark.do?&source=gale&prodId=TTDA&userGroupName=usaskmain&tabID=T003&docPage=article&searchType=BasicSearchForm&docId=CS85790985&type=multipage&contentSet=LTO&version=1.0> (last accessed 19 August 2013).

Richardson, K., and C. N. O'Gallagher (1977), *The British Motor Industry 1896–1939*, London: Macmillan.

Sachs, W. (1992), *For the Love of the Automobile: Looking Back into the History of Our Desires*, trans. D. Reneau, Berkeley: University of California Press.

Stratton-Instone (1932), 'Motor-Cars, Motor-Cycles, Lorries and Accessories', *The Times*, 8 July: 2, <http://find.galegroup.com/ttda/infomark.do?&source =gale&prodId=TTDA&userGroupName=usaskmain&tabID=T003&docPa ge=article&searchType=BasicSearchForm&docId=CS33761000&type=mult ipage&contentSet=LTO&version=1.0> (last accessed 19 August 2013).

Simpson, K. (2008), *Gifts, Markets and Economies of Desire in Virginia Woolf*, New York: Palgrave Macmillan.

Spater, G., and I. Parsons (1977), *A Marriage of True Minds: An Intimate Portrait of Leonard and Virginia Woolf*, London: Jonathan Cape and Hogarth Press.

Thacker, A. (2003), *Moving Through Modernity*, Manchester: Manchester University Press.

Wang, B. (1992), '"I" on the Run: Crisis of Identity in *Mrs Dalloway*', *MFS: Modern Fiction Studies* 38(1): 177–91.

Woolf, V. (1975–80), *The Letters of Virginia Woolf*, 6 vols, ed. N. Nicolson and J. Trautmann, New York and London: Harcourt Brace Jovanovich.

Woolf, V. (1979–85), *The Diary of Virginia Woolf*, 5 vols, ed. A. O. Bell and A. McNeillie, Harmondsworth: Penguin.

Woolf, V. [1924] (1988), 'The Cheapening of Motor-cars', in *The Essays of Virginia Woolf*, vol. 3, ed. A. McNeillie, London: Hogarth Press.

Woolf, V. [1925] (1992), *Mrs Dalloway*, ed. S. McNichol, London: Penguin.

Woolf, V. [1937] (1998), *The Years*, ed. J. Johnson, London: Penguin.

Woolf, V. [1941] (2000), *Between the Acts*, ed. F. Kermode, London: Oxford University Press.

Chapter 6

'Am I a Jew?': Woolf's 1930s Political and Economic Peregrinations

Kathryn Simpson

Woolf's troubling and contradictory attitude to Jewishness has long been seen as a source of perplexity and frustration for her readers and critics. At times she expresses her sense of identification as a Jew, aligning herself specifically with Leonard and with a more general sense of being an outsider. Yet her personal and public writing is riddled with instances of antisemitism, including pointed attacks on Leonard and his family, which are shocking in their vehemence.

The coexistence of these contradictory perceptions of her Jewish relatives and Jewishness more generally can be seen as symptomatic of a wider cultural confusion about the figure of the Jew in this historical period. Simultaneously perceived as an ancient race, outcast and alien in the modern Christian world, 'Jews were often viewed as moderns *par excellence,* ... cosmopolitan, rootless, urban' (Linett 2007: 80). The significant influx of East European Jewish immigrants during the latter part of the nineteenth century and the pre-war period heightened cultural tensions within established Jewish communities in London and in the wider society, adding further complexity to issues of identity and belonging and giving rise to the perceived sense of the 'problem' of the Jew in British society.[1] That 'the conceptual Jew' is a 'semantically overloaded entity', 'blending meanings which ought to be kept apart', as Zygmunt Bauman explains (2000: 39), seems key to understanding the Jew as a figure of contradiction and boundary-troubling complexity in Woolf's political thinking and writing.

Woolf's antisemitism was also closely bound up with class prejudice, as Michael Whitworth suggests: '[i]f social classifications motivated her distaste, class and not race was the important factor' (2005: 72). But Woolf was also critically self-aware of her 'snobbery' (particularly in her response to Leonard's family) and of the ways in which her own class privilege and racial prejudice sometimes created a myopic view and dangerous blind spots. Hermione Lee argues that 'Woolf separates herself off from the habitual, half-conscious anti-Semitism of her circle' but that she also 'spells out her complicity in bigotry and offensiveness by way of self-accusation and social critique' (1996: 680).[2] Woolf's representations of Jews and Jewishness are central to this complex stance. They signal her distance from conventional views and her critique of ideologically produced ideas of difference and distinction; she assumes the Jew's outsider status as a position from which to launch her political and social critique. Yet, she seems also complicit with racist attitudes and often creates her Jewish characters as pariah figures, as composites of racial prejudice, alien and unassailably other. As the figure of the Jew became an increasingly controversial centre around which circulated a mixture of public opinions in the 1930s, Jewish characters in Woolf's writing work to anxiously mark boundaries and signal the limits of her social and political criticism. The wandering meanings of the Jew in Woolf's writing seem to mirror her own peregrinations in relation to personal and political boundaries of belonging and, crucially, indicate her attempts to retain her status and integrity as a writer in this rapidly changing European context. Woolf's bestseller, *The Years* (1937), and two stories she published specifically for profit, 'The Duchess and the Jeweller' (1938) and 'Lappin and Lapinova' (1939),[3] will be the focus here.[4]

Woolf's antisemitism can be seen as a vehicle to articulate wider cultural anxieties and criticism than those related to only to race and ethnicity. I will examine a network of interrelated anxieties, personal, political and economic, which reach a peak for Woolf in the mid- to late 1930s and in which the figure of the Jew is inextricably enmeshed. Critics have explored potential triggers for Woolf's antisemitic representations and one of these is money. This association is unsurprising since Jewish identity is perceived as synonymous with financial matters, commerce, money-making, and greed in the cultural imaginary. As Maren Tova Linett suggests, 'Money ... is the element allosemitic discourse most commonly associates with Jews' in modernist fiction as elsewhere, so that even if Jewish characters are poor or disinterested in money, they are 'nevertheless metaphorically associated with money ... [T]he issue of money is never far from the surface when Jews are represented' (2007: 5).[5] Whitworth also notes the extremes of such thinking so that while poorer Jews were associated with criminality, 'Richer Jews ... were accused of secretly controlling international capitalist finance' (2005: 71). However, money and, more importantly, making money on the literary marketplace, take on a complex set of significances for Woolf that reverberate both positively and problematically, and with varying meanings, throughout her personal and professional experience.

From her earliest publication, Woolf's identity as a professional writer was bound up with her ability to make money from her writing and her diary entries, preoccupied with sales, indicate that this remained a marker of success. In 'Professions for Women' (1931) Woolf celebrates the ability of women to enter the literary profession and to make money and, as a successful writer and publisher, she is seen to manipulate, exploit and, Jennifer Wicke argues (1994), shape the market and our understanding of it. However, a strong distaste for popularity and the commercialisation of literature is a significant factor influencing Woolf's publishing decisions and her fictional representations of money-making success. The tensions provoked by these contradictory attitudes to the marketplace are at the heart of Woolf's 'social critique' and her 'self-accusation' is voiced through the ways in which she represents Jewishness. As Karen Leick observes, 'Woolf's anti-Semitic characterizations of Jews consistently appear in works where she was most consciously concerned with her mainstream reception and the income she might earn as a result of this success' (2010: 122–3). This connection is particularly pertinent and increasingly problematic in the context of the European crisis of the 1930s, a period coinciding with the peak of Woolf's fame, as indicated by the increasing critical attention she began to receive[6] and by the successful sales of her novels and their bestseller status (*Orlando*, *Flush*, and *The Years*).

Yet at this time she was also most stridently critical of what she saw as the pernicious influence of capitalism that provoked insatiable material desires and fed fascist thinking and the greed for political power. She objected to the pervasion of capitalist forces into all areas of life and particularly what she saw as the intrusion of market forces and political agendas in the sphere of literary writing, as she argues, for example, in 'Why Art Today Follows Politics' (1936; in *E* 6: 75–9) and 'Reviewing' (1939; in *E* 6: 195–206). This was also a personally and professionally fraught period for Woolf. While she aligned herself more closely with Leonard's Jewish identity in the mid-1930s, seeming to take on the 'accidental Jewish identity' her marriage conferred (Leick 2010: 131), her political position led to her sense of isolation as the decade wore on. Her pacifism and feminism not only distanced her from the larger political allegiances and patriotic fervour growing in Britain, but increasingly put her at odds in her intimate personal relationships with Leonard and other friends and family who gradually came to support the process of military rearmament in the struggle against Hitler. This feeling compounded her doubts about her reputation so that by the late 1930s she reflects in her diaries on a sense of her precarious position, suspecting that her 'public reputation at [that] moment' was 'secondrate', and 'likely . . . to be discarded altogether' and 'decapitated' by negative criticism (*D* 5: 188). Rather than bolstering her confidence, the increased critical attention she received served only to heighten her anxieties about her writing and its significance, and to compound her wider concerns about the place of literature and its function in an increasingly commercialised and politicised context. In 'Thoughts on Peace in an Air Raid' (1940; in *E* 6: 173–7) she asserts the power of women's creativity and the necessity for women to fight for peace and freedom 'with the mind' (173), but her anxieties about her own writing caused her to doubt the efficacy of her role as a woman writer in this increasingly masculinised, belligerent and dangerous historical moment. The corruptions of the 'money motive', which she saw increasingly interfering in literary creation, resulted in a denigrated creative field amounting to 'intellectual harlotry' and 'brain prostitution' (*TG*: 111, 114, 108).

Woolf's antisemitism could be seen, then, as a resistance to the powerful external events acting on her private experience. The complexity of forces at work in shaping Woolf's situation and her sense of her identity led to contradictions indicative of her own increasingly conflicted position in the 1930s. Her Jewish characters can be read as vehicles for her own anxieties and fears (personal, political, and professional), embodying her own sense of alienation and irreconcilable difference. A ready-made symbol for of commercialism and greed, as well as a focus of political conflict, the Jew signifies a profound sense of threat for Woolf – at once an embodiment of the forces of commercial modernity she felt to be undermining her own status as a literary writer, but also her own desire to profit from her work. Nonetheless, even as she voiced these complexly intertwined fears about the impact of market forces and political agendas on literary creativity, Woolf continued to exploit her fame and reputation to make money in the literary marketplace.

In *Three Guineas* she proposes the formation of an 'anonymous and secret Society of Outsiders' as a response to the conflicting pressures of the time, and argues that for membership '[e]lasticity is essential' (*TG*: 126, 130). Her own complex and contradictory negotiation of the modernist marketplace endorses this view. As Woolf's racial politics in relationship to Jews shift back and forth across boundaries of belonging, her writing repeatedly brings into question what it means to assume an insider/outsider position. Woolf's anxieties about commercial success seem to be played out via the antisemitism in her work, notably her representations of the greasy tallow-worker, Abrahamson; the avaricious social climber, Oliver Bacon; and the gold-obsessed Thorburns. However, Woolf's antisemitism in relation to the literary market can be seen as an axis around which a complex network of interconnected issues revolve, notably the slippery territory of complicity and belonging.

Woolf's modernist family saga, *The Years*, charts the declining fortunes of the Pargiter family from the 1880s to the 'Present Day' of the 1930s. It engages more explicitly that other of Woolf's fiction with social and political realities, including 'the continuous modern history of the Jews of London' as David Bradshaw argues (1999: 189). The final section registers the rise of antisemitism in Britain and the troubling increase in strength of the British Union of Fascists in the mid-1930s. As Bradshaw points out, Woolf's social critique is enforced by other aspects of her novel that seem to emphasise the rightful place of Jews in Britain. Although Woolf makes visible and confronts the historical zeitgeist by exposing 'the persistence of British middle-class anti-Semitism as an obstacle to anti-fascism', her social critique points also to self-accusation (Suh 2009: 126). The overt and offensive antisemitism is conveyed in the direct speech of her characters and so distanced from authorial attitudes, but still Woolf's prejudices are inferred: 'she risks a moral ambiguity that is never clarified' (Lassner 1996: 135). Although Woolf assumes the 'outsider' position from which to voice her social critique, her own middle-class privilege and 'insider' status render her status 'elastic' and her representation of her Jewish characters complex and contradictory.

The 'Present Day' section in *The Years* stages a number of encounters between groups of characters in the lead-up to Delia's family party. It is the meeting between Sara and North, however, that offers the most shocking articulation of antisemitism in the novel. The figure of the Jew acts as a vehicle for the anxieties of the characters pertaining to money, identity, and belonging, a set of interrelated anxieties also shared by Woolf. There is no question that the exchange between Sara and North is overtly antisemitic. Their discussion of Abrahamson clearly associates him with dirt, grease, and the sordid. His attempts at attaining cleanliness only result, according to Sara, in a lack of hygiene for others, signalled by the greasy line and hair he leaves in the bath, which suggest contamination, as do as his coughing and snorting. The description of Abrahamson alludes to Jewish stereotypes and his name also obviously marks his Jewish historical lineage as 'a figurative scion of the first Hebrew patriarch' (Bradshaw 1999: 185). Yet far from remaining simply the alien outsider, Abrahamson's presence brings underlying anxieties sharply into focus, connecting the problematic concerns with identity and belonging to money-making and writing. Although this exchange seems shockingly racist, the context of this scene reveals the complex contradictions and tensions in play.

The discussion takes place in Sara's 'untidy' room, in her own '"sordid"' flat in a '"low-down street"' in the East End, following a badly cooked and unappealing meal, clumsily served by the 'lodging-house skivvy' with only 'a dish of rather fly-blown fruit' to follow pudding (*TY*: 273, 271, 274, 281). Money, or rather a fall in the Pargiter family fortunes, has led to these reduced circumstances, positioning Sara as an 'outsider' to middle-class norms and eroding the financial markers of class distinction. But North's state of financial limbo is also an aspect of *his* sense of displacement as well, tied as his fortunes are to the long period of time in which he has been absent from 'home' as a colonial farmer in Africa. Although he tells Eleanor he has '"four or five thousand"' in savings (*TY*: 334), he remains vague about a permanent return to Britain. Sara and North are both social outsiders in different ways and both turn to writing for a sense of confirmation of their insider status. Their virulent exchange about Abrahamson is tellingly sandwiched between North's by-heart recital of Andrew Marvell's 'The Garden' and Sara's elaborately performed story of a visit to a newspaper office, seemingly to seek employment or possibly to contribute a story to fuel antisemitism in the press. Yet neither the great literary tradition nor commercial journalism can cement their sense of belonging or secure their status and identity, a situation that perhaps speaks of Woolf's own dilemma.

Sara's story recalls her interview at a newspaper office and her explanation of what had brought her there – '"But the Jew's in my bath, I said – the Jew . . . the Jew . . . "' (*TY*: 298). Her inability to move beyond this opening to elucidate further indicates a racist response bordering on the phobic. Her repetition of 'the Jew' stymies communication, a result perhaps of '[t]he protean instability of "the Jew" as a sign' which renders it meaningless, as Cheyette describes it (1996: 11). However, her unnerved state points also to a profound troubling of boundaries of self and other, which can be attributed to the Jew's 'semantically confusing and psychologically unnerving status of foreigner[s] inside' (Bauman 2000: 34). Although Sara is intent on divesting herself of her sense of contamination and connection with all that Jewishness signifies, the context in which she recounts this experience suggests more complex and contradictory connections. Examining Woolf's various reworkings of 'the Jew in the bath' scene, Linett persuasively demonstrates how Abrahamson, a figure synonymous with money interest, acts as a 'scapegoat' for Woolf's anxious resistance to (political and economic) external pressures that would undermine her pacifist position and stifle her imaginative freedoms as a writer (2007: 53, 55–6, 180).[7] Yet, Sara's imitation of Abrahamson's '"Pah!"' noise becomes the starting-point of her own story, thus framing and containing her narrative. That Sara's narrative is enclosed in the temporal space in which Abrahamson takes his bath keeps to the fore the sharing of this intimate amenity, which results in her need to fiercely assert her difference even as the greasy bath compounds the slipperiness of the distinctions between them. Indeed, North questions both the veracity of Sara's story and the 'truth' of Sara herself: Sara, perhaps a little intoxicated, had spoken with 'excitement' which 'created yet another person; another semblance, which one must solidify into one whole' (*TY*: 299). Like Sara, Woolf would seem to insist on distinctions between her own disinterested writing and that which is commercially produced, but these continually slip and slide and for all Woolf's 'hostility and resistance' she could not 'eradicate' the contradictions and conflicts her profession posed (Chan 2010: 602).

While analogies between Woolf and Sara are frequently the focus of discussion, North's recital of Marvell's poem in this scene is also affected by the timing of Abrahamson's bath, complicating issues of belonging and identity and suggesting Woolf's awareness that no writing, even canonical literature, can remain immune from the tensions of the present day. Although the great poets may sing of 'the dream of peace, the dream of freedom', this cannot detract from a recognition of 'the fact' of the rising tensions in Britain and Europe (*TG*: 163). North begins his recital at Sara's request and to ensure she keeps her promise to go to Delia's party and maintain the bonds of family. Since his return from Africa, North has felt displaced, 'feeling that he was no one and nowhere in particular'; he struggles to adjust to the pace and modernity of London and feels confused by the social whirl of renewing acquaintance with family and friends (*TY*: 272, 270). Via his recital, he attempts to assert his sense of belonging to his family, to British culture and to the English literary tradition.

While Linett argues that the creative harmony between Sara and North is intruded upon by a Jew here (2007: 49–50), it is actually Sara's gesture of raising her hand (evocative of a fascist salute) that halts his recital.[8] North's outburst of anger, '"Damn the Jew!"' (*TY*: 296), then derails the harmony created by Marvell's words. That Marvell's words give way to the sounds of Abrahamson in the bath suggest that the boundaries of the English literary tradition are not watertight and are no guarantee of insider identity or belonging. Woolf draws on Marvell's poems repeatedly in her own writing but, as Jim Stewart persuasively argues, '[she] had . . . a need to appropriate and rewrite him' to counter the 'masculinism' of his work (2007: 35, 33). Her 'disruptive' 'uses of Marvellian lyric' (35) are also apparent here and work to trouble boundaries of belonging. Marvell's poem, 'The Garden' creates an idealised space of 'delicious solitude', a paradisal world free from 'The busie Companies of Men' (Marvell 1952: 48). While North and Sara focus on the racial other to forge their bond and to assert their 'insider' status, Woolf's use of this particular poem, with its explicit exclusion of women, infers a connection between North and Abrahamson along gender lines.

Like Marvell's speaker, Abrahamson's ablutions signal a desire to slough off the world of money-making business, and North identifies so closely with the poem as to feel its 'words' as 'actual presences, hard and independent', which are, however, 'changed by their contact with [Sara]'(*TY*: 296). This sense of gendered connection is indicated by the fact that North does not immediately recognise the sound of Abrahamson as an interruption, but rather, momentarily, accepts it as part of Marvell's poem: 'he heard a sound. Was it in the poem or outside of it, he wondered? Inside, he thought' (*TY*: 296). The cousins are silenced by their rage and anger about 'the Jew' but, as they listen in the 'quiet' house to the sound of Abrahamson's 'bath water running away', North notices '[a] watery pattern fluctuated on the ceiling' of Sara's room (*TY*: 299). This juxtaposition of the two sentences describing the draining of the bath and the pattern suggests a metaphorical connection between the two spaces, inferring that boundaries of all kinds, material walls, social distinctions, geographical borders (for a moment North thinks he is 'in Africa, sitting on the verandah in the moonlight' (*TY*: 299), are permeable, fluid, blurred, and, importantly for Woolf's sense of belonging, 'fluctuat[ing]'.

Here and elsewhere in Woolf's writing 'the Jew' is a liminal, mobile figure, testing the insider/outsider boundary, a figure of familiar difference and of (un)belonging. Epitomising membership of the Outsider's Society, and so a counterpart in Woolf's political stance, 'the Jew' is also a figure onto which Woolf projects her own self-criticism. Woolf seeks to maintain an elastic sense of membership of the Outsiders' Society (with individuals operating simultaneously 'inside' and 'outside' norms and institutions), to privilege fluctuation over fixity in her politics and aesthetics,[9] and to resist market thinking that dominates. But, like North, she is beset by issues of '[p]olitics and money' and is unable to resist their influence on her writing (*TY*: 353). Later in the novel, at the family party, North is 'accused' by his sister, Peggy, of aspiring only to be conventional and conformist: to get married, have children and '"Make money. Write little books to make money"' (*TY*: 341). Peggy's accusation of North can also stand for Woolf's own self-accusation as she continues to '"write one little book, and then another little book . . . instead of living . . . living differently, differently"' (*TY*: 342). For Woolf herself, these 'little books' to make money include her short stories 'The Duchess and Jeweller' and 'Lappin and Lapinova'. Both continue Woolf's engagement with the issues of belonging, status, and creativity as they also foreground issues of money-making and greed articulated via antisemitic representations. Both also suggest a social critique along-side a critical self-awareness of her own complicity as they suggestively engage with Woolf's dilemma about how to maintain personal, political, and artistic integrity in this context.

Focused on selling these stories to the fashionable *Harper's Bazaar*, Woolf asserts her intention to be particularly business-like ('hard as flint') in her dealings with Jacques Chambrun, her New York agent, over negotiations about 'The Duchess and the Jeweller' (*L* 6: 173). Although Woolf responded to criticism of her offensive depiction of her central character by removing explicit references his Jewish identity (Dick 1991: 314–15), her story remains a controversial and offensively antisemitic depiction of a Jewish jeweller. In this Woolf's story and her marketing strategy suggest a repugnance for the commercial world Oliver Bacon so successfully epitomises, but also a conflicted sense of her guilty complic-ity in the monetary greed her negotiations highlight.[10] Lara Trubowitz persuasively argues for Woolf's use of a 'constellation of tropes', includ-ing the 'acquisition of rubies and diamonds', which creates a parallel between the luxurious opulence of Oliver's jewels and the conspicuous display of first editions collected by the Woolfs' acquaintance, Victor Rothschild, a wealthy Jewish aristocrat (Trubowitz 2008: 289, 290–1). In this transposition the jewels are synonymous with books and both are commodities for conspicuous display and investment.[11] This not only suggests Woolf's anxiety about the place of books in the marketplace and her own role in producing and marketing them, but also her con-flicted feelings about her own role in creating niche markets in which books are not valued and appreciated for their own sake but are prized as modernist investments (as Lawrence Rainey argues [1999: 42–5]). As Leick claims about Woolf's representation of Jews in *The Years*, 'the presence of Jews not only reveals, but also causes or is a catalyst for the new and changing marketplace that England has become, implicitly threatening the old order' (2010: 128).

By placing her story for publication in a popular magazine, Woolf's sense of this being a commercial venture is confirmed. She wrote her story to make money and, unusually for Woolf, adjusted it to suit her customer and thus allowed her artistic decisions to be compromised by the market); in effect, she 'sold out' to *Harper's Bazaar*. In what may seem to be an unexpected parallel, it would seem that, like Oliver, she is aware of her own complicity in dealing in 'false pearls' and so shoring up a social, political, and economic system she finds increasingly despicable and inhuman. Both Woolf and Oliver recognise their 'treasures' carry worth (emotional, associative, and political) beyond their market value. As Oliver assesses the jewels he trades in:

> 'Tears!' said Oliver, looking at the pearls.
> 'Heart's blood!' he said, looking at the rubies.
> 'Gunpowder!' he continued, rattling the diamonds so that they flashed and blazed. (*CSF*: 250)

Yet both betray this understanding: Oliver, insatiable for social and sexual satisfaction, willingly puts aside his professional expertise and skills in discerning authentic gems in order to capitalise on the privileges of the rich social and sexual bounty the Duchess offers; Woolf similarly compromises her professional integrity to make money and consolidate her reputation on the competitive literary market.[12] During the process of negotiating her deal with Chambrun, Woolf reflects on the pleasure of writing out her story, the 'extravagant flash' experienced as 'a moment of the old rapture' (*D* 5: 107). However, she also considers her own integrity as she wonders whether she ever writes just for herself, for her own private consumption and not for an audience or for profit in any way, even in her diary: 'Do I ever write, even here, for my own eye? If not, for whose eye? An interesting question, rather' (*D* 5: 107).[13] Creating a character willing to turn a blind eye to the Duchess's trick in order to satisfy his greedy social aspirations is one way in which Woolf directs her self-scrutiny outward onto her offensive depiction of her Jewish character. This highly stereotyped character (a caricature, no less[14]) acts as both a repository for her own guilty complicity and a smokescreen shielding her own professional compromise. However, the parallels between the risks that his greedy venture entails and those that Woolf also undertakes are very apparent: both allow greed and ambition to override their professional judgement and the unease registered in this story, the literal and metaphorical dealing in 'fake pearls', pinpoints this explicitly.

Similar concerns and anxieties about markets, belonging, and the value and valuing of integrity also resonate strongly in 'Lappin and Lapinova', a story in which (private) imaginative creativity is set in opposition to the (public) worship of gold. What is also very apparent here is the way in which Woolf's class prejudice coloured her perception of Jews in general and intensified the antisemitism in her writing. Woolf loathed what she perceived as the middle-class ostentation, vulgarity, showy displays of emotion, and senseless chatter of her Jewish acquaintances and relatives. Rosalind's distaste for her husband Ernest's family echoes Woolf's own antithetical, if not at times offensive and hostile, feelings towards Leonard's family, and her difficult relationship with his mother, Marie Woolf, that she expressed in letters and diaries.[15] Like Leonard's family, there are ten Thorburn siblings[16] and Rosalind is repelled by the way they seem to 'breed so' (*CSF*: 265). This criticism is echoed in Woolf's responses to the large Woolf family gatherings she found so irritating and distasteful, and which brought out her antisemitic prejudices, articulated through exaggerations of numbers of family members (Lee 1996: 314).

Yet in this story 'breeding' has a dual meaning that signals both class and racial prejudice. Suggestively breeding like rabbits, the Thorburns have no 'breeding' and this slur on their manners and demeanour takes on a specifically monetary turn so central to antisemitic stereotypes. They are represented as crass and preoccupied with ostentatious display of their wealth and their family values are focused only on increase and profit. These values are exaggerated in the central event of the story, the Thorburn's golden-wedding anniversary party, where '[e]verything was gold' (*CSF*: 264). The party's obsession with flashy gold and excessive opulence serves to expose more fully the shallow greed and desire for profit which forge the Thorburn family bond, and the abundant and lavish gifts the Thorburns are given emphasise this more fully: these are all 'gold, hall-marked, authentic' and so readily translatable into, in fact synonymous with, money (*CSF*: 264).

In this context, Rosalind feels herself to be not only an outsider, but profoundly overwhelmed and under threat. Distinguishing herself from Ernest's prolifically fertile family by wearing her white wedding dress, her intense discomfort and feeling of isolation are signalled by her gaze, which 'seemed insoluble as an icicle' (*CSF*: 264). But the power of gold, associated the overbearing heat of the party, leads to a sensation of disintegration: 'She was being melted; dispersed; dissolved into nothingness' (*CSF*: 265). This thawing and potential burning that the Thor(thaw)burns seem to represent are experienced as powerful threats, eroding Rosalind's sense of autonomy. However, recourse to the private fantasy world she and Ernest have created saves her temporarily. The importance of the imagination to sustain existence and relationships is emphasised here and their creative collaboration seals an exclusive bond in which they assume a privileged position, as King Lappin (a rabbit) and Queen Lapinova (a hare), from which they mock and criticise Ernest's family. They feel 'in league together, *against* the rest of the world' (*CSF*: 263; my emphasis). However, the 'real' world intrudes and this utopian fantasy cannot be sustained and, with the loss of Ernest's co-operation, Rosalind experiences a sense of doom with her own metaphorical death and the death of her marriage.

Reading through a biographical lens, this loss of being in league with Ernest may reflect Woolf's own feelings of political discord with her own 'earnest' husband, Leonard, in the 1930s context of the story's publication.[17] When this emphasis on creativity and narrative is considered alongside the literary associations of Rosalind's golden-anniversary gift, there emerges a complex and contradictory perspective on Woolf's feelings about her role in the literary marketplace that sheds new light on her representation of the Jewish Thorburns. Rosalind's gift is an 'eighteenth-century relic', 'an old sand caster' (*CSF*: 264), something outmoded and not gold which marks her difference from Ernest's family and their monetary values that the other gifts confirm. The sand caster's role in fixing words on the page invites comparisons with the Hogarth Press, which, utilising hand-printing and other outdated modes and traditions of literary production, signalled its refusal of mechanised efficiency and the profit motive as key to literary production, valuing the intellectual and creative work itself rather than seeing writing simply as a commodity for sale.

While this reading obviously looks back to the period of the story's original composition, the turn to outmoded practices of publication takes on a more radical political purpose in *Three Guineas* where, as Collier points out, 'Woolf . . . urges her readers to use such anachronistic means of production and distribution as the private printing press and the hand-distributed leaflet' as a counter to the mass communications of 'her society's dominant media channels' (2010: 319). However, while Woolf stands in opposition the ethos of acquisitiveness dictating the operation of the commercial literary marketplace, wanting her writing to be distinct from the popular proliferation of words that are mechanically produced, politically aligned and closely associated with propaganda, she, nonetheless, produced a racially provocative story that she exchanged for its equivalent in gold. Like the Thorburns' gifts her story is also 'hall-marked', a commodity readily traded for cash.

Woolf's fiction of the mid- to late 1930s speaks, in different ways, to her position as a writer, feminist, and a pacifist in a context in which she both sought success on the literary market but opposed what she saw as the distortions and corruptions accompanying the commercialisation of literature. On the one hand, like Rosalind, Woolf felt her self overwhelmed, dissolved, by the political and commercial heat of the late 1930s as European tensions increased. She found herself an unwilling member of a society intent on a war that, as she argues in *Three Guineas*, is fuelled by greed. She may long to elude the mechanisms of the literary marketplace, to be 'the hare, a long way ahead of the hounds [her] critics' (*D* 4: 45), to privilege the life of the imagination as vital to existence, and to foster collaboration and co-creation, but 'Lappin and Lapinova' reveals the complexity (and perhaps the impossibility) involved in striving for these goals. Yet, like Oliver Bacon, Woolf was also willingly complicit in the commercial world, seeming to risk her professional and artistic integrity for profit.

The antisemitism in Woolf's work is indicative of her anxieties resulting from her publication practices, namely the tension created by her hostile criticism of the literary marketplace and the commercialisation of literature, and her own deliberate strategy of making money from her writing. In this particular period, as her doubts about her role as a professional writer increased, her ability to make money from her writing and thereby to assert her success and efficacy became even more pressing. The stereotypical Jewish figures in her writing, associated with commerce, greed, and conspicuous consumption, become repositories for her conflicted feelings and responses to this situation. But the figure of the Jew also becomes a more complex and contested site of meaning, a vehicle for a tangled web of contradictory impulses. Jewishness is at once the focal point for Woolf's personal, political, and professional anxieties, but also a more ambiguous symbol of the slipperiness of notions of belonging. Emphasising racial otherness works to keep the anxieties her Jewish characters embody at a distance and they also bear the brunt of Woolf's hostile class and racist prejudice. However, they also epitomise membership of the Society of Outsiders associated as they are with mobility, fluctuation, and a certain elasticity conferring the capacity to transgress boundaries.

The discomfort generated by Woolf's antisemitism seems to mirror Woolf's own unease in her present moment. Like the stereotypical Jew, Woolf feels that she cannot fully assimilate into contemporary society and considers herself to be 'fundamentally . . . an outsider' (*D* 5: 189). Woolf cannot comply with the belligerence and patriotism of the wider society, nor adhere to what in *Three Guineas* she calls 'unreal loyalties' of pride, patriotism, honour, and loyalty to corrupt institutions (*TG*: 93). Woolf felt her claiming of the outsider status in *Three Guineas* had 'queered the pitch' and enabled her to publicly register her resistant and critical stance (*D5*: 188). However, although like her Jewish jeweller, she recognises the revolutionary potential of the materials at their disposal – Oliver's hoard of diamonds are '"Gunpowder!"' enough to blow up Mayfair, and Woolf's hoard of newspaper cuttings and other evidence are enough to blow up St Paul's (*CSF*: 250; *D* 4: 77)[18] – she does not seek to radically explode the social edifice.

It is perhaps North, however, who most evocatively encapsulates the paradox of Woolf's predicament. Standing accused of simply conforming to expectations by writing for money, North, like Woolf, recognises the dangerous impact of 'money and politics' on language itself in his awareness of 'a gap, a dislocation, between the word and the reality' as different political groups and societies represent it (*TY*: 354). His recognition of the severe compromise that 'belonging' entails echoes Woolf's own. Membership of social and political groups involves conformity and loss of individuality, leading to a compulsion to 'march[ing] in step after leaders, in herds, groups, societies, caparisoned' (*TY*: 358). But when he considers the effect of 'simplify[ing]' and breaking down barriers between such groups, he sees the danger of 'a world . . . that was all one jelly, one mass, . . . a rice pudding world, a white counterpane world' (*TY* 358–9). Like North, Woolf wants 'to make other sentences', to articulate a sense of autonomy 'but at the same time spread out, make a new ripple in human consciousness' (*TY*: 359). She wants to belong to the flow of society and the historical moment as well as to retain individuality, to 'be the bubble and the stream, the stream and the bubble – myself and the world together' (*TY*: 359). Woolf frequently feels that she is 'writing against the current', which she finds 'difficult entirely to disregard' (*D* 5: 189). Jewishness provokes her irrational anger but also focuses her critical zeal, including her criticism of her own complicity in antisemitic prejudice. Like North, Woolf is an insider with an outsider's sometimes critical and defamiliarising perspective, a perspective she also adopts in her scrutiny of her own position.

In *Three Guineas* Woolf notes the dream of harmony proffered by Literature – 'the voices of the poets, answering each other, assuring us of a unity that rubs out divisions as if they were chalk marks only' (*TG*: 163) – yet the chalk marks of this historical period, used to enforce the difference between Jew and non-Jew, are neither so easily erased nor so readily ignored. Indeed, they severely threaten this idealised notion of harmony in multiplicity that literature has the capacity to create. She understands that all writing is open to question and manipulation and although she may, as Jed Esty argues in relation to *Between the Acts*, seek 'to celebrate the right kind of English civilization' through celebrating the English literary tradition, she is aware that this runs the risk of 'fueling the wrong kind of English patriotism' (2004: 90). As others have argued, Woolf's antisemitism remains a troubling element in her life and work, seeming to severely undermine her political stance in relation to her feminism, pacifism, and broadly socialist thinking. However, Ruth Gruber's early analysis astutely sums up Woolf's position: 'Between these two extremes, between exaggerated integrity and self-betrayal, Virginia Woolf attempts to steer her way' (2005: 65), an attempt made only more fraught and complex as the extremes of the 1930s pressed ever more heavily on her. Woolf recognised that boundaries dividing groups and individuals are simply ideologically endorsed conventions; in giving them tangible form – the greasy line, the string of fake pearls, the chalk marks – she makes visible their impermanence and precariousness and sets in their place the ideal of the bubble's thin skin – its molecules in tension with each other and ready to burst and reform perpetually.

Notes

1. See Whitworth (2005: 70–2) and Deborah L. Parsons (2000: 101–4). See also Schröder (2013) and Lassner and Spiro (2013), who discuss antisemitism, assertions of Englishness and the perceived threat to British culture that Jews represented.
2. Other critics also see that Woolf's antisemitic prejudices 'co-existed with respectful, informed, engaged responses to Jews and Jewish culture', as Emma Sutton argues (2013: 135, n.44). See also Bradshaw (1999).
3. Both published in *CSF*.
4. Short sections of my discussion of these two stories have appeared in the *Selected Papers from the Twenty-first Annual Conference on Virginia Woolf* (Simpson 2012) and in the *Virginia Woolf Miscellany* (Simpson 2011).
5. 'Allosemitism' is the Jewish literary critic Artur Sandauer's term to refer to the ways in which Jews are perceived as 'other' and set apart, 'regardless of the ostensible level of approval' (Linett 2007: 3).
6. See, for example, Roberts (1934), Holtby ([1932] 1978), and Gruber ([1935] 2005). Holtby's study includes a biographical chapter.
7. Not only is Milton Street where Sara lives indirectly associated with Jewishness (see Bradshaw 1999: 187–8), but was 'previously known as "Grub Street" [and] notorious for its hack writers and commercial literary pursuits', as Lassner and Spiro note (2013: 68). Other critics, including Evelyn Chan (2010: 600–1) and Maren Linett (2007: 63–70), view Sara's resistance to the pressures and/or temptations to 'prostitute' her brain to male-dominated commercial journalism as indicative of Woolf's repugnance for such enterprises, as well as her reflections on the problematic place of women in the professions.
8. Bradshaw comments that this is a familial gesture shared with other Pargiter women but that in this context it is 'disquieting' (1999: 184).
9. See Linett (2007) and Snaith (2000) for discussion of these issues in relation to the form of *The Years*.
10. That ultimately Chambrun got the best 'deal' may also suggest an atonement on Woolf's part. Initially offering Woolf $1,000 for a story in July 1937, following negotiations over the content of her story, this sum was reduced to $960 for both 'The Duchess and the Jeweller' plus 'The Shooting Party' (*D* 5: 107, n.6).

11. Rodríguez also discusses Woolf's contradictory position and the questioning of artistic value arising from the 'double dimension' of representation of Oliver's gems (2001–2: 126).
12. Both also compromise their family values, which, in different ways, were felt to have played a large role in ensuring their success.
13. Rodriguez cites this entry too in relation to Woolf's sense of marketplace competition (2001–2: 120).
14. Indeed, Woolf included a first draft, 'The Great Jeweller', in her list of 'Caricatures' written in 1932 (Dick 1991: 314).
15. Woolf complains of the incessant 'readymade reach me down chatter' from relatives with 'hearts of gold, eyes brimming with sympathy' when she longs, like Rosalind/Lapinova, only to be is 'alone by herself . . . walking on some solitary distant shore . . . [under] a rising moon or a setting sun' (*L* 5: 209). She anticipates that Marie Woolf's eighty-fourth birthday will 'be as hot as the monkey house', echoing the overbearing heat of the Thorburn party (*L* 5: 239).
16. Though one of Leonard's siblings 'died in infancy' (Glendinning 2006: 3).
17. The story was written at Asheham, therefore before 1919 (*D* 5: 188), and so invites a dual perspective on Woolf as a writer and publisher in this earlier post-war context as well as the later context of publication (April 1939) with fears of a second European war looming.
18. Trubowitz (2008: 293, 302 n.5) also notes this connection.

Bibliography

Bauman, Z. [1989] (2000), *Modernity and the Holocaust*, Cambridge: Polity.

Bradshaw, D. (1999), 'Hyams Place: *The Years*, the Jews and the British Union of Fascists', in *Women Writers of the 1930s: Gender, Politics and History*, ed. M. Joannou, Edinburgh: Edinburgh University Press, pp. 179–91.

Chan, E. T. (2010), 'Professions, Freedom and Form: Reassessing Woolf's *The Years* and *Three Guineas*', *The Review of English Studies*, New Series, 61(251): 591–613.

Cheyette, B., ed. (1996), Introduction, 'Unanswered Questions', *Between 'Race' and Culture: Representations of 'the Jew' in English and American Literature*, Stanford: Stanford University Press, pp. 1–15.

Collier, P. (2010), 'Virginia Woolf and the Art of Journalism', in *The Edinburgh Companion to Virginia Woolf and the Arts*, ed. M. Humm, Edinburgh: Edinburgh University Press, pp. 314–31.

Dick, S., ed. [1985] (1991), *Virginia Woolf: The Complete Shorter Fiction*, London: Triad Grafton Books.

Esty, J. (2004), *A Shrinking Island: Modernism and National Culture in England*, Princeton and Oxford: Princeton University Press.

Glendinning, V. (2006), *Leonard Woolf: A Life*, London: Simon and Schuster.

Gruber. R. [1935] (2005), *Virginia Woolf: The Will to Create as a Woman*, New York: Carroll and Graf Publishers.

Holtby, W. [1932] (1978), *Virginia Woolf: A Critical Memoir*, Chicago: Academy Press.

Lassner, P. (1996), '"The Milk of Our Mother's Kindness Has Ceased to Flow": Virginia Woolf, Stevie Smith, and the Representation of the Jew', in *Between 'Race' and Culture: Representations of 'the Jew' in English and American Literature*, ed. B. Cheyette, Stanford: Stanford University Press, pp. 129–44.

Lassner, P., and M. Spiro (2013), 'A Tale of Two Cities: Virginia Woolf's Imagined Jewish Spaces and London's East End Jewish Culture', *Woolf Studies Annual*, 19; 59–82.

Lee, H. (1996), *Virginia Woolf*, London: Chatto and Windus.

Leick, K. (2010), 'Virginia Woolf and Gertrude Stein: Commerce, Bestsellers and the Jew', in *Virginia Woolf and the Literary Marketplace*, ed. J. Dubino, New York and London: Palgrave Macmillan, pp. 159–75.

Linett, M. T. (2007), *Modernism, Feminism, and Jewishness*, Cambridge: Cambridge University Press.

Marvell, A., [1681] (1952), *The Poems and Letters of Andrew Marvell*, vol. 1, ed. H. M. Margoliouth, Oxford: Clarendon Press, pp. 48–50.

Parsons, D. L. (2000), *Streetwalking the Metropolis: Women, the City and Modernity*, Oxford: Oxford University Press.

Rainey, L. (1999), 'The Cultural Economy of Modernism', in *The Cambridge Companion to Modernism*, ed. M. Levenson, Cambridge: Cambridge University Press, pp. 33–69.

Roberts J. H. (1934), 'Toward Virginia Woolf', *The Virginia Quarterly Review*, 10: 587–602.

Rodríguez, L. M. L. (2001–2), 'Contradiction and Ambivalence: Virginia Woolf and the Aesthetic Experience in "The Duchess and the Jeweller"', *Journal of English Studies*, 3: 115–29.

Schröder, L. K. (2013), '"A question is asked which is never answered": Virginia Woolf, Englishness and Antisemitism', *Woolf Studies Annual*, 19: 27–57.

Simpson, K. (2011), '"Lappin and Lapinova: The Hares and the Woolves', *Virginia Woolf Miscellany*, 79, Spring: 19–21.

Simpson, K. (2012), '"Come buy, come buy": Woolf's Contradictory Relationship to the Marketplace': in *Contradictory Woolf: Selected Papers from the Twenty-First International Conference on Virginia Woolf*, ed. D. Ryan and S. Bolaki, Clemson: Clemson University Digital Press, pp. 186–93.

Snaith, A. (2000), *Public and Private Negotiations*, Basingstoke: Palgrave Macmillan.

Stewart, J. (2007), 'Woolf and Andrew Marvell: The Gendering of Modernism', in *Woolfian Boundaries: Selected Papers from the Sixteenth Annual International Conference on Virginia Woolf*, ed. A. Burrells, S. Ellis, D. Parsons, and K. Simpson, Clemson: Clemson University Digital Press, pp. 30–5.

Suh, J. (2009), *Fascism and Anti-Fascism in Twentieth-Century British Fiction*, Basingstoke: Palgrave Macmillan.

Sutton, E. (2013), *Virginia Woolf and Classical Music: Politics, Aesthetics, Form*, Edinburgh: Edinburgh University Press.

Trubowitz, L. (2008), 'Concealing Leonard's Nose: Virginia Woolf, Modernist Antisemitism and "The Duchess and the Jeweller"', *Twentieth-Century Literature*, 54(3): 273–306.

Whitworth, M. (2005), *Authors in Context: Virginia Woolf*, Oxford: Oxford University Press.

Wicke, J. (1994), 'Mrs Dalloway Goes to Market: Woolf, Keynes, and Modern Markets', *Novel: A Forum on Fiction*, 28(1): 5–23.

Woolf, V. (1974–84), *The Diary of Virginia Woolf*, 5 vols, ed. A. O. Bell and A. McNeillie, New York: Harcourt Brace Jovanovich.

Woolf, V. (1975–80), *The Letters of Virginia Woolf*, 6 vols, ed. N. Nicolson and J. Trautmann, New York: Harcourt Brace Jovanovich.

Woolf, V. [1985] (1991a), *Virginia Woolf: The Complete Shorter Fiction*, ed. S. Dick, London: Triad Grafton Books.

Woolf, V. [1938] (1991b), *Three Guineas*, London: Hogarth Press.

Woolf, V. [1937] (1992), *The Years*, London: Vintage.

Woolf, V. [1931] (2003), 'Professions for Women', in *Women and Writing*, ed. and intro. M. Barrett, San Diego: Harvest/Harcourt, pp. 57–63.

Woolf, V (2011), *The Essays of Virginia Woolf*, vol. 6: 1933–41, ed. S. N. Clarke, London: Hogarth Press.

Part Four

Human, Animal, and Nonhuman

Chapter 7

The Bispecies Environment, Coevolution, and *Flush*

Jeanne Dubino

So that to know her, or any one, one must seek out the people who completed them; even the places. Odd affinities she had with people she had never spoken to, some woman in the street, some man behind a counter – even trees, or barns.

somehow in the streets of London, ... here, there, she survived, Peter survived, lived in each other, she being part . . . of the trees at home; of the house . . .; part of people she had never met; being laid out like a mist between the people she knew best, who lifted her on their branches as she had seen the trees lift the mist, but it spread ever so far, her life, herself.

Virginia Woolf, *Mrs Dalloway*

The first headnote emphasises identity; our identity is dependent on our relations with others, including those we have not met, and even objects, whether they are edifices like barns or alive like trees. The second headnote links this interdependent identity to survival. It is through our tree-like linkage – our branching out – to other people that we survive. Trees are, or can be, a lattice, a network.[1] Woolf here suggests that our survival is dependent on this kind of network. It is not just through a one-on-one connection that we continue on after death, but rather through a mesh of multiple connections. More than half a century later, in their song, 'Touch of Grey', the Grateful Dead acknowledge this multiple dimension of survival too. This song, about growing old – much like *Mrs Dalloway* – is wistful in tone. The voice is that of a middle-aged man behind in his rent – that is, someone who has not made the most of his life, like, perhaps, Peter Walsh. Yet through the song the music remains upbeat, and the first-person pronoun of the refrain, 'I will get by', changes to 'we' in the last line of the song.[2] We will survive, 'get by', through our connections with each other.

We survive, as scientists now prove, through 'coevolution', or through interacting with other people, species, and groups, and through changing in response to these interactions.[3] This process is a fluid one, with 'everything . . . always on its way to becoming something else' (Holland 2011: 53). Coevolutionary approaches, as the sociologist Myra Hird writes, 'consider selective pressures as more involved with each other, more enmeshed' (2010: 740). Coevolutionary histories 'privilege species interdependence' (McHugh 2009: 160). Though 'co' might suggest binary, coevolution is not binary, but rather heterogeneous. As Donna Haraway colourfully characterises the coevolutionary scene, 'living critters' – and we humans are part of this 'bestiary of agencies' too[4] – 'form consortia in a baroque medley of inter- and intra-actions' (2006: 112). The environmentalist Anders Pape Møller notes that coevolution involves 'interactions among interactions'; scientists thus recognise that 'any single case of interaction between two parties may be affected by an entire range of additional interacting factors' (2008: 180). The ecologist Geerat Vermeij hypothesises four main ways in which species coevolve: predator-prey, competitors, host-guest, and mutual beneficiaries (this last is also termed symbiosis) (1994: 224). The zoologist James Thomson complicates this taxonomy with his term 'diffuse evolution' (2003: S1), whereby a species can 'function as a mutualist . . . in some ecological circumstances and as a parasite in others' (2003: S2), and other scientists[5] agree that relationships may shift.

In *Flush*, Virginia Woolf reminds us of the connection between biography and biology in her portrayal of the life of a dog. She imagines the ways that Elizabeth Barrett Browning's spaniel Flush shifts among these four forms of species' interactions – predator-prey, competitors, host-guest, and mutual beneficiaries – over the course of his life. While her focus, in this feeling-filled novel, is on the emotional dimensions of these interrelations, Woolf also represents the physical ways species interact with each other. In *Being Animal* Anna L. Peterson asks, 'What do . . . cross-species relationships ultimately mean?' (2013: 7). We understand these relationships, writes Peterson, by attending to animals' lived experiences. In *Flush* Woolf teases out these meanings through representing Flush's cross-species encounters, especially those relating to eating and to intimacy. Procreating and obtaining food are, of course, essential for evolutionary survival. In a novel that gestures toward Darwinianism, Woolf includes scenes of eating or of seeking food, and of those alluding to sex, or as *Flush*'s narrator euphemistically tells us, 'love' (119).[6]

Woolf points to the contexts in which these encounters take place. Like a scientist, she shows acute awareness of the significance of the environment. Scientists who now work within the framework of coevolution often include a consideration of the ecosystem in which these interactions take place; indeed, some conceive of coevolution as the interaction between the species and their environments.[7] Like twenty-first-century scientists, Woolf sees the interactions among species, and among species and their environments, as multidirectional (Haraway 2006: 112). The worlds in which Flush lives out the chapters of his existence – rural Reading, metropolitan London, and the streets of Italy – are, primarily, domesticated ones. At the same time, Woolf often reminds her readers, even in London, an epitome of civilisation, this domestication is, at times, little more than a thin veneer; the wild is ever present. Like ecofeminists now, including Carol J. Adams and Josephine Donovan (2006: 6), Woolf depicts these spheres as gendered, with the domestic associated with the feminine and the wild with the masculine. As this paper will show, these gendered associations have bearing on the development of Flush's character.

But first, a word on development. This term might suggest an evolutionary, forward process, but Woolf, like Jakob von Uexküll, an Estonian biologist and ethologist whose dates overlapped with hers (1864–1944), resisted a 'teleological narrative of progression' (see p. 156 this volume). Derek Ryan explains in his essay, 'Posthumanist Interludes: Ecology and Ethology in *The Waves*', located in this collection, that Woolf shared affinities with Uexküll, who developed the concept of 'umwelt', or environment, and whose writings addressed the meanings that animals make of their environments. These meanings unfold through a series of relationships; both meanings and relationships are multiform, and interwoven into one another. Uexküll's 'umwelt', indeed, resembles Darwin's 'inextricable web of affinities' (Darwin 1985: 415).

In *Darwin's Plots* Gillian Beer notes that in Victorian England 'web' referred not to a spider's web but rather to the weave of a fabric (1985: 168). In *Flush*, 'web' also specifically refers to fabric – when Flush first enters a shopping arcade he observes 'webs of tinted gauze' (28) – but more significantly, *Flush* is a novel filled with textiles: 'gleaming silk', 'ponderous bombazine', 'thin white muslin', the stuff of skirts and trousers, banners and shawls, tapestry and plush, carpets and runners, knitting and needlework (28, 120, 149, 154, 166, 18, 19, 158, 123). These webs whirling around Flush are suggestive of the interwoven worlds[8] within the novel, and a reminder of Woolf's lifelong desire to defy linearity and to render the manifold textures of life in all its plenitude and profusion. In this essay I focus on the life of the world of the companion animal. Woolf populates *Flush* with wild and tamed species: a menagerie of lions and tigers and cobras, partridges and parrots and rooks, elephants and fish and fox, black beetles and blue bottles, hares and fleas, and dogs (purebreds and mixed breeds, generations of greyhounds, and of course breeds of spaniels). I will address the interconnections she makes between the two prominent species of the book – dogs and humans – two species, as Donna Haraway writes, that 'have always had a vast range of ways of relating' (2003: 33). Along with expanding upon the four types of bispecies interactions (predator-prey, competitors, host-guest, and mutual beneficiaries), I will look at the significance of the environments – primarily domestic with the wild not far removed – in which these interactions take place. I will attend to the gendered dimensions of these environments, and to the activities themselves, especially those relating to food and intimacy, that characterise the interactions and thus illustrate how densely Woolf weaves a web of coevolution in a layered and interconnected world.

Predator-Prey

The first page of *Flush* introduces the first of the relationships identified by Vermeij, that between the predator and its prey: 'where there is vegetation the law of Nature has decreed that there shall be rabbits; where there are rabbits, Providence has ordained there shall be dogs' (3). In this one sentence Woolf not only sets forth the 'life-dinner principle' (Vermeij 1994: 227), but she also illustrates the way '[b]eings do not preexist their relatings' (Haraway 2003: 6); we only come into being within the context of, and by relating to, other beings.[9] At the same time Woolf parodies the notion of divine intervention: Providence here does become the means by which beings enter into 'co-constitutive relationships' (Haraway 2003: 12). This particular relationship, as Vermeij reminds us, is an asymmetrical one; success for the prey – escape from the predator – means life, or survival, while capture means injury or death. Failure for the predator, on the other hand, may mean just waiting that much longer to acquire a meal, and, possibly, ultimately death if too much time passes before it can eat again (Vermeij 1994: 227). Clearly, in *Flush*, the predator – the spaniel – does prevail, and does go on to propagate and develop into lines and families, 'the Clumber, the Sussex, the Norfolk, the Black Field, the Cocker, the Irish Water and the English Water' (5). Later, when Flush is in London, he dreams of hares – but then opens his eyes to the harsh reality that '[t]here [are] no hares'; they have been displaced by the Victorian world in which Elizabeth Barrett lives, with 'only Mr Browning in the armchair talking to Miss Barrett on the sofa' (59). Woolf does not tell us what happened to the hares; by implication, like the rabbits who have disappeared in Spain,[10] they seem to have vanished.

But Woolf would never settle for just an easy eat-or-be-eaten relationship; she complicates it in the following scene from early on in the novel, of Flush walking with Mary Russell Mitford in Three Mile Cross. Here she reminds us of how 'plants and animals interact in much more sophisticated and intricate ways than nonspecialists could imagine from a walk in a field or forest' (Thompson 1985: 596):

> The cool globes of dew or rain broke in showers of iridescent spray about his nose; the earth, here hard, here soft, here hot, here cold, stung, teased and tickled the soft pads of his feet. Then what a variety of smells interwoven in subtlest combination thrilled his nostrils ... But suddenly down the wind came tearing a smell sharper, stronger, more lacerating than any – a smell that ripped across his brain stirring a thousand instincts, releasing a million memories – the smell of hare, the smell of fox. Off he flashed like a fish drawn in a rush ... He forgot his mistress; he forgot all humankind ... He raced; he rushed. At last he stopped bewildered; the incantation faded ... And once at least the call was even more imperious; the hunting horn roused deeper instincts, summoned wilder and stronger emotions that transcended memory and obliterated grass, trees, hare, rabbit, fox in one wild shout of ecstasy. Love blazed her torch in his eyes; he heard the hunting horn of Venus. Before he was well out of his puppy-hood, Flush was a father. (*F*: 12–13)

A 'variety of smells interwoven in subtlest combination' trigger Flush's flight, but this sensory intermingling of textures and smells is overtaken by a lightning-like bolt of predatorial instinct shooting through his brain and releasing atavistic, prehistoric memories of the chase. This scene reminds us that dogs are, after all, 'domesticated predators' (Peterson 2013: 2). The call of the wild, growing more imperious, rouses yet deeper and stronger instincts, but not, as we might expect, the instinct to kill; rather, it ignites the flame of 'love'. Like Chaucer's monk, Flush 'lovede venerie' (Chaucer 2000: 219), and it is the venery of love rather than the venery of hunting that here leads to Flush's survival: that is, he does not capture the prey, but rather, he becomes a father and perpetuates the species.

Once Flush is in the city, he becomes prey to the dognappers Taylor and his gang. The London world that Flush enters is a cutthroat one, not so much dog-eat-dog as it is human-eat-human. The contrasts emerge most forcefully in the Whitechapel chapter, where Wimpole Street 'live[s]' – and note the anatomical language here – 'cheek by jowl' with St Giles (81). Wealth is dependent on squalor. On the other hand, the terms upon which the arch-respectable neighbourhood of the Barrett family lives side by side with 'one of the worst slums in London' (79–80) are also reversible, the narrator tells us: 'St Giles's stole what St Giles's could; Wimpole Street paid what Wimpole Street must' (81). London is also a human-eat-dog world, because what St Giles steals, is, of course, Wimpole's pets. If Wimpole Street does not pay the ransom demanded by Mr Taylor, the 'jaws of Whitechapel' (93), inside of which 'demons pawed and clawed' (85), will chew up dogs like Flush, spitting out body parts, 'head[s]' and 'paws' (81). Elizabeth heroically rescues Flush, intact, though her pet's faith in the 'solidity and security' (77) of Wimpole Street has been shaken; Elizabeth's

> room was no longer the whole world; it was only a shelter; only a dell arched over by one trembling dock-leaf in a forest where wild beasts prowled and venomous snakes coiled; where behind every tree lurked a murderer ready to pounce. (101)

But Flush eventually gets over his status as quarry who starts every time a door opens and a whip cracks (109, 101). When he begins a new life in Italy, he has, in effect, returned to a freer version of his life in Reading; all of 'his old fetters' have fallen from him, including the fetters of class (the Spaniel Club), danger (dog-stealers), and immobility (the chain); he is entirely at liberty to run (117). But rather than resuming his old role as a would-be predator chasing after pheasants, we see him, in Pisa's Cascine gardens, racing, as Elizabeth notes in one of her letters, *with* '"the pheasants all alive and flying"' (117).[11]

Competitors

Flush's sense of freedom, most marked when he is 'rac[ing] free through the emerald grass of the Cascine gardens where the pheasants fluttered red and gold' (123), is checked, however, with another sensation that increasingly takes the shape of 'jealous anxiety' (124). When this 'awful event' (125) happens – when Elizabeth gives birth to Penini – Flush is '[t]orn with rage and jealousy and some deep disgust' (126) at the thought of a competitor for Elizabeth's attentions. But Flush eventually gets used to Penini, and soon 'return[s] the baby's affection' (127).

Penini is not the first human rival whom Flush encounters; Flush had already been schooled in the art of competition years before when Robert Browning disrupted the life that he and Elizabeth had established together in the back bedroom. Woolf complicates and even mocks Flush's attempts to block the advances of his challenger by portraying Robert as indifferent to his adversary. Woolf builds up the suspense leading to Flush's attack on his rival. Flush can detect that something dangerous is looming simply by a gesture; as he later could tell the anticipated arrival of Penini by the way Elizabeth 'became busy with her needle' (123), he could earlier sense 'some danger menacing his safety' (51) by the way Elizabeth picks up a letter (50–1). Soon this anticipated danger takes shape; Flush comes to envision a contemporary version of his enemy, a Victorian-looking figure resembling the vampire Count Dracula, a 'man in a cloak, . . . a cowled and hooded figure' (52). When this figure physically appears in the shape of Robert, Flush, overcome by feeling, flings himself at his target and bites his trousers. Flush's attack is met not by an assault in kind, but far worse, by 'a flick of the hand' and not even a beat in the action: Robert continues talking with Elizabeth (63). The 'arms race scenario' that has been used to characterise competition, 'with each side continually deploying new defenses and counterdefenses' (Thompson 1985: 596), is quickly made ridiculous, becoming that of a gnat pestering a giant. Flush's second attack on Robert is met by the same indifference. After his exile from the sofa to the carpet, where he undergoes 'whirlpools of tumultuous emotion' (69), he overcomes his hatred and, by the end of the novel, becomes the 'best of friends' (117) with his former rival.

Host and Guest

If Flush is similar to a guest, or a troublesome gnat flicked off by a large member of another species, he takes on the opposite role in the third of the bispecies relationships. This time, Flush is the host to a plague of fleas who, in feeding upon his blood, torture him; his suffering, wrote Barrett Browning herself, is comparable to '"Savonarola's martyrdom"' (133). Flush cannot, of course, as easily flick off his tormenters as Robert can flick him off; he requires human agency to remove his scourge. As a pet, he depends upon a human for his care. Indeed, in his role as pet, one may argue that he himself is a parasite – and certainly there are those who do. Stephen Budiansky attributes the dog's 'brilliant evolutionary success' to its parasitic 'shrewd adaptation' (2002: 5, 14). He argues that 'dogs loom as a huge net biological burden upon mankind, competing for food, diverting vast economic assets in the form of labor and capital, spreading disease, causing serious injury' (7). No doubt, as the zoologist James Serpell notes, the costs of pet-keeping alone are 'staggering' (1986: 122); in 2010 $55 billion was spent on pets in the United States alone (Martin 2011). Flush may have been a gift to Elizabeth, but his maintenance requires effort on her part; those purple drinking jars and collars alone, apart from the luxurious dinners she feeds him, cost something. In addition, to save his life when he is kidnapped, she must pay a sizeable ransom, and, moreover, a price of another kind – a willingness to risk her family's censure and even her relationship with Robert.

As Elizabeth's dependant, Flush is under her control. The host–guest relationship takes on more ominous connotations when one adds the element of power to the parasitic and the physical. Yi-Fu Tuan notes the connection between domestication and domination: 'the two words have the same root sense of mastery over another being – of bringing it into one's house or domain' (2007: 143). The dog, writes Tuan, is 'the pet par excellence'; with the dog, the human can carry one relationships based on 'dominance and affection, love and abuse, cruelty and kindness' (145). The most successful training results in getting the dog to fight against its own wishes and desires and to submit to a human's.[12] In *Flush*, Woolf repeatedly shows the contrast between Flush's instincts and the domesticated life to which he has submitted, as we see in this tableau:

> For the rest of the day he kept his station on the sofa at Miss Barrett's feet. All his natural instincts were thwarted and contradicted. When the autumn winds had blown last year in Berkshire he had run in wild scampering across the stubble; now at the sound of the ivy tapping on the pane Miss Barrett asked Wilson to see to the fastenings of the window. (33)

According to Peterson, 'Pet-keeping underlines the larger fact that relationships between people and nonhuman animals are always fraught with power imbalances, dependence, and vulnerability' (2013: 110). At best, she writes, humans should employ the ethic of care, one that 'acknowledges the inequalities in power and ability that typify relationships between humans and domestic animals' (103).[13] Elizabeth recognises the sacrifices that Flush makes; she 'was too just not to realize that it was for her that he had sacrificed his courage . . . [and] the sun and the air' (*F*: 48; see also 70). One might argue that Elizabeth's chaining Flush is her acknowledgement of his relative vulnerability; when she forgoes that care, and forgets to collar him, he is susceptible to danger, and is, in fact, stolen (77).

On the other hand, in *Flush*, the most obvious symbol of the power that humans hold over their pets is the chain, a word that appears twenty-six times throughout the novel. In the domestic world, 'where there are flower-beds and asphalt paths and men in shiny top-hats, dogs must be led on chains' (30). Wearing the chain, in 'Wimpole Street and its neighbourhood', is the 'law' (77) for purebreds, including purebred women like Elizabeth, who is herself 'chained to the sofa' (35). Once he enters Elizabeth's domesticated world, Flush, as a purebred pet, bends his will to this law: 'he bent his head quietly to have the chain fixed to his collar' (32). Woolf emphasises the stress of this captivity on Flush: 'At first the strain was too great to be borne . . . many battles [that is, to submit one's will] have been won that cost their generals not half such pain' (34–5). Woolf would agree with other ethologists that dog love is not unconditional love.[14] Haraway and others note that being a pet is 'a demanding job for a dog, requiring self-control and canine emotional and cognitive skills matching those of good working dogs' (2003: 38). Roger Grenier writes that 'too close a proximity to humans makes domestic animals unhappy . . . Everything is a sign: a cough, a glance at a watch . . . Every minute carries its ration of anguish' (2002: 32). After long years of training in the bedroom school, Flush has learned to 'read signs that nobody else could even see' (*F*: 51). But though he has now, in this scene, overcome the initial pain that he felt when he first moved into Elizabeth's house, his move to Florence gives him leave to break out of his confined existence. At last, he is free to roam about the city without the protection of his chain, and so we are reminded, as the behavioural ecologist Barbara Smuts writes, that 'most dogs are perfectly capable of negotiating and managing many aspects of their world without us' (2006: 124). Both Elizabeth's and Flush's joy in the liberation they experience in Italy – 'freedom and life and the joy that the sun breeds' (*F*: 115; see also 116) – contrasting as starkly as it does to his life on the chain, vivifies the pressure that the host-guest relationship has put on the guest, and perhaps the host as well.

Flush's plunge into the life on Italian streets, where the 'threads of his old fetters fell from him' (117), also serves to remind readers of how tenuous the chains of domesticity are; once Flush has the opportunity to break free, he does. 'He ran, he raced; his coat flashed; his eyes blazed . . . He had no need of a chain in this new world; he had no need of protection' (117). Flush has so adapted to his life in Italy that when he returns to England for a short visit, with Elizabeth and Robert upon the death of Elizabeth's father, 'the old trumpet blew; the old ecstasy returned' as he goes ripping after 'hare or . . . fox' (140). The novel is filled with reminders that, as a domesticated animal, Flush is a creature 'poised between the social and natural world' (Peterson 2013: 7).[15] Flush also inhabits an ambiguous, bordered position, one between 'wild nature and human culture' (101), two gendered realms, with the wild perceived as masculine and the domestic as feminine (Peterson 2013: 104).[16]

In the wild, Flush takes on a dominant persona – he is, above all, a hunter and a lover, 'follow[ing] the horn wherever the horn blew' (119), and fathering offspring (113, 119). In the back bedroom, he is in an obviously submissive position, similar to that of his mistress, one of resignation and the suppression of the 'most violent instincts of his nature' (34). We see Flush repeatedly fluctuating between these positions throughout the novel, diverging from his domesticated role, and submitting to but also gravitating towards it, for example, in 'The Back Bedroom':

He longed for air and exercise; his limbs were cramped with lying on the sofa. He had never grown altogether used to the smell of eau de cologne. But no – though the door stood open, he would not leave Miss Barrett. (35)

Here we also see a clear contrast between female loyalty set against male sexual freedom.

Mutual Beneficiaries

Even though Flush seems, in Italy, to be veering away from his domestic role, free from the 'need of a chain in this new world' (117) as he grows more 'independent' (118), he continues to define himself in relation to other beings. Initially, in Italy, Flush's new comrades are members of his own species, but his circle has expanded to 'all the world now' (117).[17] Flush's world is an inclusive one, and, though reminiscent of the wild, where Flush can run free with his canine 'brothers', it is also populated by women to whom he is drawn, such as the old market woman who, in return for his 'guard[ing] her melons . . . scratche[s] him behind the ear' (158). This tit for tat, which takes place at the end of Flush's life, is a miniaturised version of the most important relationship in this novel, or that of mutual beneficiaries and its possibilities for 'an ever-widening acceptance of kinship across boundaries' (Weil 2012: 92). As such, the ontological dimension of mutual beneficiaries, such as Flush's companionable relationship with the market woman, who like Flush is well into old age, produces a new kind of epistemology, queer knowledges, or a 'more inclusive sense of the social as enriched by abundance beyond reproductive calculation' (McHugh 2009: 162).

Starting with the biologist Lynn Margulis in the 1960s, scientists have stressed the importance of this interrelation in evolution. They argue that 'cooperation, symbiosis, and coevolution' are as important as competition in the 'emergence and development of the earth's life forms' (Bateson 2012: 37). Organisms that are not in direct competition with each other 'have evolved so that their lives interlock' (37). In *Flush*, we see how, in the manner of food and affection, Flush and his fellow humans alternate between both competition and cooperation in all four forms of relationships: predator-prey, eat-or-be-eaten; competitors for Elizabeth's attention; host-guest, with Flush as both guest (to Elizabeth) and host (to fleas); and, in this final category of mutual beneficiaries, companion species who eat together. Donna Haraway reminds us that the word companion comes from the Latin *cum panis*, which refers to breaking bread together (2008: 322). In *Flush*, food becomes a means of exchange that demonstrates mutual harmony, or its lack. In Elizabeth's back bedroom, we see Flush demonstrating exquisite cooperation. He assists Elizabeth – who is too tired and depressed to eat, and who wants to hide that fact from her father – in forgoing her dinner. In turn, she obliges his appetite:

> She held up her fork. A whole chicken's wing was impaled upon it. Flush advanced. Miss Barrett nodded. Very gently, very cleverly, without spilling a crumb, Flush removed the wing; swallowed it down and left no trace behind. Half a rice pudding clotted with thick cream went the same way. Nothing could have been neater, more effective than Flush's co-operation. (42)

But when Robert enters her life, Elizabeth eats with vigour; 'she ate her chicken to the bone. Not a scrap of potato or of skin was thrown to Flush' (57). Withholding food breaks the bonds of companionship, and Flush knows that; 'Never had such wastes of dismal distance separated them. He lay there, ignored' (57). Robert, seeking to establish ties of friendship with Flush, offers him cake, but Flush rejects that offering, and instead attacks him (67). When, eventually, Flush swears 'to love Mr Browning and not bite him for the future' (72), he signals his sincere contrition by eating the cakes – now 'stale', 'distasteful', 'mouldy', 'flyblown', 'sour'– because 'they were offered by an enemy turned to friend, because they were symbols of hatred turned to love' (72). This act expresses Flush's change of heart toward Robert and is, as Kari Weil writes, one of 'symbolic communion' (2012: 91), turning competition into cooperation. In the transformation of Flush's relationships with Robert (and also Penini, as we saw earlier), we can see an instance of how, to use the words of the biologist John N. Thompson, 'mutualisms ... have evolved from initially antagonistic interactions' (1985: 596). Food becomes the means to signify these emotional mutualisms. While David Eberly rightly notes that *Flush* is 'the emotional story of the adults who tower above', my focus is not on the story behind the story – on Vita's abandonment of Virginia (Eberly 1996: 24, 22) – but rather on the story of a human and her dog – on dog love.[18]

Flush is reflective of the emotional bonds between humans and dogs since the earliest beginnings of civilisation, as encapsulated by the anthropologist Mary Elizabeth Thurston in the title of her book, *The Lost History of the Canine Race: Our 15,000-Year Love Affair with Dogs* (1996).[19] Soon after Flush arrives in the Barrett household, he and Elizabeth become soul mates: 'She loved Flush, and Flush was worthy of her love' (49). Elizabeth is Flush's Cleopatra; for her, he would in the style of Antony, renounce the world:[20] 'Flush, to whom the whole world was free, chose to forfeit all the smells of Wimpole Street in order to lie by her side' (35). With Robert in the picture, the possibility of being exiled from her affections puts him into a state of 'tense and silent agony' (56), and his rejoining the circle of love, and lying on the sofa at Elizabeth's feet, causes 'glory and delight [to] course through his veins' (73). Even though his grand passion for Elizabeth abates once they move to Italy, 'the tie which bound them together was undeniably still binding' (123), and at the end of the novel, before the end of his life, he returns to be with Elizabeth so that he can die in the presence of his beloved (160–1).

But even more broadly, throughout the novel, it was 'human sympathy' he preferred, and 'the human scene that stirred him' (47, 129). The novel bears out what Darwin writes in *The Origin of Species*, 'It is scarcely possible to doubt that the love of man has become instinctive in the dog' (1985: 240).[21] As Flush benefits from the mutual exchanges he has with Elizabeth and the other humans in the novel, and as he seeks to please and is drawn to the humans in his life, he becomes more like them. Indeed, we are reminded, early on, that as a spaniel, Flush is 'by nature sympathetic' (11), eager to please. As Flush goes on to spend much of his life lying 'upon human knees and hear[ing] men's voices', he comes to be afflicted by the same suffering that affects humans; his 'flesh' comes to be 'veined with human passions; he kn[ows] all grades of jealousy, anger and despair' (133). Flush, that is, becomes more human. It would seem that the novel dramatises what scientists now call the controversial theory of 'convergence', or the concept 'that living closer to humans has made dogs more *like* humans' (Vatter 2013). Woolf plays with this theory several times throughout the novel; for example, when Flush's world consists of the back bedroom, he feels 'strange stirrings at work within him', and longs to mimic Elizabeth: on seeing her 'delicately lifting some silver box or pearl ornament from the ringed table, his own furry paws seemed to contract and he longed that they should fine themselves to ten separate fingers' (38).

The bispecial relationship between humans and their pets is coconstitutive. 'Canine science', Walter Vatter writes, 'is intended to shed light not only on what makes dogs dogs but also on what makes people people' (2013).[22] For Peterson, 'The evolutionary relationship between humans and domesticated species is increasingly understood as one of mutual shaping rather than unidirectional human influence' (2013: 95); she emphasises the way that '[i]nteractions with animals are . . . mutually transformative encounters between active subjects' (2013: 14).[23] Covering a range of genres and disciplines, the number of dog books testifying to the way this emotional creature make humans emotional is legion. Linda Hogan, Deena Metzger, and Brenda Peterson write: 'From them we have even learned about love and the depths of community and familial bonding . . . We are animated by animals. Their lives have transformed our lives' (1998: xi–xii). Vicki Hearne describes the way dogs specifically are 'domesticated to, and into, us, and we are domesticated to, and into, them' (2000: 28). Jeffrey Moussaieff Masson believes that 'dogs make us human' (2010: xi); they heighten our 'capacity for love' (2010: 14). Caroline Knapp rhapsodises, in moments, about dogs, who are able 'lead us into . . . a place that can transform us' (1998: 7). Falling in love with a dog, she continues, is like 'enter[ing] a new orbit' (1998: 7). Elizabeth Barrett Browning herself made this claim in her sonnet to Flush; he is one of those '"low creatures"' who '"lead to heights of love"' (qtd in *F*: 160). Flush's entry into Elizabeth's life does momentarily send her out of her grief; in an early scene, when she is crying, he presses his head against her and looks into her eyes:[24] 'Was it Flush, or was it Pan?', she thinks, 'Was she no longer an invalid in Wimpole Street, but a Greek nymph in some dim grove in Arcady? . . . For a moment she was transformed; she was a nymph and Flush was Pan' (38). In her typical way, Woolf immediately deflates this intensity: 'But suppose Flush had been able to speak – would he not have said something sensible about the potato disease in Ireland?' (38). Yet the entirety of the book speaks to the way, as Weil writes:

> Elizabeth's love of Flush empowers her to turn against those structures and institutions of domestication that are founded on abusive forms of domination and to stand up to her father's 'civilization' in its refusal to recognize the value of love. (2012: 92)

Even if, finally, the novel ends on not a note of convergence, but divergence – 'she was woman; he was dog' (161) – the power of dog love convinces us also that Elizabeth and Flush 'completed what was dormant in the other' (161).

Wendy Doniger insists that 'art must illustrate science' (2012: 352). I have hoped to conjoin the worlds of literary studies and animal studies – or, more broadly, the humanities and the sciences – in an effort to enrich our understanding of a novel that captures a spectrum of human-animal relations. Woolf's writing in particular is nothing if not, to include a phrase from Haraway, demonstrative of a 'layered and distributed complexity' (2003: 63). To understand this complexity means we need to go to other disciplines, and to that end I have consulted the work of evolutionary biologists, cognitive ethologists, sociologists, and other scientists.[25] Writes Haraway, 'Dogs are about the inescapable, contradictory story of relationships' (2003: 12), and in studying these relationships, Anders Pape Møller insists on an integrative approach (2008: 181). Edward O. Wilson calls for a 'consilience' of knowledges, or a synthesis of disciplines across the spectrum, from the humanities to the sciences, to create a new groundwork of explanation (1998: 12; see also Nordlund 2002). A coevolutionary approach to literary studies, one that analyses four forms of bispecies relationships, shows how Woolf, ever attuned to the fluidities, volatilities, and disruptions that are a part of human relationships, was also sensitive to the ebbs and flows of the patterns of interactions among nonhuman and human animals.

Notes

1. See Nakazawa, who writes about the way Woolf often 'superimposes human life on the image of trees' (2012: 11).
2. There are other versions of this song, some of which have the final line of the refrain repeating the first-person singular pronoun.
3. Vermeij (1994: 219). See also Blondel (2006), Hird (2010), Laland John Odling-Smee, and Marcus W. Feldman (2001), Møller (2008), Thompson (1985), Thomson (2003), and Bateson (2012).
4. Haraway (2003: 6). Rohman highlights Darwin's genius in linking human life species with other animal forms (2009: 22). Hird reinforces humans' symbiotic relationship with the world; we must, she insists, learn from this '"filthy lesson" of our connection with the world' (2010: 740).
5. For example, see Thompson (1985) and Møller (2008).
6. All references are to *Flush* unless otherwise indicated.
7. For example, according to the 'Red Queen hypothesis', evolutionary changes in a species cause the environment to deteriorate unless the species continues to evolve (Vermeij 1994: 220). See also Blondel (2006), who reports on the ways human societies and Mediterranean landscapes have interacted through the millennia; Laland et al. (2001), who describe how organisms modify their environment; and Stone, who argues on behalf of 'dual inheritance' theory (2008: 146), or the coevolutionary, dialectic interaction of genetic make-up and cultural conditioning, and their effect, in turn, on environment and culture.
8. The word 'world' appears thirty-two times in the novel.
9. See also Smuts, who writes that her relationships with her dogs is a 'perpetual improvisational dance, co-created and emergent, simultaneously reflecting who we are and bringing into being who we will become' (2006: 115).
10. See David and DeMello, who have written about the way the population of rabbits in Spain has been considerably diminished (2003).
11. Flush has not, of course, entirely abandoned his predatorial identity; his teeth nearly sink into a pheasant when he is with the Brownings for a return visit to England (140). He dreamt of hunting even when he was in the most domesticated phase of his life with Elizabeth, in the back bedroom (59), and at the very end of his life, when he atavistically dreams of hunting rabbits in Spain (158–9).
12. See Thurston (1996: 7).

13. See also Hird, who recommends an 'ethics of vulnerability' which 'begins from the starting point of entangled relationality, radical asymmetry, and indissoluble openness' (2012: 332).
14. Haraway insists that 'belief in "unconditional love" is pernicious' (2003: 33).
15. See Angeliki Spiropoulou, who writes of the ways Woolf, as a modernist, 'multiply interrogat[es] the validity of set borders between human and nonhuman nature' (2010: 15).
16. Of course, as Peterson writes, '"nature" and "culture" are not mutually exclusive' (2013: 8).
17. One is reminded here of the narrator of *Three Guineas* who declares, as 'a woman my country is the whole world' (1966: 109).
18. See Garber's *Dog Love* (1996).
19. See also Thomas (2010: viii).
20. The specific reference to *Antony and Cleopatra* and its grand passion does make a very brief appearance in the novel, but at the period of his life when, for Flush, smell is his be-all and end-all (130).
21. Updating Darwin, the ethologist Ádám Miklósi, in his recent research, confirms that 'if dogs have a choice they seem to prefer to join human groups' (2007: 165). See also Gopnik (2011: 47).
22. Pet-keeping can, as James Serpell writes (1986: 187), make us aware of our biological affinities with other species.
23. See also Peterson (2013: 14, 115) and Hird (2012: 338).
24. For an astute discussion on the many mirror scenes in *Flush*, see Ferguson (2014: 96), who notes that 'Woolf toys with reflected animals to show how they stand as signifiers of some unknowable secret of selfhood'.
25. But literary theory certainly provides useful frameworks; for example, Raymond Williams's notion of 'structures of feeling', with its emphasis on relations, particularly on the relations, over time, between lived and felt experience, and 'formal and systematic beliefs', would be another window through which to consider coevolution (Williams 1977: 132).

Bibliography

Adams, C. J., and J. Donovan, eds (2006), Introduction, *Animals and Women: Feminist Theoretical Explorations*, Durham, NC: Duke University Press, pp. 1–8.
Bateson, M. C. (2012), 'Darwin's Half-Truth', *Boston College Magazine*, Winter: 37–8.
Beer, G. [1983] (1985), *Darwin's Plots: Evolutionary Narrative in Darwin, George Eliot and Nineteenth-Century Fiction*, Boston, MA: Ark.
Blondel, J. (2006), 'The "Design" of Mediterranean Landscapes: A Millennial Story of Humans and Ecological Systems during the Historic Period', *Human Ecology*, 34(5): 713–29.
Budiansky, S. [2000] (2002), *The Truth about Dogs: The Ancestry, Social Conventions, Mental Habits and Moral Fibre of Canis Familiaris*, London: Phoenix.

Chaucer, G. [1478] (2000), *The General Prologue*, in *The Norton Anthology of English Literature*, 7th edn, vol. 1, gen. ed. M. H. Abrams, New York: W. W. Norton, pp. 214–35.

Darwin, C. [1859] (1985), *The Origin of Species*, ed. J. W. Burrow, London: Penguin.

David, S. E., and M. DeMello (2003), *Stories Rabbits Tell: A Natural and Cultural History of a Misunderstood Creature*, New York: Lantern Books.

Doniger, W. (2012), 'Epilogue: Making Animals Vanish', in *Animals and the Human Imagination*, ed. A. Gross and A. Vallely, New York: Columbia University Press, pp. 349–53.

Eberly, D. (1996), 'Housebroken: The Domesticated Relations of *Flush*', in *Virginia Woolf: Texts and Contexts: Selected Papers from the Fifth Annual Conference on Virginia Woolf*, ed. B. R. Daugherty and E. Barrett, New York: Pace University Press, pp. 21–5.

Ferguson, K. (2014), 'Pets in Memoir', in *Representing the Modern Animal in Culture*, ed. J. Dubino, Z. Rashidian, and A. Smyth, New York: Palgrave Macmillan, pp. 81–99.

Garber, M. (1996), *Dog Love*, New York: Touchstone.

Gopnik, A. (2011), 'Dog Story', *The New Yorker*, 8 August: 46–53.

Grateful Dead (n.d.), Song, 'Touch of Grey', <http://www.lyricsfreak.com/g/grateful+dead/touch+of+grey_20062412.html> (last accessed 30 May 2013).

Grenier, R. [1998] (2002), *The Difficulty of Being a Dog,* trans. A. Kaplan, Chicago: University of Chicago Press.

Haraway, D. J. (2003), *The Companion Species Manifesto: Dogs, People, and Significant Otherness*, Chicago: Prickly Paradigm Press.

Haraway, D. J. (2006), 'Encounters with Companion Species: Entangling Dogs, Baboons, Philosophers, and Biologists', *Configurations*, 14(1–2): 97–114.

Haraway, D. J. (2008), *When Species Meet*, Minneapolis: University of Minnesota Press.

Hearne, V. [1982] (2000), *Adam's Task: Calling Animals by Name*, Pleasantville, NY: Akadine Press.

Hird, M. (2010), 'Coevolution, Symbiosis and Sociology', *Ecological Economics*, 69(4): 737–42.

Hird, M. (2012), 'Animal, All Too Animal: *Blood Music* and an Ethic of Vulnerability', in *Animals and the Human Imagination*, ed. A. Gross and A. Vallely, New York: Columbia University Press, pp. 331–48.

Hogan, L., D. Metzger, and B. Peterson, eds (1998), *Intimate Nature: The Bond Between Women and Animals*, New York: Fawcett.

Holland, J. (2011), 'A Fragile Empire', *National Geographic*, 219, 5 May: 30–53.

Knapp, C. (1998), *Pack of Two: The Intricate Bond between People and Dogs*, New York: Delta.

Laland, K. N., J. Odling-Smee, and M. W. Feldman (2001), 'Cultural Niche Construction and Human Evolution', *Journal of Evolutionary Biology*, 14(1): 22–33.

Martin, A. (2011), '"For the Dogs" Has a Whole New Meaning', <http://www.nytimes.com/2011/06/05/business/05pets.html?pagewanted=all> (last accessed 5 June 2011).

Masson, J. M. (2010), *The Dog Who Couldn't Stop Loving: How Dogs Have Captured Our Hearts for Thousands of Years*, New York: HarperCollins.

McHugh, S. (2009), Review essay, 'Queer (and Animal) Theories', *GLQ: A Journal of Lesbian and Gay Studies*, 15(1): 153–69.

Miklósi, A. (2007), *Dog: Behaviour, Evolution, and Cognition*, Oxford: Oxford University Press.

Møller, A. P. (2008), 'Interactions between Interactions: Predator-Prey, Parasite-Host, and Mutualistic Interactions', *Annals of the New York Academy of Sciences*, 1133: 180–6.

Nakazawa, M. (2012), '"A Million Atoms": Virginia Woolf's Primeval Trees in *The Waves*', *Virginia Woolf Miscellany*, 81, Spring: 10–11.

Nordlund, M. (2002), 'Consilient Literary Interpretation', *Philosophy and Literature*, 26(2): 312–33.

Peterson, A. L. (2013), *Being Animal: Beasts and Boundaries in Nature Ethics*, New York: Columbia University Press.

Rohman, C. (2009), *Stalking the Subject: Modernism and the Animal*, New York: Columbia University Press.

Serpell, J. (1986), *In the Company of Animals: A Study of Human–Animal Relationships*, Oxford: Blackwell.

Smuts, B. (2006), 'Between Species: Science and Subjectivity', *Configurations*, 14(1–2): 115–26.

Spiropoulou, A. (2010), 'Woolf on Nature, History and the Modern Artwork', *Virginia Woolf Miscellany,* 78, Fall–Winter: 15–17.

Stone, B. L. (2008), 'The Most Unique of All Unique Species', *Society*, 45: 146–51.

Thomas, E. M. [1993] (2010), *The Hidden Life of Dogs*, Boston, MA: Mariner.

Thompson, J. N. (1985), Review of Susan Grant's *Beauty and the Beast: The Coevolution of Plants and Animals*, *BioScience*, 35(9): 594–6.

Thomson, J. (2003), 'When Is It Mutualism?' *The American Naturalist,* Supplement, 162: S4, S1–S9.

Thurston, M. E. (1996), *The Lost History of the Canine Race: Our 15,000-Year Love Affair with Dogs*, Kansas City, MO: Andrews and McMeel.

Tuan, Y.-F. [1984] (2007), *Dominance and Affection: The Making of Pets*, repr. as 'Animal Pets: Cruelty and Affection', in *The Animals Reader: The Essential Classic and Contemporary Writings*, ed. L. Kalof and A. Fitzgerald, New York: Berg, pp. 141–53.

Vatter, W. (2013), Review of John Homans's *What's a Dog For? New York Times Book Review*, 6 January: 20.

Vermeij, G. J. (1994), 'The Evolutionary Interaction among Species: Selection, Escalation, and Coevolution', *Annual Review of Ecology and Systematics*, 25: 219–36.

Weil, K. (2012), *Thinking Animals: Why Animal Studies Now?* New York: Columbia University Press.

Wilson, E. O. (1998), *Consilience: The Unity of Knowledge*, New York: Vintage.

Williams, R. (1977), *Marxism and Literature*, Oxford: Oxford University Press.

Woolf, V. [1925] (1953), *Mrs Dalloway*, New York: Harcourt Brace Jovanovich.

Woolf, V. [1938] (1966), *Three Guineas*, New York: Harcourt Brace Jovanovich.

Woolf, V. [1933] (1983), *Flush*, New York: Harcourt Brace Jovanovich.

Chapter 8

Posthumanist Interludes:
Ecology and Ethology in *The Waves*

Derek Ryan

For some years now critics have demonstrated that *The Waves* (1931) is not solely concerned with the internal workings of the human mind.[1] Sections of Woolf's most experimental novel that clearly reach outside human psychology are the ten – if we include the final line of the novel, *'The waves broke on the shore'* (*TW*: 248) – italicised interludes, which have been read by critics in three primary ways: as a formal structuring device, linked to Woolf's concern with visual art and music; as an allegory of empire, demonstrating Woolf's anti-imperialist politics; and as a representation of the natural world, evincing Woolf's interest in nonhuman environments. In the first approach the interludes are seen to alternate between an Impressionist and Post-Impressionist aesthetic (McLaurin 1973: 84; Goldman 1998: 189), or to resemble a 'musical symphony' (Henke 2007: 128).[2] The second approach points to the solar imagery of the interludes as a retort to the popular nineteenth-century expression 'the sun never sets on the British Empire', in which they offer an allegory either of 'how the imperial impulse continues' (Dickinson 2007: 26), or of imperial decline (Marcus 1992: 137, 155). The third approach – which will be my central focus – finds Woolf's depiction of the natural world in the interludes re-emerging as a concern for critics in recent years. While conceiving of *The Waves* Woolf famously wrote that she wanted to 'saturate every atom' (*D* 3: 209), and the interludes are definitely 'nature-saturated' (Scott 2012: 123). Critics have considered their depiction of a natural world that escapes human capture: the interludes show 'there is much that is out of reach of human intelligence and perception' (Monaco 2008: 160), and they reveal 'inhuman rhythms' or 'cosmological forces' (Rohman 2011: 14). Such readings return us to Frank McConnell's influential essay on *The Waves*, which suggested that 'the "nature" of the italicised passages is neither the anthropomorphic and sympathetic nature of the pastoral nor its malevolent but equally anthropomorphic contrary'; the interludes do not merely reflect human concerns, but illustrate a 'self-sufficient *unhu-manity*' (1986: 63).

This essay explores in more detail Woolf's drawing of the natural world and argues that our readings of *The Waves* in the twenty-first century should take seriously her interest in nonhuman animals and nature. But the concern in the interludes with natural environments is especially important because this also signals how the formal, political, and ecological combine in Woolf's writing. After all, such a combination is seen in *A Room of One's Own* (1929) when, amid her discussion of the sexual politics of writing, Woolf emphasises the importance of viewing

> human beings not always in their relation to each other but in relation to reality; and the sky, too, and the trees or whatever it may be in themselves . . . [O]ur relation is to the world of reality and not only to the world of men and women. (*AROO*: 149)

Woolf's call here to see men and women in 'relation to reality' is an affirmation that human beings are always already embedded within a material world where the entanglements of human bodies and non-human environments are foregrounded. Published two years after Woolf's modernist feminist (ecological?) manifesto, but with the first draft written concurrently with her revisions of *A Room of One's Own* (Graham 1976: 30), *The Waves* finds Woolf more directly interested in an ecological, ethological, and posthumanist politics of writing. To demonstrate this, my essay is divided into two sections that put forward the following claims: first, that Woolf's ecological interludes offer a *nonanthropocentric* anthropomorphism that recognises the primacy of nonhuman events over cultural attempts to master life through language; and second, that the animals inhabiting these interludes illuminate Woolf's interest in nonhuman 'Umwelten' – the term Jakob von Uexküll used to describe animal environment-worlds – and that this helps us to situate Woolf's response to Darwinian evolution and her interest in nature and animality more broadly.

Anthropomorphism without Anthropocentrism: Writing Sun/Sea/Landscapes

In purely quantitative terms, there is more attention to nonhuman animals and natural elements in the interludes of *The Waves* than there is to human figures: we find the sun, sea, sky, and fire; trees, rocks, flowers, and grass; horses, fish, mules, slugs, and numerous different birds; a black cat, a worm, a dragonfly, and a cow; and woods, rivers, clouds, and snow. Even in the human-made environment of the house, there is little sign of the human presence that we might expect, with the focus firmly on objects including chairs, cupboards, and a bookcase. But qualitatively too, when human figures do appear in the interludes they are often somewhat vague presences, a feature that Woolf decided on early in her drafting of the novel (on the very first drafted pages she names characters in the opening interlude only to then score them out [Graham 1976: 3]). The human figures who find a role in the interludes most often appear as figures of speech, contributing to their ambiguity. In the first interlude there are similes comparing the undulations of the waves with the breathy sighs of a '*sleeper*' and the sunrise with '*the arm of a woman*' lifting a lamp, with the latter developing into an extended metaphor (*TW*: 3).[3] In the second interlude a simile compares the wild singing of birds to '*skaters*' (21). The figure of the girl in the third interlude may continue the same extended metaphor as in the first (the past perfect tense of '*who had shaken her head*' suggests we have been introduced to this '*girl*' figure in a previous interlude, even though it is a '*woman*' who now appears), and there are also similes that include a '*sailor*' (58) and '*turbaned warriors*' (60), which are important markers of the colonial context *The Waves* engages. We also have here the first human figure to appear more literally, outside the dense patterning of similes and metaphors: '*the cook*' startles the birds by throwing '*cinders on an ash heap*' (58). The simile with '*turbaned soldiers*' (89) returns in the fourth interlude, and in the fifth the simile of the girl from the third interlude returns (121) along with the simile with a '*warder*' (122). The second example of human figures (albeit still vague ones) not employed as simile or metaphor is found here, too: there are the '*long-breasted, white-haired women*' and the '*washerwomen*' lit up by the sun (121), as well as '*passengers*' aboard ships (121). But rather than heralding a turn towards the human in these interludes, we have to wait until the eighth interlude for human figures to reappear, by which time they have again returned to simile: the erratic and variegated 'rays of light' emanating from the sinking sun are compared to '*laughing boys*' running through shrubbery (173). Finally, when we find more literal human figures in the ninth interlude – '*couples clasped . . . under elm trees*' and '*girls, sitting on verandahs*' – they are soon blotted out by darkness (198).

To be sure, human qualities in the interludes are not only ambiguous due to their infrequent appearances, but also because of the specific way they appear in both figurative and more literal language. This appearance becomes clear if we look in more detail at the opening interlude:

Gradually the dark bar on the horizon became clear as if the sediment in an old wine-bottle had sunk and left the grass green. Behind it, too, the sky cleared as if the white sediment there had sunk, or as if the arm of a woman couched beneath the horizon had raised a lamp and flat bars of white, green and yellow spread across the sky like the blades of a fan. (3)

Within her own sentence, the figure of the woman only appears as part of the second simile, yet even as she does so she merely sneaks in, covertly entering this natural scene by hiding '*couched beneath*' a horizon that soon takes centre stage again as we read of the whites, greens, and yellows in the sky. The specific use of 'as if' also stresses the precariousness of the human; this bifocal connective reveals a less certain, more conditional comparison being drawn between the natural sunscape and the woman figure. Importantly, however, when there are signs of human presence in the later interludes that are not dependent upon Woolf's more figurative language in order to enter the text, they are also 'couched' in that they are far from being presented with the same detail as the sun, sea, and landscape. Moreover, they are almost literally couched in their positions; certainly none of these bipedal humans are standing upright: the '*washerwomen*' are '*kneeling*' and the passengers '*dozing*' in the fifth interlude (122), and the '*couples*' are '*clasped*' under elm trees and '*girls*' are '*sitting*' on verandas '*shading*' their faces in the ninth interlude (198).[4] In all cases, Woolf's intricate deployment of metaphor, simile, imagery, and allusion[5] points to a human presence couched *in language*. And yet, the language of the interludes appears to bring together the human and the nonhuman in a way that is not human-centred; Woolf challenges the view, long held in the Western scientific and philosophical tradition, that language is the capacity that hierarchically divides meaning- and world-making humans from nonhuman environments and animals. This feature coincides, perhaps, with Woolf's anti-imperialist impulse; she does not wish to continue in the tradition of inflating the sense of human entitlement over either human *or* nonhuman territories. But a number of paradoxes are evident here: how can language be used *by* the human in order to *de-centre* the human? How can a highly experimental form be employed by a human agent (the writer) in order to present a more humble form of human agency?

Woolf's figurative use of 'as if' offers crucial clues in answering these questions. Laura Doyle has noted that Woolf's recourse to 'as if' in the opening interlude functions so that the sun, sea, and sky are always already metaphors to the reader. First, Doyle views the metaphorical as primary in the interlude, and argues that 'the sun appears in *reflection*, in metaphor, before it emerges as visible fact . . . [T]he very sun's appearance is openly entangled in metaphoric effects.' Second, she sees this figurative manipulation of the natural world as an illustration of her wider argument about Woolf's attempts to write an anti-imperialist text while speaking from an imperialist position, where 'this figural mode is one Woolf does not herself escape and so she remains tied to the aesthetic economy of imperialism which she exposes' (1996: 341). In her subtle reading, Doyle is quite right to link Woolf's exploration of the natural world to her concern with imperialism's subjugating proper-ties, but it is also possible to argue that the figurative explorations in the interludes become disentangled from the 'aesthetic economy of imperi-alism'. For example, Woolf's metaphorical figurations come only *after* the solar scene has plainly and concretely been introduced in monosyl-labic words: '*The sun had not yet*' appeared. The sun may not reach the '*horizon*' until it is embedded in metaphor, but the '*not yet*' signals that its existence in the text, and for the reader, is far from being in doubt. Moreover, while it is true to say that the appearance of nature is entan-gled in figures of speech, it seems important that Woolf inverts the more common order when drawing further figurations: natural elements are frequently mentioned in the interludes *before* entering into figurative entanglements with the human. We see this pattern in the first interlude of the sea and sky (*TW*: 3) and birds (4), and we see it in the other nonhuman elements listed above. Indeed there are no examples in the interludes of nature used as a simile or metaphor to explain or enhance a human feature, despite the fact that this use is commonplace in Woolf's modernist aesthetics and is evident early on in the soliloquy sections of *The Waves*, such as when we read about Jinny's 'heart jumping . . . like the leaves' under her dress (8). In the interludes Woolf is careful not to always already write from within this cultural – we might say imperial-istic and anthropocentric – appropriation of the natural world through language. Complicated figurations allow Woolf to explore complicated natural and cultural dynamics, but they do not aim to 'master' (Doyle 1996: 341) either nature or the colonised subject.

The articulation of nature in the interludes demonstrates that *The Waves* is not only concerned with 'the symbols, the poetic symbols, of life', as one well-known contemporary review charged (Kronenberger 1931). Woolf's exploration of the natural world may be entangled in an intricate and vibrant arrangement of figurative language, but she is careful not to relegate (or elevate) nature to 'symbolic' status. As Gillian Beer warns, symbolism 'is the means by which we make *things* serve the human' thereby granting 'primacy to the human because it places the human at the centre' (1996: 41), but in *The Waves* we find moments when 'words bear some kind of unsymbolical meaningfulness independent of the human subject', or at least irreducible to the human (Chun 2012: 61). We should hesitate before concluding that the interludes offer a rendering of nature that is purely captured and controlled by the human; Woolf is certainly engaged in experimental word-making and an innovative modernist aesthetics in the interludes, but the human capacity to shape language is not her only concern. As she notes in a letter to Goldie Dickinson, after receiving praise from him for the book:

> I wanted to give the sense of continuity, instead of which most people say, no you've given the sense of flowing and passing away and that nothing matters. Yet I feel things matter quite immensely. What the significance is, heaven knows I cant guess; but there is significance . . . I'm annoyed to be told that I am nothing but a stringer together of words and words and words. (*L* 4: 397)

Woolf seeks in the interludes to explore 'things' that 'matter quite immensely'; she wants to articulate something that is firmly real rather than ethereal, something that comes before the 'words and words and words' that she is praised for, even if her only way of documenting this 'something before' is through such words. This concern with what comes before words is emphasised in a well-known letter Woolf wrote to Vita Sackville-West on 16 March 1926:

> Now this is very profound, what rhythm is, and goes far deeper than words. A sight, an emotion, creates this wave in the mind, long before it makes words to fit it; and in writing (such is my present belief) one has to recapture this, and set this working (which has nothing apparently to do with words). (*L* 3: 247)

Like the rhythm that mattered so much to Woolf's writing – and crucially that mattered *before* her writing – the interludes of *The Waves* remind us that we are affected by our relationship with the external world before we try to translate that affect into language. In this view humanity does not transcend nature through language or the workings of the mind; rather, language helps explore how the human is entangled with/in an active, material world. Woolf's 'as if' attempts, along with her other figurative connectives, to find a rhythm that expresses the relationship between human and nonhuman without simply conflating them within the cultural realm. Woolf is interested in how words become worlds but also in how worlds become words.

Reversing the expected order of human and nonhuman in these figures of speech does not, however, entirely avoid the issue of anthropomorphism. Woolf's figurations in the interludes still involve an equating of some human features with the nonhuman world, and necessarily include a form of human appropriation of the nonhuman through language. But what is important is that Woolf's reversal of the human (contained within the figure of speech) and the nonhuman (which appears before this act of figuration) demonstrates a *nonanthropocentric* anthropomorphism. This nonanthropocentric anthropomorphism allows Woolf to articulate nonhuman worlds – to use language to create environments that are nonetheless not centred on humans – but to do so while acknowledging that some anthropomorphism may be necessary in any attempt to make sense of these worlds. This practice is recognised today by many ecologists, ethologists, and philosophers who suggest that 'an anthropomorphic element in perception can uncover a whole world of resonances and resemblances . . . revealing similarities across categorical divides', thereby helping to challenge human claims to privilege over nonhuman worlds (Bennett 2010: 99). Refusing to run the risk of anthropomorphism at all simply allows the perceived hierarchy between human and nonhuman, and settled anthropocentric understandings of agency, to remain unchallenged. Returning to *The Waves*, we can consider the following example from the eighth interlude: '*Erratically rays of light flashed and wandered, like signals from sunken islands, or darts shot through laurel groves by shameless, laughing boys*' (173). Anthropomorphism may be present in this seascape description, yet 'the effect is not the humanization of the landscape, but the assimilation of the human into the nonhuman' (Chun 2012: 57). Expressing the shared vibrancy of life between human bodies and nonhuman environments, this passage is an example of the kind of nonanthropocentric anthropomorphism I am suggesting we find throughout the interludes, where Woolf risks anthropomorphism precisely in order to consider multiple nonhuman agencies. It is through this nonanthropocentric anthropomorphism that the interludes entangle nonhuman and human while avoiding a purely sentimental identification with the natural world or dismissive rejection of humanity. In contrast to Bernard, who towards the end of *The Waves* wants to trade in his human language for a 'bark' or 'howl' (210, 246), the interludes retain a challenging paradox: namely, it is precisely Woolf's sophistication of language that expresses a humanity, language, and culture more deeply embedded in the natural world. Language, Woolf seems to suggest, need not ultimately divide humans from nature.

This nonanthropocentric exploration of nonhuman bodies and environments in the interludes brings Woolf into conversation with posthumanist approaches to life, which, alongside related fields such as ecocriticism and animal studies, have played a significant role in critical debates in the twenty-first century.[6] Such posthumanist debates are not about imagining a world after or without the human, but about better accounting for the entanglement of humans with nonhuman animals, objects, and environments. Posthumanism urges humans to respect and respond to nonhuman worlds, and to reject essentialist and hierarchical divisions between culture and nature, but it also enables us, as Cary Wolfe illustrates, 'to describe the human and its characteristic modes of communication, interaction, meaning, social significations, and affective investments with *greater* specificity once we have removed meaning from the ontologically closed domain of consciousness, reason, reflection' (2010: xxv). The remainder of this essay will consider the distinctly nonanthropocentric and posthumanist approach to life conceptualised in Woolf's interludes by focusing on the relationship between her modernist ecological and ethological aesthetics and developments in the life sciences.

Animal Umwelten: Woolf, Darwin, and Uexküll

From their first appearances in *The Waves*, characters observe the finer details of various nonhuman environments: Susan hears the 'cheep, chirp' of birds *(TW:* 5); Bernard sees the 'spider's web on the corner of the balcony' (5); Rhoda notices a 'grey-shelled snail' (6); and Neville listens as a 'bee booms' in his ear (7). These are just a few of the many examples of Woolf's characters in the novel perceiving animal worlds. Similar observations of nonhuman animals are recorded in the interludes, but what is distinct in these passages is that there is no discernible human observer. Indeed there is no first-person 'I' or third-person 'he' or 'she' that the perception can be linked to, reinforcing the fact that the focus is not primarily on the human. Such nonanthropocentric explorations of animal worlds in the interludes can add to our broader understanding of how Woolf's modernism, as Christina Alt convincingly demonstrates, is attuned to the shift in late-nineteenth- and early-twentieth-century natural science away from taxonomic research and towards observational studies of animals as living organisms with internal functioning who interact with their environments (2010: 39).[7]

Unsurprisingly, Darwin has played an important role in critical attention to Woolf's interest in animals. While there is evidence of the importance of taxonomic classification in Darwin's work, Alt has shown how Darwin – whose writings Woolf knew well[8] – was not content with simply ordering the natural world but wanted to theorise 'the implications of taxonomic classifications for the relationships among organisms' (Alt 2010: 39). Yet, as critics, including Alt, also note, Woolf's relationship to Darwin is ambivalent. Woolf finds limitations in his theorisation of how animals and their environments relate: she resisted the linear view of 'development' and the focus on 'descent' (Beer 1996: 13); she was not interested in a discourse of development (as improvement) or degeneration, or in a teleological narrative of progression (Lambert 1991: 6). Of course, Woolf is often taking issue with the Victorian reception of Darwinism rather than providing a sustained reproach to Darwin himself, but there are also aspects of his writings that, despite his own anti-imperialism, are at odds with her anti-imperialist politics and, as I will argue here, her nonanthropocentric ethology: some of his texts can be said to 'encourage the belief that northern European men are the apex of evolution' (Lambert 1991: 2). We can see this belief, and how Woolf's ambivalence towards Darwinism might have come about, in the conclusion to *The Descent of Man* (1871). Here Darwin on the one hand emphasises the persistence of the past in the present and the animality of the human (something that Beer has shown Woolf to be interested in), but on the other hand he displays a concern with the elevation of humanity:

> Man may be excused for feeling some pride at having risen, though not through his own exertions, to the very summit of the organic scale; and the fact of his having thus risen, instead of having been aboriginally placed there, may give him hope for a still higher destiny in the distant future . . . We must, however, acknowledge . . . that man with all his noble qualities, with sympathy which feels for the most debased, with benevolence which extends not only to other men but to the humblest living creature, with his god-like intellect which has penetrated into the movements and constitution of the solar system – with all these exalted powers – Man still bears in his bodily frame the indelible stamp of his lowly origin. (2003: 619)

There is a discourse of *ascent* here, a sense of the human (who for Darwin is always 'man') rising from a 'lowly origin' to reach the pinnacle in the hierarchy of life. There is a privileging of certain 'qualities': 'man' is 'noble', he has 'god-like intellect' that is able to penetrate as far as the solar system, and he has sympathy for 'the humblest living creatures'.

Woolf was aware of challenges to a purely Darwinian view of evolution, such as the Mendelian 'laws of inheritance', which showed that hereditary characteristics were passed on as discrete entities (Alt 2010: 40–1). But while alternative or additional paradigms modified evolutionary theory in Woolf's lifetime, the limitations she felt in evolutionary discourse went further, as shown above, than the finer details of patterns of descent. I want to suggest here that Woolf's interest in animality shares affinities with an early-twentieth-century critic of Darwinism, one who has been overlooked by scholars interested in Woolf's writings on nature and nonhuman animals – namely, the Estonian-born German biologist and ethologist Jakob von Uexküll. Uexküll's theory of the 'Umwelt' (or 'environment-world' as it is sometimes translated) of each animal takes seriously the meaningfulness of its territories, of each animal's development and attunement within its world that does not rely on a teleological concept of progress. Development, as Uexküll stresses in *A Theory of Meaning* (1940), is non-linear and contains a fundamentally different *meaning* based on different animal worlds: in nature we see

> hundreds of variations, but never showing any transitions from the imperfect to the perfect. Environments were certainly simpler at the beginning of the world-drama than they were later. But, in them, each carrier of meaning faced a recipient of meaning. Meaning ruled them all. Meaning bound changing organs to the changing medium ... Everywhere there was progression, but nowhere progress in the sense of the survival of the fittest, never a selection of the better by a planlessly raging battle for existence. (2010: 196)

In *A Foray into the Worlds of Animals and Humans* (1934) he underlines this point: 'All animal subjects, from the simplest to the most complex, are inserted into their environments to the same degree of perfection. The simple animal has a simple environment; the multiform animal has an environment just as richly articulated as it is' (2010: 50). The meaning derived from animal Umwelten comes about through the animal's ability to discern what aspects of its surroundings help it to function, what objects are of significance to it. Uexküll firmly rejects the mechanistic model of animal behaviour and focuses on how animals meaningfully behave in their respective environment-worlds. What is emphasised is that meaning-making is not restricted to the human's cultural realm: '*The question as to meaning must therefore have priority in all living beings*' (Uexküll 2010: 151; italics in original).

Uexküll responds to the subjectivity of the animal, countering the predominance of methodologies in physiology, which

> posited one objective environment for all life forms and, subsequently, proceeded to analyze animals from the outside in, that is, by torturing them with selected stimuli in order to elicit mechanical responses. The new (and true) biology required a radical reorientation on the part of the researcher. The blind reliance on an indifferent environment had to be replaced by the recognition of species-specific Umwelten, a shift in perspective which required that human researchers forego what is of significance to them for what is significant to the animal. (Winthrop-Young 2010: 231)

In order to offer his nonanthropocentric account of the inner and outer worlds of animals, Uexküll does, like Woolf, risk the charge of anthropomorphism. An example of this can be seen in his description of a jackdaw and a grasshopper:

> The jackdaw is completely unable to see a motionless grasshopper and only snaps at it when it hops. Here, we shall first suppose that the jackdaw is well familiar with the form of the grasshopper at rest but cannot recognize it as a single unit due to the blades of grass which crisscross over it, just as we have trouble finding the familiar form in ambiguous picture puzzles. (Uexküll 2010: 79)

In drawing an analogy between the jackdaw seeking the grasshopper and the human trying to solve a problem, Uexküll suggests that human mental activities share something in common with the jackdaw, but he does so in order to bring to life the jackdaw's perceptual capacities and to show the limits of human perceptual processes at the same time. There is a twofold movement away from anthropocentrism, and towards posthumanism, here: 'Animals are promoted by virtue of their human-like ability to construct their own environment; humans are demoted by virtue of our animal-like inability to transcend our Umwelt' (Winthrop-Young 2010: 222). Uexküll therefore offers an immanent ontological mapping of life where, as Brett Buchanan explains, the concern is with 'rules that extend horizontally across time and space' rather than 'lineages descending historically through time' (2008: 20). Uexküll's approach has not only led to the assessment of him as 'one of the greatest zoologists of the twentieth century' (Agamben 2004: 39), but he also influenced key twentieth-century philosophers and this has resulted in his Umwelt research gaining new theoretical currency in twenty-first-century debates about posthumanism.[9] It is Uexküll's markedly posthumanist vision that shares affinities with Woolf's exploration of animal worlds.

The interludes of *The Waves* are full of details of nonhuman Umwelten, where Woolf's own foray into the worlds of animals is characterised by a studied, observational tone that respects and responds to different animal environments.[10] We see this in her representation of the birds:[11] in the first interlude we read of how '*one bird chirped high up; there was a pause; another chirped lower down*', but rather than informing us of what these birds are singing about the narrative acknowledges the human's position outside the birds' Umwelten and simply records their song as '*blank melody*' (*TW*: 4). In the description of the birds in the second interlude we are given further detail – their '*breasts were specked canary and rose*' – but in getting closer to these birds we might say that Woolf begins to anthropomorphise. Again simile functions to bring together human and nonhuman while also registering the anthropomorphising of the birds who '*sang a strain or two together, wildly, like skaters rollicking arm-in-arm*' (21). Similarly, in the third interlude the connective 'as if' reappears: the birds '*now sang together in chorus, shrill and sharp; now together, as if conscious of companionship, now alone as if to the pale blue sky*' (58). We see the movement from simply documenting an observation to trying to probe deeper into the Umwelt of the birds, a probing that leads to an increased element of anthropomorphism, but which is always negotiated tentatively. Having made this attempt to understand the world inhabited by these birds, the narrator then considers the meaning that the elements (including other nonhuman animals as well as the human figure of the cook who disturbs them) in the birds' Umwelten might create:

> *They swerved, all in one flight, when the black cat moved among the bushes, when the cook threw cinders on the ash heap and startled them. Fear was in their song, and apprehension of pain, and joy to be snatched quickly now at this instant. Also they sang emulously in the clear morning air, swerving high over the elm tree, singing together as they chased each other, escaping, pursuing, pecking each other as they turned high in the air. And then tiring of pursuit and flight, lovelily they came descending, delicately declining, dropped down and sat silent on the tree, on the wall, with their bright eyes glancing, and their heads turned this way, that way; aware, awake; intensely conscious of one thing, one object in particular.* (58)

The anthropomorphising of the birds appears to be clearer here than in the earlier interludes: we read of their experience of '*fear*', '*pain*' and '*joy*' – indeed their ability to *apprehend* this pain and joy. Significantly, there has been a shift from the birds earlier in the interlude who acted '*as if conscious*' to now being '*intensely conscious*'.

In the paragraph that follows, however, the awareness of the birds' Umwelten, of the meaningful relations between them and their environment-world, results in a narrative that does not finally capture this '*one object*' that the birds are so '*intensely conscious of*'. Having recognised the birds' capacity for world-making, Woolf is hesitant to fully anthropomorphise these birds. The word 'perhaps' is key: '*Perhaps it was a snail shell . . . Or perhaps they saw the splendour of the flowers . . . Or they fixed their gaze on the small bright apple leaves . . . Or they saw the rain drop on the hedge*' (58). When detail is then added that seems to further anthropomorphise – for example, the birds would judge the flowers to have the '*splendour*' that the human sees them as having due to their '*flowing purple*' and they would witness the '*dancing*' and '*sparkling*' apple trees – this addition does not foreclose the possible meaning of the birds' perceptions or subsume them within a human realm. Rather, it puts into action (and note the frequent use of the gerund above) the distinctly muddy and messy Umwelt of the bird swooping to the '*monstrous body of the defenceless worm, pecked again and yet again, and left it to fester*' (59), as well as of the birds in the following interlude that '*descended, dry-beaked, ruthless, abrupt*', and that '*swooped*' and '*tapped ferociously, methodically*' at a snail's shell '*until the shell broke and something slimy oozed from the crack*' (89). In addition, although the interludes are focused on the specific environment-world of the birds, they are not homogenised, nor is their presence totalised into some emblematic or symbolic meaning. This is evident in the fourth interlude which accounts for the different objects that are, at that moment, significant to each bird: '*the birds sang in the hot sunshine, each alone. One sang under the bedroom window; another on the topmost twig of the lilac bush; another on the edge of the wall*' (88).

Although these swooping birds are less prominent in later interludes, further details of their Umwelten are provided, alongside even smaller creatures:

> *The birds sat still save that they flicked their heads sharply from side to side. Now they paused in their song as if glutted with sound, as if the fullness of midday had gorged them. The dragon-fly poised motionless over a reed, then shot its blue stitch further through the air.* (136)

These additions allow us to draw a further comparison with Uexküll, who specifically includes dragonflies alongside birds in a passage from his *Foray into the Worlds of Animals and Humans*. Here Uexküll describes the Umwelt as a 'soap bubble':

> We must therefore imagine all the animals that animate Nature around us, be they beetles, butterflies, gnats, or dragonflies who populate a meadow, as having a soap bubble around them, closed on all sides, which closes off their visual space and in which everything visible for the subject is also enclosed . . . Only when we can vividly imagine this fact will we recognise in our own world the bubble that encloses each and every one of us on all sides. (2010: 69)

Uexküll's account of nonhuman and human animal worlds (and it is worth noting that beetles and butterflies find their way into *The Waves*, too) emphasises a multiplicitous experience of space, and warns against enclosing the animal's perceptual world within our own. For Uexküll 'there is no space independent of subjects', and these subjects include nonhuman animals, so that any human concept of a holistic, 'all-encompassing world-space' is an anthropocentric 'fiction' or 'fable' (2010: 70). Woolf, I would suggest, has vividly imagined these different

Umwelten in the interludes, balancing her foray into anthropomorphism with a foray into a nonanthropocentric, posthumanist aesthetic. Crucially, in imagining these different perceptual-worlds, Woolf seems to be more concerned here with the materially embedded, affective territories of animals than she is with features that would classify them under one category or another. This concern is another example of how the interludes provide more than a simple documentation of nonhuman life as merely a background to the main human action of the novel. Woolf's 'interludes' do not, as the etymology of the word suggests, signal a break for the reader between the acts of *The Waves*; instead, they return us to the other meaning of the 'inter' in 'interlude', which comes from the Proto-Indo-European root 'enter' meaning 'among' (as well as 'between'). Language and nature *collude* in the interludes to offer a nonanthropocentric and non-hierarchical model of life. Again, we could view this as consistent with Woolf's anti-imperialist politics; her concern is that we recognise the multiplicity of worlds rather than trying to territorialise or homogenise them into one.

Whether or not we agree that *The Waves* explores something akin to Uexküll's Umwelt, and whether or not we fully concur with Uexküll's theory, both the material-semiotic Umwelten of animals and Woolf's literary animal environments prompt us to confront the notion of non-anthropocentric worldviews – the possibility of meaning-making and world-making that, even though humans will inevitably use language to try to communicate such worldly meaning, is not solely reduced to human word-making. Of course, Woolf does not directly engage with or rewrite Uexküll's ethology in the same way as she addresses Darwin's work in some of her texts, but there are several avenues through which Woolf may well have been aware of Uexküll. We know that she was familiar with contemporary scientific developments in quantum physics, astronomy, and the life sciences[12] – all of which radically unsettled anthropocentric worldviews – and Uexküll's developing ethology was known among leading scientists and those who popularised science in newspapers and magazines. One early citation of Uexküll (which occurs before he fully articulates his Umwelt theory in 1909) comes in a book review of *The Cambridge Natural History* in the *Times Literary Supplement* of 3 May 1907, titled 'Form and Life in Lower Animals'. The reviewer, geologist Francis Arthur Bather, notes a new school of 'experimental naturalists' returning to observational methods of studying animals and considering their meaning-making actions:

> We have restricted ourselves too long to the description of the animal in itself. This is only half the matter. An animal is a bit of the universe, no more to be

studied apart than is the sun . . . [W]e must see the animal alive, not set to work as a machine on the bench of the physiologist, but living and working for its life in its own home. (1907: 138)

Bather singles out for praise the passages concerning Uexküll's early work in the volume: 'It is particularly pleasing to see the use made of Baron von Uexküll's researches on the nervous physiology of these creatures [sea urchins and starfish], for these have illuminated many fundamental features in the morphology of the group' (1907: 138).

In the following years Uexküll developed his Umwelt research and it was written about by English scientists, including the zoologist Frederick William Gamble, whose book *The Animal World* (1911) the Woolfs had in their library.[13] Gamble does not engage with Uexküll directly in that book, but he did write a review in *Nature* on 19 May 1910 of *Umwelt und Innenwelt der Tiere* (1909), which was where Uexküll first wrote about his study of animal Umwelten. Gamble praises Uexküll's 'analytic skill . . . in delineating the inwardness of animal movement' and finds his work on animal Umwelten to be 'illuminating'. Gamble concludes that Uexküll's study is 'one of the most interesting summaries of biological work that has appeared recently' and that 'if translated (with a glossary appended) would be eagerly read by a much larger public than will appreciate it in its present form'. To this day a full English translation of this text has not appeared, but Uexküll did become more familiar in England with his later publications and Woolf may have heard of his work from her Bloomsbury circle and especially the Cambridge Apostles. For example, Bertrand Russell and Uexküll both contributed essays to the same volume of the journal *Psyche* in 1924–5.[14] Russell's essay, titled 'Materialism, Past and Present', does not mention or endorse an Uexküllian worldview, but it does contain a telling passage which acknowledges that Descartes' view of animals as automata is no longer plausible: 'Nowadays no one would dream of drawing such a distinction between men and animals' (Russell 1924–5: 114).

But even if Woolf never heard of Uexküll's ideas, the affinities between his modern ethology and her modernist animals reveal an attentiveness to nonhuman Umwelten that is important in considering her relationship with the natural sciences and her literary renderings of animal life. This adds a layer of complexity to our understanding of Woolf's concern with the natural world and her response to Darwinian evolution. Yet it does not mean that Woolf's exploration of animal environments cannot also maintain affinities with Darwin. We might even claim that some of Darwin's writings are themselves Uexküllian, where he focuses on the inner worlds of animals in relation to their environments, and the way that animals perceive in terms of functions rather than always in terms of features (Sagan 2010: 17).[15] For example, in the first chapter of *The Expression of the Emotions in Man and Animals*, which among other things looks at how dogs and cats deal differently with their excrement(!), it is clear Darwin is attuned both to multiple animal Umwelten and the 'different state of mind' of different animals (Darwin 1965: 44). More significantly in relation to *The Waves*, his famous description in the closing section of *The Origin of Species* (1859) of an 'entangled bank' bears a striking resemblance to the interludes:

> It is interesting to contemplate an entangled bank, clothed with many plants of many kinds, with birds singing on the bushes, with various insects flitting about, and with worms crawling through the damp earth, and to reflect that these elaborately constructed forms, so different from each other, and dependent on each other in so complex a manner, have all been produced by laws acting around us. (1985: 459)

In contemplating the complex entanglements of nonhuman worlds in *The Waves*, we might reflect that Woolf's interludes present nonanthropocentric, posthumanist articulations of nature.

Notes

1. For a critical account of approaches to *The Waves* as apolitical and about internal workings of the individual mind, see Tratner 1995: 217–40.
2. For a discussion of classical music in relation to the interludes, see Clements 2005.
3. Quotations from the interludes of *The Waves* will be in italics throughout.
4. Another way humans are 'couched' is that characters in the soliloquy portions of the text are associated with certain images in the interludes (see Vandivere 1996).
5. We could say that human figures are also covertly present in the interludes through allusions to the likes of Shakespeare (Herbert and Sellers 2011: 363), Shelley (Herbert and Sellers 2011: 240; 242; 373), and Tennyson (Herbert and Sellers 2011: 296).
6. For recent critical developments on Woolf and ecocriticism, animal studies, and posthumanist theory, see Swanson 2012; Goldman 2007; Scott 2012; Ryan 2013.
7. See Alt's discussion of 'The Lady in the Looking-Glass', which captures Woolf's awareness of, and positive view towards, observational approaches to animals in nature (1–2).
8. Lambert notes that as well as reading Darwin's writings throughout her youth, Woolf was also 'surrounded by luminaries of evolutionary thought, including her father, Leslie Stephen, and evolution's primary evangelist, T. H. Huxley' (1991: 3).

9. See Buchanan (2008), who provides a study of Uexküll's influences on Heidegger, Merleau-Ponty, and Deleuze.
10. Woolf's drafts of *The Waves* show much time and care was spent on perfecting the depiction of nature in the interludes (Graham 1976).
11. Diane F. Gillespie (2011) has suggested that Woolf's birds draw inspiration from the naturalist writer W. H. Hudson.
12. For Woolf and the new physics, see Beer 1996; for Woolf and astronomy, see Henry 2003: 93–107.
13. See King and Miletic-Vejzovic (2003).
14. Both essays appear in the fifth volume, with Russell's printed in issue 2 and Uexküll's in issue 4. Uexküll's essay is titled 'Time, Number and Measurement' and is extracted from his *Theoretical Biology*, published in English translation in 1926.
15. Indeed Uexküll might be more Darwinian than his critique of Darwinism often allows. For a discussion of the importance of the German context in Uexküll's critique of Darwin, see Winthrop-Young 2010: 211–13.

Bibliography

Agamben, G. (2004), *The Open: Man and Animal*, trans. K. Attell, Stanford: Stanford University Press.

Alt, C. (2010), *Virginia Woolf and the Study of Nature*, Cambridge: Cambridge University Press.

Bather, A. F. (1907), 'Form and Life in Lower Animals', Review of *The Cambridge Natural History*, vol 1', *Times Literary Supplement*, 3 May: 138.

Beer, G. (1996), *Virginia Woolf: The Common Ground*, Edinburgh: Edinburgh University Press.

Bennett, J. (2010), *Vibrant Matter: A Political Ecology of Things*, Durham, NC: Duke University Press.

Buchanan, B. (2008), *Onto-Ethologies: The Animal Environments of Uexküll, Heidegger, Merleau-Ponty, and Deleuze*, Albany: State University of New York Press.

Chun, M. (2012), 'Between Sensation and Sign: The Secret Language of *The Waves*', *Journal of Modern Literature*, 36(1): 53–70.

Clements, E. (2005), 'Transforming Musical Sounds into Words: Narrative Method in Virginia Woolf's *The Waves*', *Narrative*, 13(2): 160–81.

Darwin, C. [1872] (2003), *The Expression of the Emotions in Man and Animals*, Chicago and London: University of Chicago Press.

Darwin, C. [1859] (1985), *The Origin of Species*, London: Penguin.

Darwin, C. [1871] (2003), *The Descent of Man and Selection in Relation to Sex*, London: Gibson Square Books.

Dickinson, R. (2007), 'Exposure and Development: Re-imagining Narrative and Nation in the Interludes of Virginia Woolf's *The Waves*', *Woolf Studies Annual*, 13: 25–47.

Doyle, L. (1996), 'Sublime Barbarians in the Narrative of Empire: Or, Longinus at Sea in *The Waves*', *Modern Fiction Studies*, 42(2): 323–47.

Gamble, F. W. (1910), 'Review: *Umwelt und Innenwelt der Tiere*', *Nature*, 83: 331–2.

Gillespie, D. F. (2011), '"The Bird Is the Word": Virginia Woolf and W. H. Hudson, Visionary Ornithologist', in *Virginia Woolf and the Natural World: Selected Papers from the Twentieth International Conference on Virginia Woolf*, ed. K. Czarnecki and C. Rohman, Clemson: Clemson University Digital Press, pp. 133–42.

Goldman, J. (1998), *The Feminist Aesthetics of Virginia Woolf: Modernism, Post-Impressionism, and the Politics of the Visual*, Cambridge: Cambridge University Press.

Goldman, J. (2007), '"Ce chien est à moi": Virginia Woolf and the Signifying Dog', *Woolf Studies Annual*, 13: 49–86.

Graham, J. W. (1976), *The Waves: The Two Holograph Drafts*, London: Hogarth Press.

Henke, S. (2007), '*The Waves* as Ontological Trauma Narrative', in *Virginia Woolf and Trauma: Embodied Texts*, ed. S. Henke and D. Eberly, New York: Pace University Press, pp. 123–55.

Henry, H. (2003), *Virginia Woolf and the Discourse of Science: The Aesthetics of Astronomy*, Cambridge: Cambridge University Press.

Herbert, M. and S. Sellers, eds (2011), *The Waves*, Cambridge: Cambridge University Press.

King, J. and L. Miletic-Vejzovic (2003), *The Library of Leonard and Virginia Woolf: A Short-title Catalog*, Pullman: Washington State University Press, <http://ntserver1.wsulibs.wsu.edu/masc/onlinebooks/woolflibrary/woolflibraryonline.htm> (last accessed 19 August 2013).

Kronenberger, L. (1931), 'Poetic Brilliance in the New Novel by Mrs Woolf', review of *The Waves*, *New York Times*, 25 October, <http://www.nytimes.com/books/97/06/08/reviews/woolf-waves.html> (last accessed 31 August 2013).

Lambert, E. G. (1991), '"and Darwin says they are nearer the cow": Evolutionary Discourse in Melymbrosia', *Twentieth-Century Literature*, 37(1): 1–21.

Marcus, J. (1992), 'Britannia Rules *The Waves*', in *Decolonizing Tradition: New Views of Twentieth-Century 'British' Literary Canons*, ed. K. Lawrence, Urbana: University of Illinois Press, pp. 136–62.

McConnell, F. D. [1968] (1986), '"Death Among the Apple Trees": *The Waves* and the World of Things', *Modern Critical Views: Virginia Woolf*, ed. H. Bloom, Philadelphia, PA: Chelsea House Publishers, pp. 53–65.

McLaurin, A. (1973), *Virginia Woolf: The Echoes Enslaved*, Cambridge: Cambridge University Press.

Monaco, B. (2008), *Machinic Modernism: The Deleuzian Literary Machines of Woolf, Lawrence and Joyce*, Basingstoke: Palgrave Macmillan.

Rohman, C. (2011), '"We Make Life": Vibration, Aesthetics, and the Inhuman in *The Waves*', in *Virginia Woolf and the Natural World: Selected Papers from the Twentieth International Conference on Virginia Woolf*, ed. K. Czarnecki and C. Rohman, Clemson: Clemson University Digital Press, pp. 12–23.

Russell, B. (1924–5), 'Materialism, Past and Present', *Psyche*, 5(2): 111–20.

Ryan, D. (2013), *Virginia Woolf and the Materiality of Theory: Sex, Animal, Life*, Edinburgh: Edinburgh University Press.

Sagan, D. (2010), Introduction, 'Umwelt after Uexküll', *A Foray into the Worlds of Animals and Humans* with *A Theory of Meaning*, Minneapolis: University of Minnesota Press, pp. 1–34.

Scott, B. K. (2012), *In the Hollow of the Wave: Virginia Woolf and Modernist Uses of Nature*, Charlottesville: University of Virginia Press.

Swanson, D. (2012), 'Woolf's Copernican Shift: Nonhuman Nature in Virginia Woolf's Short Fiction', *Woolf Studies Annual*, 18: 108–25.

Tratner, M. (1995), *Modernism and Mass Politics: Joyce, Woolf, Eliot, Yeats*, Stanford: Stanford University Press.

Uexküll, J. von (1924–5), 'Time, Number and Measurement', *Psyche* 5(4): 315–26.

Uexküll, J. von [1934; 1940] (2010), *A Foray into the Worlds of Animals and Humans* with *A Theory of Meaning*, trans. J. O'Neil, Minneapolis: University of Minnesota Press.

Vandivere, J. (1996), 'Waves and Fragments: Linguistic Construction as Subject Formation in Virginia Woolf', *Twentieth-Century Literature*, 42(2): 221–33.

Winthrop-Young, G. (2010), Afterword, 'Bubbles and Webs: A Backdoor Stroll through the Readings of Uexküll', *A Foray into the Worlds of Animals and Humans* with *A Theory of Meaning*, Minneapolis: University of Minnesota Press, pp. 209–43.

Wolfe, C. (2010), *What is Posthumanism?*, Minneapolis: University of Minnesota Press.

Woolf, V. (1975–80), *The Letters of Virginia Woolf*, 6 vols, ed. N. Nicolson and J. Trautmann, New York: Harcourt Brace Jovanovich.

Woolf, V. (1977–84), *The Diary of Virginia Woolf*, 5 vols, ed. A. O. Bell and A. McNeillie, New York: Harcourt Brace Jovanovich.

Woolf, V. [1929] (1998a), *A Room of One's Own*, Oxford: Oxford University Press.

Woolf, V. [1931] (1998b), *The Waves*, Oxford: Oxford University Press.

Part Five

Genders, Sexualities, and Multiplicities

Chapter 9

Indecency:
Jacob's Room, Modernist
Homosexuality, and the
Culture of War

Eileen Barrett

In a famous scene at the centre of Virginia Woolf's *Jacob's Room*, Jacob Flanders with assistance from his friend Richard Bonamy composes his 'essay upon the Ethics of Indecency' (*JR*: 79) to challenge the sexual repression, control, and censorship of Edwardian society and its institutions. Enraged by Professor Bulteel who 'disembowelled' 'indecent words and some indecent phrases' (70) from his edition of Wycherley, Jacob and Bonamy invoke Lucretius, Aristophanes, and Shakespeare throughout to condemn the idiocy of Bulteel and all he represents. Conveying the kind of outrage, scorn, and derision that Woolf would later employ in *Three Guineas*, Jacob reverses Bulteel's defence of these excisions to expose the 'sheer prudery', 'lewd mind[s]', 'disgusting nature' (70), and fundamental indecency of modern morality.

Celia Marshik analyses the tension in Woolf's writing between disdain for censorship and ambivalence about indecency, showing how Woolf defends and transvalues indecency in *Jacob's Room* by humanising the characters who are prostitutes and denouncing moral purity. Marshik concludes that Woolf remains 'unwilling to put "raw" indecency in her novel' (2006: 112). Susan C. Harris contends that Woolf deliberately includes as one of her multiple narrative voices a censorious narrator to reflect the policing of sexuality as a central theme in Edwardian literature. Through this voice, Woolf shows how homophobia 'operates in *Jacob's Room* both within and outside the academy. To protect itself, the academy must conceal from itself and from outsiders the redirection of sexual desire on which its continued dominance depends' (Harris 1997: 432). Thus the academy refuses to publish Jacob's essay that instead is sealed in a coffin-like box that anticipates Jacob's own death as a catastrophe of war. 'The lid shut upon the truth' in the 'black wooden box, upon which his name was still legible in white paint' (*JR*:

71). Poignantly, in the holograph draft of the novel, Jacob's wooden box also contains 'a great many photographs of ~~young men~~' (Woolf 2010: 79), the generation of Cambridge lovers who will be lost in the war.[1]

Vara Neverow opens the lid of the wooden box to decode the homoerotic throughout *Jacob's Room*, showing that not simply Jacob's essay but the whole novel 'is explicitly engaged in a debate about indecency' (2010: 154).[2] I will illustrate how Jacob's essay on the ethics of indecency conveys on multiple levels how repressed, closeted, and untold stories of late-nineteenth- and early-twentieth-century male homosexuality challenged the attitudes towards masculinity that contributed to militarisation and war. Jacob's essay suggests other clandestine homosexual writing of the period with which Woolf was familiar. Jacob's ethics, for example, might derive from John Addington Symonds's essays in defence of homosexual love, 'A Problem in Greek Ethics' (1883) and 'A Problem in Modern Ethics' (1891).[3] I argue that Woolf draws on Lytton Strachey's early-twentieth-century essays on politics, sex, and war, especially 'Art and Indecency', in shaping Jacob's analysis of indecency in the so-called civilised world.[4]

As numerous critics and biographers note, Woolf was thoroughly engaged with social, political, economic, and cultural issues of her time. Her connections included high-level politicians and leading intellectuals. Prior to and during the First World War, she attended political meetings, avidly read newspapers, and conversed with a range of friends and associates. Her close male friends – Duncan Grant, Lytton Strachey, E. M. Forster – were gay pacifists, conscientious objectors, or noncombatants; her brother Adrian Stephen, whose male lovers during the pre-war period included Grant, organised, advised, and defended other conscientious objectors throughout the war. Other gay male friends such as Goldsworthy Lowes Dickinson and John Maynard Keynes worked tirelessly with Leonard Woolf on speeches, meetings, and writing for the peace movement, promoting a practical vision that led to the founding of the League of Nations. While writing *Jacob's Room* in the early 1920s, Woolf and many of these friends met regularly in the Memoir Club to share and encourage truth-telling in their autobiographical writing.

I read *Jacob's Room* as a coming-of-age novel, based on the experiences of Woolf's male friends, that provides insight into how the social control of gender and sexuality contributes to war. I expand upon Christina Froula's argument that Woolf 'unwrites' Jacob's story 'to expose the social forces that initiate him into masculinity and leave him dead on the battlefield' (2005: 69), and I explore the ongoing repression of homosexuality as one of those social forces. The passage of the Criminal Law Amendment Act in 1885, a turning point in gay male history, defined and criminalised male homosexuality as 'gross indecency' (see Cook 2003: 42). Woolf's novel in general and Jacob's indecency essay in particular reflect the context of this legalised persecution of gay men. Her narrative strategies enable her to 'unwrite' both the sexual secrets of gay men and the story of a young man who becomes masculinised and militarised into the indecency of war. Late-nineteenth-century scandals and trials in London, including those of Oscar Wilde, spread fear among gay men and social intolerance for homosexuality under the infamous rubric of 'gross indecency'. In the first decade of the twentieth century, Woolf's reading of newspapers would have kept her informed about scandals and trials in Germany that exposed the homosexuality of Kaiser Wilhelm's innermost circle, which historians suggest led to Germany's military build-up. Woolf embeds these scandals and their ramifications in *Jacob's Room* revealing the charged context that culminated in the First World War.

Jacob's Room opens with a plethora of sexual secrets, and Woolf suggests how maintaining secret sexuality requires orderly social discipline and control. On the Scarborough beach, the young Jacob encounters the shame of sexuality when he stumbles upon heterosexual lovers, 'their faces very red, an enormous man and woman' (*JR*: 6). His mother, Betty Flanders, keeps secret from her three sons the nature of her long-term affair with Captain Barfoot. Captain Barfoot conceals his involvement with Mrs Flanders from his wife, although as the narrator indicates 'Mrs Barfoot knew that Captain Barfoot was on his way to Mrs. Flanders' (26). The women in the community also repress their knowledge of Barfoot's transgression and believe that 'Here is law. Here is order. Therefore we must cherish this man' (26). Thus from the beginning Woolf reveals how the social complicity of Mrs Barfoot and these other local women maintains Captain Barfoot's sexual secrets and reinforces his masculine authority.

When as a young man of nineteen Jacob arrives at university, the narrator emphasises the institutionalised order and control of Cambridge. Each participant in the King's College convocation ritual, for example, is assigned a role 'so inside the Chapel all was orderly' (*JR*: 30). The narrator describes the young men in the procession as passive, ghost-like figures, who, as though devoid of bodies and sexuality, are grounded by their militaristic marching boots and groomed for war: 'Look, as they pass into service, how airily the gowns blow out, as though nothing dense and corporeal were within. What sculptured faces, what certainty, authority controlled by piety, although great boots march under the gowns' (30). Jacob embraces this elite masculine environment and admires how 'the cities which the elderly of the race have built upon the skyline showed like brick suburbs, barracks, and places of discipline against a red and yellow flame' (34). The description of these 'places of discipline' illustrates parallels among suburbs, military, prisons, and churches, all of which are products of social and political as well as architectural construction. London's marvels such as St Paul's Cathedral, a place that Jacob visits later, also enclose the 'order; the discipline' (66), protecting the tombs of military heroes such as the Duke of Wellington and Admiral Nelson and aligning religion with war. The spatial imagery reinforces the lessons Jacob imbibes from the copy he carries of Finlay's *Byzantine Empire*, a monumental text that chronicles an earlier militaristic culture (66).

But throughout the Cambridge chapters, Woolf depicts the homoerotic energy pervading the rooms of Jacob and his friends in Neville's Court as disrupting order and control, writing that 'gestures of arms, movements of bodies, could be seen shaping something in the room' and then interrupting the narration to wonder, 'What was shaped by the arms and bodies moving in the twilight room?' (*JR*: 43). Woolf's elusive narrator answers such questions ambiguously. 'But intimacy', we are told a few pages later, 'the room was full of it, still, deep, like a pool' (45). With meaningful pauses and aptly placed questions, this narrative calls attention to the silences surrounding the homoerotics that these young men shape and perform. It conveys the communal light of same-sex love, the intimacy and the physicality of same-sex friendship, yet stops at the bedroom door: 'young men rising from chairs and sofa corners, buzzing and barging about the room, one driving another against the bedroom door, which giving way, in they fell' (44).

The narrator crosses the bedroom threshold to reveal, for example, a moment between Jacob and Simeon in which intimacy 'rose softly and washed over everything, mollifying, kindling, and coating the mind with the luster of pearl, so that if you talk of a light, of Cambridge burning, it's not languages only. It's Julian the Apostate' (*JR*: 45; see Neverow 2010: 154–5). With its reference to Julian, this passage evokes the early modern homosexual values that submerge the homoerotic within the heroic warrior. Yet in this instance, Woolf's narrator lifts the curtain to reveal intimacy and aroused sexuality with their potential to challenge social control for, as Neverow writes, 'Jacob is almost drunk with pleasure and there is a strong suggestion that he has an erection' (2010: 154). Neverow cites descriptions from the novel of Jacob 'rising and standing over Simeon's chair . . . as if his pleasure would brim and spill down the sides if Simeon spoke' (2010:154; *JR*: 45).

This moment echoes Lytton Strachey's descriptions of sexual feelings for a fellow member of the Cambridge 'Midnight Society'[5] – none other than Clive Bell: 'He was divine – in a soft shirt, & hair & complexion that lifted me & my penis to the heights of heaven. Oh! Oh! Oh!' (qtd in Holroyd 1995: 59). Well known and sometimes feared by his friends for his flamboyant and openly queer identity, Strachey refused to associate homosexuality with the homoerotic male warrior. Woolf revelled in Strachey's sexual iconoclasm, famously recalling the moment when the 'long and sinister figure' of Strachey appeared on her Bloomsbury threshold and said the word 'semen'.

> Can one really say it? I thought and we burst out laughing. With that one word all barriers of reticence and reserve went down. A flood of the sacred fluid seemed to overwhelm us. Sex permeated conversation. The word bugger was never far from our lips. (*MOB*: 194–5)

Descriptions of Jacob and Timmy Durrant are permeated with the explicit homoerotic that breaks down some barriers of reticence and reserve. '[T]he sight of [Timmy] sitting there, with his hands on the tiller, rosy gilled, with a sprout of beard ... would have moved a woman', the narrator observes; she then reminds us, 'Jacob, of course, was not a woman' (*JR:* 46). At the same time, as Timmy watches the naked Jacob sunning himself in the boat, he realises '[t]here are things that can't be said' (49). Walking at dawn arm-in-arm through London, Jacob and Timmy Durrant 'were boastful, triumphant'; 'they had read every book in the world; known every sin, passion, and joy' (77). Jacob implies the scope of their sins when he announces that probably 'we are the only people in the world who know what the Greeks meant' (77). The narrator interrupts to ponder 'this love of Greek, flourishing in such obscurity, distorted, discouraged, yet leaping out, all of a sudden' (77) and traces its homoerotic source. Although Jacob 'seldom thought of Plato or Socrates in the flesh' (157), the narrator assures us 'if Socrates saw them coming he would bestir himself and say "my fine fellows"' (78).

With the references to intimacy, Plato, Socrates, and 'what the Greeks meant', Woolf alludes to the history of the homoerotic familiar to her and her Bloomsbury friends. The Cambridge chapters of *Jacob's Room* celebrate Platonic and heroic homoerotic ideals analysed, revised, and re-envisioned in the works of Symonds and Woolf's friend Goldsworthy Lowes Dickinson. Symonds, father of Woolf's own early lesbian love Madge Vaughan, privately published essays that held enormous sway among Woolf's Cambridge friends.[6] In 'A Problem in Greek Ethics' (1883), Symonds traces the underlying homoerotic throughout the literature of the Greeks with particular attention to the *Phaedrus* and *Symposium*. Comparing homoerotic passion to a madness of desire 'not different in quality from that which inspires poets', Symonds writes that 'after painting that fervid picture of the lover', Socrates elides the sexual and declares that 'a noble life can only be attained by passionate friends, bound together in the chains of close yet temperate comradeship, seeking always to advance in knowledge, self-restraint, and intellectual illumination' (Symonds 2012: 94). 'The doctrine of the *Symposium* is not different', Symonds continues, 'except that Socrates here takes a higher flight. The same love is treated as the method whereby the soul may begin her mystic journey to the region of essential beauty, truth, and goodness' (94). But six years later in a letter to a colleague, Symonds emphasises the evidence of overt homosexuality in Plato, arguing that 'Such passion is innate in some persons no less than the ordinary sexual appetite is innate in the majority.' For Symonds the effect upon gay men of reading Plato 'has the force of revelation' (1984: 100). Symonds concludes his defence of their love by writing, 'Greek love for Plato was no "figure of speech", but a present poignant reality' (1984: 102).

A Cambridge don and an intimate friend of Virginia and Leonard Woolf, Dickinson also described reading the *Symposium* and *Phaedrus* as revelatory (Forster 1973: 36). With candid celebrations of the love of one man for another, Dickinson's early books *The Greek View of Life* (1896) and *A Modern Symposium* (1905) profoundly influenced Forster, Strachey, and their Apostle friends at Cambridge. The 'passion for a particular body and soul', Dickinson argues, leads 'to an enthusiasm for that highest beauty, wisdom, and excellence' (1957: 189–90). Rather than confined to the pedagogues, philosophers, and poets, Dickinson's erudition reveals that this sexual love of one man for another was commonly practised among all levels of Greek society, and that homosexuality 'was not invented but interpreted by Plato' (1957: 190). Sharing these ideas with his disciples at Cambridge, as Forster writes in his biography, Dickinson strove to create a university where '[p]eople and books reinforced one another, intelligence joined hands with affection, speculation became a passion, and discussion was made profound by love' (Forster 1973: 30). During one of his frequent visits with Woolf, when she was writing *Jacob's Room*, Dickinson described his work on a dialogue about homosexuality and on an autobiographical poem, which he called 'Body and Soul', about his own homosexual experiences. But as Woolf recorded in a 1921 letter, prevailing homophobia meant that both works would remain unpublished during his lifetime 'for fear of the effect upon parents who might send their sons to Kings' (*L* 2: 485).

Symonds and Dickinson influenced Strachey's rapturous description of his 'mingled pleasure and pain' upon discovering the *Symposium* at Cambridge: '"That day of surprise, relief, and fear to know that what I feel now was felt 2000 years ago in glorious Greece"' (qtd in Taddeo

1997: 201–2). Strachey incorporated 'what the Greeks meant' into his own fictional depiction of homosexuality. In his 'Diary of An Athenian, 400 B.C.' (1974), written when he was in his early twenties, he borrowed characters from Plato's dialogues to write his defence of same-sex love:

> I love because I love – not because it is right or wrong; and so I dare swear, do you . . . You think of my love impure: is yours so pure as that? Speak not of what you do not understand! . . . Men call my love 'the love of boys' . . . I would rather name it 'The Love of Souls'. (Strachey 1974: 141)

Several critics notice how Forster interweaves the dialogues of the *Phaedrus* and *Symposium* with the romantic narrative of *Maurice*, moving beyond the restriction of Platonic love embedded in the relationship between Maurice and Clive to the fully realised sexual relationship between Maurice and Alec.[7] Reading the *Phaedrus* awakens the youthful Clive: "He saw there his malady described exquisitely, calmly, as a passion which we can direct, like any other, towards good or bad' (Forster 1971: 70). Despite the warning from their Dean to "'Omit: a reference to the unspeakable vice of the Greeks"' (51), Clive urges Maurice to read the *Symposium*, leading Maurice to acknowledge that he 'loved men and always had loved them. He longed to embrace them and mingle his being with theirs' (62).

The homosexuality in *Jacob's Room* echoes the longing found in the early-twentieth-century homoerotic writing and the correspondence of Strachey and Forster, whose Cambridge experiences form the basis for those of the young male characters in *Jacob's Room*. Jacob's early sexual explorations foster a love of souls that is concealed within cloistered rooms and narrative censorship. Jacob's own sexuality is indeterminate. He is an object of desire for both sexes, and his 'sins' include sexual adventures with several female characters. At the Guy Fawkes dinner, Jacob is wreathed in paper flowers and seated on a white, gilt chair, and seemingly admired by both genders: 'We think', said two of the dancers, breaking off from the rest, and bowing profoundly before him, 'that you are the most beautiful man we have ever seen' (*JR*: 76). The end of Jacob's affair with Florinda is 'a violent reversion towards male society, cloistered rooms, and the works of the classics' (83). Yet, unlike Symonds, Dickinson, Strachey, Forster, and other gay students of the classics who read Plato with the force of revelation, Jacob finds that 'The *Phaedrus* is very difficult' (114). Although 'momentarily' Jacob becomes 'part of this rolling, imperturbable energy, which has driven darkness before it since Plato walked the Acropolis', in the end, he remains encased in darkness (114–15): 'The dialogue draws to its close.

Plato's argument is done. Plato's argument is stowed away in Jacob's mind, and for five minutes Jacob's mind continues alone, onwards, into the darkness' (115). Rather than fully illuminate Jacob's homoerotic tendencies, the novel – to use Froula's verb – unwrites them, leaving them instead in the darkness. 'One word is sufficient', the narrator claims, only to qualify with an unanswered question. 'But if we cannot find it?' (71).

> Even the exact words get the wrong accent on them. But something is always impelling one to hum vibrating, like the hawk moth, at the mouth of the cavern of mystery, endowing Jacob Flanders with all sorts of qualities he had not at all – for though, certainly, he sat talking to Bonamy, half of what he said was too dull to repeat; much unintelligible (about unknown people and Parliament); what remains is mostly a matter of guess work. Yet over him we hang vibrating. (*JR*: 74)

On one level, Woolf pairs mundane details – unknown people and Parliament – with an exquisite analogy – this cavern of mystery. On another level, she pairs Jacob's dull conversation with Bonamy about the lawmaking of government with the vibrating hawk moth. The hawk moth cannot enter but instead vibrates at the mouth of the anus-like cavern of mystery that is Jacob. The laws of Parliament legislate that love between men dare not speak its name; instead it remains either hidden in the impenetrable space of the cavern of mystery or publicly condemned as gross indecency.

Throughout the London chapters, Jacob walks the streets of the metropolis, free to explore and fantasise yet always under the watchful eye of the police. In daylight Jacob finds life tolerable 'when the policeman holds up his arm and the sun beats on your back' (*JR*: 65), and at night, Jacob roams, 'passing at length no one but shut doors, carved door-posts, and a solitary policeman' (83). 'Holborn straight ahead of you', says the policeman' (99) later in the novel. But what if Jacob refuses to go straight and evades the surveillance of the police? The narrator duly warns, 'The streets of London have their map; but our passions are uncharted. What are you going to meet if you turn this corner?' (99):

> Ah, but where are you going if instead of brushing past the old man with the white beard, the silver medal, and the cheap violin, you let him go on with his story, which ends in an invitation to step somewhere, to his room, presumably off Queen's Square and there he shows you a collection of birds' eggs and a letter from the Prince of Wales's secretary, and this (skipping the intermediate stages) brings you one winter's day to the Essex coast, where the little boat makes off to the ship, and the ship sails and you behold on the skyline the Azores; and the flamingoes rise; and there you sit on the verge of

the marsh drinking rum-punch, an outcast from civilization, for you have committed a crime, are infected with yellow fever as likely as not, and – fill in the sketch as you like. (*JR*: 99)

This strange scene of seduction, lawlessness, and flight appears near the middle of a chapter that digresses about letters – the legal letters that require the signature of Jacob, literary letters of Bryon and Cowper, philosophical letters of Jacob, and domestic letters of Mrs Jarvis, Clara Durrant, Florinda, and Betty Flanders that elide sexual secrets (*JR*: 93–7). Although the narrator invites us to fill in the unwritten sketch as we like, there is an historical source for this encounter and its enigmatic reference to a letter from the Prince of Wales's secretary. The elderly man in the street with his mysterious story and evidentiary letter recalls the infamous Cleveland Street homosexual affair of the early 1890s.

Well reported in the press, this scandal occurred between 1889 and 1890, focused on a brothel frequented by British aristocrats, and reinvigorated calls for prosecution of 'gross indecency'. In the course of investigating petty theft in the London post office, police discovered that several telegraph messengers supplemented their incomes with earnings from their work as male prostitutes at a Cleveland Street address in the West End. The press correctly suspected that high-ranking aristocrats were the clients of Cleveland Street and elicited testimony from the young men. Theo Aronson (1994), Matt Cook (2003), and Morris B. Kaplan (2005) have analysed this protracted scandal and its extensive coverage in the press showing that Lord Arthur Somerset, Extra Equerry to the Prince of Wales, was one of several aristocrats accused of sexual acts of gross indecency at this infamous address. The 'affair led to speculation that members of the royal family itself might be involved . . . Criticism in the radical press and in Parliament led to widespread debate about moral standards, law enforcement, and equal justice' (Kaplan 2005: 167). Somerset's attorney threatened that if the prosecution continued 'a very distinguished person [would] be involved' and then hinted in coded initials that '(P.A.V.)' was at risk (Kaplan 2005: 169). The initials, Kaplan notes, refer to Prince Albert Victor, the eldest son of the Prince of Wales and next in line to the throne after his father.

Although not actually 'the Prince of Wales's secretary', Somerset served the Prince in the manner that the title of *secret*ary (my italics) etymologically implies: he kept the secrets. An outcast of civilisation, Somerset resigned his post and fled the country to avoid a public trial and to protect the royal family. Foolishly, perhaps, he continued to share confidences with his adviser Reginald Brett, who collected numerous letters from a range of clients implicated in the Cleveland Street scandal. As the situation worsened, correspondents anxiously requested that Brett destroy their letters. Instead, Brett bound all the letters in a leather volume marked 'The Case of Lord Arthur Somerset'. This trove includes correspondence from Somerset and his family to Brett and is full of intrigue about the involvement of Prince Albert and fear of reprisals from the Prince of Wales (Aronson 1994: 162–77; Cook 2003: 42–52; Kaplan 2005: 166–72).

The Cleveland Street male prostitution scandal exposed the secret lives of British aristocrats and criminalised the young telegraph workers, one of whom complained, '"I think it is very hard that I should get into trouble while men in high positions are allowed to walk about free"' (qtd in Kaplan 2005: 168). Most of the upper-class participants in the Cleveland Street scandal escaped prosecution, but those who were tried were convicted under section 11 of the Criminal Law Amendment Act. Beginning in 1895, about five years after these West End scandals, Oscar Wilde's trials and imprisonment for gross indecency shifted the attention to artists and literary figures. The impact of these homosexual trials continued for generations, and Julie Anne Taddeo thoroughly analyses their effect on Strachey and his fellow Apostles who 'did not deliberately cultivate a queer, Oscar Wilde type of identity. In fact, Wilde's legacy was a reminder to Bloomsbury to practice discretion and not arouse the suspicion of outsiders' (Taddeo 1997: 221). Wendy Moffat similarly notes the significance of the Victorian era scandals, writing, 'Forster came of age sexually in the shadow of the 1895 Wilde trials, and he learned their lessons well' (2010: 46–7). In *Jacob's Room*, Woolf represents this shadow as the 'cavern of mystery' and hints at homosexuality in the private room and the public market, noting that 'part of this is not Jacob but Richard Bonamy – the room; the market carts; the hour; the very moment of history' (*JR*: 74).

An infamous homosexual scandal in Germany, whose duration from 1906 to 1908 was a moment in history that coincides with the time period of *Jacob's Room*, had enormous implications for international politics. Like the Wilde trials the decade before, this scandal and its subsequent trials were regularly reported in the *Daily Telegraph*, the *Daily Mail*, *The Star* and other London newspapers that various characters in the novel read. Isabel V. Hull provides fascinating background on the homoerotic circle that played such a significant part in the lead-up to the First World War. As a young man, the future German Kaiser Prince Wilhelm II fell in love with the older and charismatic Philipp Eulenburg. Hull describes their romantic first meeting: 'What instantly drew Wilhelm and Eulenburg together was not politics or power, but personality. Each had found a boon companion, soul mate, and friend who seemed so suitable' that their friendship 'took on the character of a whirlwind courtship'. For Eulenburg, 'His love of men was the central, shaping impulse of his private and public self', a great attraction for the Kaiser who, Hull writes, 'basked in male comradeship and attention unencumbered by demands that he be kingly or warrior-like' (1982: 45, 47, 63).

But enemies within this highly charged political circle prevailed, ending this homosexual idyll and exposing the loves and lives of Eulenburg and his associates. John Röhl documents evidence from 'secret reports of the political and vice police in Vienna, Munich, Berlin' 'so overwhelming that it would be virtually hopeless for Phili [Eulenburg] to contest it [homosexual affairs] in open court, and that at the very least it would mean a disastrous scandal for the Kaiser' (1987: 59). Wilhelm distanced himself from his former friend, 'paralyzed between his conventionality, which labeled male homosexuals weakly effeminate non-men, and his fear that he could not live up to society's masculine stereotype' (Hull 1982: 64).

James D. Steakley describes how the Eulenburg lawsuits and countersuits exposed homosexuals not only among the closest political allies of Kaiser Wilhelm II but also in the German military. Historians link the outing of the Kaiser and his entourage 'to a far-reaching shift in German policy that heightened military aggressiveness and ultimately contributed to the outbreak of World War I' (Steakley 1990: 235). Hull concludes that those who feared Eulenburg's power attacked him on all fronts because he favoured a pacific foreign policy: 'Eulenburg became a symbol of unmanly weakness and pacifism. His fall removed one more voice against sabre-rattling and against military influence on foreign affairs. Inside the entourage, the balance now tipped decisively in favor of the military' (Hull 1982: 145). Well publicised in England, these scandals catapulted 'sexual conduct out of the private sphere into the public arena' (Steakley 1990: 235).

A daily reader of newspapers, Woolf would have known of the Eulenburg scandal. In 1908, Wilhelm conducted an intemperate, ill-advised interview with the *Daily Telegraph* that published his incoherent utterances, leading to increased tensions between the two countries. Woolf followed news of the Kaiser during and after the war, and she likely would have seen in the London papers the obituaries on Eulenburg's death in 1921, when she was working on *Jacob's Room*. Woolf understood how politics feeds upon scandal and propaganda. In *Jacob's Room* the onset of the war is announced when the 'wires of the Admiralty shivered with some far-away communication. A voice kept remarking that Prime Ministers and Viceroys spoke in the Reichstag; . . .

Papers accumulated, inscribed with the utterances of Kaisers' (*JR*: 182, my emphasis). The novel describes how the machinations of bureaucracy are manfully determined to shape events and impose coherence on the incoherent utterances of unmanly Kaisers:

> His head – bald, red-veined, hollow-looking – represented all the heads in the building. His head, with amiable pale eyes, carried the burden of knowledge across the street; laid it before his colleagues, who came equally burdened; and then the sixteen gentlemen, lifting their pens or turning perhaps rather wearily in their chairs, decreed that the course of history should shape itself this way or that, being manfully determined, as their faces showed, to impose some coherency upon Rajahs and Kaisers and the mutterings in bazaars, the secret gatherings, plainly visible in Whitehall ... to control the course of events. (*JR*: 182)

As if echoing the German scandal and its aftermath, *Jacob's Room* describes how anonymous figures – the bald, red-veined, hollow heads that multiply in the halls of power – turn gossip, trials, and sexual secrets of Kaisers into policy, war, and the decree of history.

Jacob and Bonamy's relationship outlines the divergence between those who accept and those who reject the 'manfully determined' course of events that leads to war. Strachey loved *Jacob's Room*, describing it to Woolf as 'a most wonderful achievement' – 'I occasionally almost screamed with joy at the writing. Of course you're very romantic – which alarms me slightly – I am such a Bonamy' (Woolf and Strachey 1956: 103–4). It's not surprising that Strachey saw himself in Bonamy. Although Woolf relegates Jacob's sexuality and sexual identity to the unwritten and undefined space of the 'cavern of mystery' (*JR*: 73), her narrative makes Bonamy's same-sex love explicit. Bonamy, in fact, is 'fonder of Jacob than of anyone in the world' (148). Expression of this attraction for Jacob remains permissible only as playful activity when, for example, they are 'two bulls of Bashan driving each other up and down, making such a racket', with 'Bonamy, all his hair touzled and his tie flying' (107) or when 'Bonamy would play around [Jacob] like an affectionate spaniel; and that (as likely as not) they would end by rolling on the floor' (174). For Jacob, an ideal London evening would be:

> to take the air with Bonamy on his arm, meditatively marching, head thrown back, the world a spectacle, the early moon above the steeples coming in for praise, the sea-gulls flying high, Nelson on the column surveying the horizon, and the world our ship. (*JR*: 93)

The militaristic language of the conventional Jacob – marching, Nelson on the column, and the world our ship – associates Jacob's homoeroticism with the classical traditions of war.[8] Moreover, depictions of Jacob in his law offices imply the tension he feels between legislating and reciprocating explicit homosexuality.

Jacob's travels through Greece increase his need for Bonamy as he tries to resist the seduction of Sandra Wentworth Williams. After all '[i]t was to Bonamy that Jacob wrote from Patras – to Bonamy who couldn't love a woman and never read a foolish book' (*JR*: 147). The narrator conveys Jacob's ambivalence: 'When bedtime came the difficulty was to write to Bonamy, Jacob found . . . Poor old Bonamy! No, there was something queer about it. He could not write to Bonamy' (155). Jacob's queer longing and confusion continues:

> But on Wednesday he wrote a telegram to Bonamy, telling him to come at once. And then he crumpled it in his hand and threw it in the gutter.
> 'For one thing he wouldn't come', he thought. 'And then I daresay this sort of thing wears off'. 'This sort of thing' being that uneasy, painful feeling, something like selfishness – one wishes almost that the thing would stop – it is getting more and more beyond what is possible. (*JR*: 157)

For Bonamy, this sort of thing does not wear off, and he is distraught by the distance he senses from Jacob upon his return from Greece: '"he has not said a word to show that he is glad to see me", thought Bonamy bitterly', who yet remains in love, finding Jacob 'more sublime, devastating, terrific than ever' (*JR*: 173). Bonamy's unrequited love leaves him 'tossed like a cork on the waves' (174). When Jacob finally admits to being in love with another, Bonamy sees the devastating combination of the statuesque homoerotic warrior and the contemporary military leader as Jacob 'stared straight ahead of him, fixed, monolithic – oh, very beautiful! – like a British Admiral, exclaimed Bonamy in a rage' (174).

While the Eulenburg scandals were unfolding, Lytton Strachey was writing essays in which he grappled with the connections between politics, sexuality, and war as well as with his own ethics of indecency. Lasciviousness is a favourite Strachey topic which he also claims as 'one of the essential attributes of mankind' (Strachey 1974: 73), and many of his pieces are humorous, ribald, and boldly sexual. Strachey not only felt free to use the word 'semen' in mixed company for the amusement of his friends; he invented examination topics in sex education with instructions such as 'Distinguish clearly, with diagrams, between the clitoris and the vagina' (Strachey 1971: 111). 'Art and Indecency' incorporates this sexual playfulness, including a sly reference to the Eulenburg scandals – 'The Kaiser's delinquencies have really nothing to do with his moustaches' (Strachey 1974: 83). At the same time, Strachey raises serious questions about the relationship between the artistic and the indecent.

Like Jacob in his essay, Strachey excoriates Victorian prudery that 'regard[s] with horror, detestation, and anger any introduction of indecency into works of art' (Strachey 1974: 84). Whereas Jacob challenges the excisions and censorship of Bulteel, Strachey eviscerates the arrogance, prudery, and stupidity of Mr Bowdler – 'Shakespeare contains indecencies; indecency is bad; the inference is obvious: remove the indecencies, and you will improve Shakespeare' (1974: 85). But somewhat surprisingly Strachey also objects to the defence of indecency set forth by the naturalists – Edward Carpenter, Walt Whitman, and Symonds, for example – who deny the existence of indecency, arguing that it is the result of 'ignorant traditions and the artificialities of civilization' (1974: 86)· What the world identifies as indecent is for these theorists a product of nature. What is even more surprising is that Strachey would challenge such a persuasive argument in defence of homosexuality, which is anything but indecent since it is a result of bodily, natural urges. But for Strachey,

> It is not a question of properties and functions, or of glands and ducts, or of movements of living tissue: it is a question of mental states – of extraordinary agitations, of unexpected and dominating impulses, of intensifying excitements, of unparalleled joys. (1974: 88)

Strachey refuses to deny the possibility of a dangerous indecency. Instead he claims an ethical argument that some things – military leaders and the wars they represent – are not only indecent but have horrific and unimaginable effects. In 1916, Strachey challenged this indecency in the raw when he professed his conscious objection to the war: 'I am convinced that the whole system by which it is sought to settle international disputes by force is profoundly evil' (1971: 135). In *Jacob's Room*, Woolf describes the tragic death of young men such as Jacob who accept the masculine role they are assigned to play in this profoundly evil system of war: 'With equal nonchalance a dozen young men in the prime of life descend with composed faces into the depths of the sea; and there impassively (though with perfect mastery of machinery) suffocate uncomplainingly together' (*JR*: 164). But Strachey refused to join the battleships; he refused to train a gun at a target; he refused to descend into the depths of the sea; he refused to suffocate and die impassively with these tragically misinformed young men. Indeed throughout these essays Strachey seeks, as Woolf does in her novel, to illustrate the intrinsic passivity at the heart of the manliness required for war. In the end, Bonamy and Strachey embody a pacifist unmanliness to counter virile masculinity and the machinery of war.

Why would the lesbian Woolf write the modernist male homoerotic? In some ways the answer is simple. Woolf loved her gay male friends; she shared their pacifist convictions; discussing and understanding their lives and loves allowed her the freedom to explore the excitement and mysteries of her own sexual life.[9] Yet her path was not always easy, as a telling comment to Strachey in a 1912 letter reveals:

> How difficult it is to write to you! It's all Cambridge – that detestable place; and the ap-s-les [Cambridge Apostles] are so unreal, and their loves are so unreal, and yet I suppose it's all going on still – swarming in the sun – and perhaps not as bad as I imagine. But when I think of it, I vomit – that's all – a green vomit, which gets into the ink and blisters the paper. (*L* 1: 498)

The self-censorship of Woolf's Bloomsbury friends and their precursors was something Woolf contended with throughout her life. Forster never shared with her the *Maurice* manuscript (Moffat 2010: 194); she wanted a 'full & outspoken life' of Lytton (*D* 4: 296); and in the 1930s, she urged Katharine Furse, Symonds's daughter, to write openly about her father's sexuality (see Fowler 1990: 205–30). She did, however, write about her own sexual abuse and throughout her work she celebrates lesbian desires. Woolf's passionate truth-telling fed her commitment to redefine as well as name indecency in the raw. She exposed the complex homosexuality closeted in the youthful experiences of her pacifist male friends and narrated the extraordinary agitations, the unexpected and dominating impulses, and the intensifying excitements of their unparalleled and unmanly homosexual loves.

Notes

1. Other work on *Jacob's Room* that informs my reading includes Bishop (1992); Handley (1992); Phillips (1994: 121–53); Zwerdling (1986: 62–83).
2. See also Neverow's Introduction to the Harcourt edition of *Jacob's Room* (Neverow 2008). For a discussion of lesbianism in the novel, see Neverow (2004).
3. Both of these essays are republished in *John Addington Symonds and Homosexuality: A Critical Edition of Sources* (2012), listed in the bibliography.
4. Levy believes Strachey wrote 'Art and Indecency' sometime before 1908 for reading at one of the Cambridge societies (Levy 1974: 82). On Symonds, see Brady (2005: 157–94). For insightful work on Strachey see Avery (2004), Taddeo (2002), and Taddeo (1997).

5. The Society was so named because members met Saturdays at twelve o'clock (Holroyd 1995: 58–9).
6. Brady describes the publishing history and influence of Symonds's essays (Brady 2012: 1–38). In 'Unmasking Lesbian Passion' (Barrett 1997), I discuss the influence of Symonds on Woolf and the significance of Woolf's relationship with his daughter Madge Vaughan. As I note in this article even Quentin Bell acknowledged the profundity of Woolf's love for Madge Vaughan, who was a model for Sally Seton in *Mrs Dalloway*. Ruth Vanita (1997) also discusses the influence of Symonds and Dickinson on Woolf.
7. See Martin (1983) and Raschke (1997).
8. See Phillips (1994: 123) for a similar reading of Jacob's complicity with the culture of war.
9. As Vanita argues, 'talking about the relatively more visible phenomenon of male homosexuality was the route whereby Woolf was able to express her own anxieties and finally her own desire for a Sapphic relationship' (1997: 167).

Bibliography

Aronson, T. (1994), *Prince Eddy and the Homosexual Underworld*, New York: Barnes and Noble.

Avery, T. (2004), '"This intricate commerce of souls": The Origins and Some Early Expressions of Lytton Strachey's Ethics', *Journal of the History of Sexuality*, 13(2): 183–207.

Barrett, E. (1997), 'Unmasking Lesbian Passion: The Inverted World of *Mrs Dalloway*', in *Virginia Woolf: Lesbian Readings,* ed. E. Barrett and P. Cramer, New York: New York University Press, pp. 146–64.

Bishop, E. (1992), 'The Subject in Jacob's Room', *Modern Fiction Studies,* 38(1): 147–75.

Brady, S. (2005), *Masculinity and Male Homosexuality in Britain, 1861–1913,* New York: Palgrave Macmillan.

Brady, S. (2012), Introduction, *John Addington Symonds and Homosexuality: A Critical Edition of Sources,* ed. S. Brady, New York: Palgrave Macmillan, pp. 1–38.

Cook, M. (2003), *London and the Culture of Homosexuality, 1885–1914,* Cambridge: Cambridge University Press.

Dickinson, G. L. [1905] (1922), *A Modern Symposium*, Garden City, NY: Doubleday, Page & Co.

Dickinson, G. L. [1896] (1957), *The Greek View of Life*, London: Methuen & Co.

Forster, E. M. [1913–14] (1971), *Maurice*, New York: W. W. Norton.

Forster, E. M. [1934] (1973), *Goldsworthy Lowes Dickinson and Related Writings,* London: Edward Arnold Publishers.

Fowler, R., ed. (1990), 'Virginia Woolf and Katharine Furse, an Unpublished Correspondence', *Tulsa Studies in Women's Literature*, 9(2): 205–30.

Froula, C. (2005), *Virginia Woolf and the Bloomsbury Avant-Garde: War, Civilization, Modernity,* New York: Columbia University Press.

Handley, W. R. (1992), 'War and the Politics of Narration in *Jacob's Room*', in *Virginia Woolf and War: Fiction, Reality, and Myth*, ed. M. Hussey, Syracuse, NY: Syracuse University Press, pp. 110–33.

Harris, S. C. (1997), '"The Ethics of Indecency": Censorship, Sexuality, and the Voice of the Academy in the Narration of *Jacob's Room*', *Twentieth-Century Literature*, 43(4): 420–38.

Holroyd, M. [1994] (1995), *Lytton Strachey: The New Biography*, New York: Farrar, Straus and Giroux.

Hull, I. V. (1982), *The Entourage of Kaiser Wilhelm II, 1888–1918*, Cambridge and New York: Cambridge University Press.

Kaplan, M. B. (2005), *Sodom on the Thames: Sex, Love, and Scandal in Wildean Times*, Ithaca, NY: Cornell University Press.

Levy, P. (1974), *The Really Interesting Question and Other Papers*, by L. Strachey, ed. and commentary P. Levy, New York: Capricorn Books.

Marshik, C. (2006), *British Modernism and Censorship*, Cambridge: Cambridge University Press.

Martin, R. K. (1983), 'Edward Carpenter and the Double Structure of *Maurice*', *Journal of Homosexuality*, 8(3/4): 35–46.

Moffat, W. (2010), *A Great Unrecorded History: A New Life of E. M. Forster*, New York: Farrar, Straus and Giroux.

Neverow, V. (2004), 'The Return of the Great Goddess: Immortal Virginity, Sexual Autonomy and Lesbian Possibility in *Jacob's Room*', *Woolf Studies Annual*, 10: 203–31.

Neverow, V. (2008), Introduction, *Jacob's Room* by V. Woolf, New York: Houghton Mifflin Harcourt, pp. xxxvii–xciv.

Neverow, V. (2010), 'Contrasting Urban and Rural Transgressive Sexualities in *Jacob's Room*', *Virginia Woolf and the City: Selected Papers from the Nineteenth Annual Conference on Virginia Woolf*, ed. E. F. Evans and S. E. Cornish, Clemson: Clemson University Digital Press, pp. 154–60.

Phillips, K. J. (1994), *Virginia Woolf Against Empire*, Knoxville: University of Tennessee Press.

Raschke, D. (1997), 'Breaking the Engagement with Philosophy: Re-envisioning Hetero/Homo Relations in *Maurice*', in *Queer Forster*, ed. R. K. Martin and G. Piggford, Chicago: University of Chicago Press, pp. 151–66.

Röhl, J. C. G. (1987), *The Kaiser and His Court: Wilhelm II and the Government of Germany*, Cambridge: Cambridge University Press.

Steakley, J. D. (1990), 'Iconography of a Scandal; Political Cartoons and the Eulenburg Affair in Wilhelmin Germany', in *Hidden from History: Reclaiming the Gay and Lesbian Past*, ed. M. Duberman, M. Vicinus, and G. Chauncy, New York: Meridan, pp. 233–57.

Strachey, L. (1971), *Lytton Strachey by Himself: A Self-Portrait*, ed. and intro. M. Holroyd, New York: Holt, Rinehart and Winston.

Strachey, L. [1972] (1974), *The Really Interesting Question and Other Papers*, ed. P. Levy, New York: Capricorn Books.

Symonds, J. A. (1984), *The Memoirs of John Addington Symonds: The Secret Homosexual Life of a Leading Nineteenth-Century Man of Letters*, ed. P. Grosskurth, Chicago: University of Chicago Press.

Symonds, J. A. (2012), *John Addington Symonds and Homosexuality: A Critical Edition of Sources*, ed. S. Brady, New York: Palgrave Macmillan.

Taddeo, J. A. (1997), 'Plato's Apostles: Edwardian Cambridge and the New Style of Love', *Journal of the History of Sexuality*, 8(2): 196–229.

Taddeo, J. A. (2002), *Lytton Strachey and the Search for Modern Sexual Identity: The Last Eminent Victorian*, New York: Haworth Press.

Vanita, R. (1997), 'Bringing Buried Things to Light: Homoerotic Alliances in *To the Lighthouse*', in *Virginia Woolf: Lesbian Readings,* ed. E. Barrett and P. Cramer, New York: New York University Press, pp. 165–79.

Woolf, V. (1975–80), *The Letters of Virginia Woolf,* 6 vols, ed. N. Nicolson and J. Trautmann, New York and London: Harcourt Brace Jovanovich.

Woolf, V. (1982), *The Diary of Virginia Woolf*, vol. 4: 1931–1935, ed. A. O. Bell and A. McNeillie, New York: Harcourt Brace Jovanovich.

Woolf, V. (1985), *Moments of Being*, 2nd edn, ed. J. Schulkind, New York: Harcourt Brace Jovanovich.

Woolf, V. [1938] (2006), *Three Guineas*, annot. and intro. J. Marcus, New York: Harcourt.

Woolf, V. [1922] (2008), *Jacob's Room*, annot. and intro. V. Neverow, New York: Harcourt.

Woolf, V. [1998] (2010), *Virginia Woolf's* Jacob's Room: *The Holograph Draft*, transcr. and ed. E. L. Bishop, New York: Pace University Press.

Woolf, V. and L. Strachey (1956), *Virginia Woolf and Lytton Strachey: Letters*, ed. L. Woolf and J. Strachey, London: Hogarth Press.

Zwerdling, A. (1986), *Virginia Woolf and the Real World*, Berkeley: University of California Press.

Chapter 10

Multiple Anonymities:
Resonances of Fielding's *The Female Husband* in *Orlando* and
A Room of One's Own

Vara Neverow

For we think back through our mothers if we are women. It is useless to go to the great men writers for help, however much one may go to them for pleasure. Lamb, Browne, Thackeray, Newman, Sterne, Dickens, De Quincey – whoever it may be – never helped a woman yet, though she may have learnt a few tricks of them and adapted them to her use. The weight, the pace, the stride of a man's mind are too unlike her own for her to lift anything substantial from him successfully.

Virginia Woolf, *A Room of One's Own*

The question marks and ellipses, to which we supply silent assent and fill in the blanks, seal the pact of our conspiracy.

Jane Marcus, *Virginia Woolf and the Languages of Patriarchy*

In the first paragraph of *A Room of One's Own*, Virginia Woolf's narrator states, '"I" is only a convenient term for somebody who has no real being. Lies will flow from my lips, but there may perhaps be some truth mixed up with them.' The narrator asserts: 'Here then was I (call me Mary Beton, Mary Seton, Mary Carmichael or by any name you please – *it is not a matter of any importance*)' (*AROO*: 5; my emphasis).[1, 2] This evasive phrasing reveals the same sly intentionality as the first epigraph above in which the narrator asserts that 'whoever it may be', a male author is 'useless' to women writers. But I will argue that this statement is one of the narrator's lies. Although Henry Fielding[3] is not mentioned in her list of male British literary luminaries, Woolf seems to parody and indeed pillory one of his works in both *Orlando* and *A Room of One's Own*: his semi-factual 23-page pamphlet, *The Female Husband: Or The Surprising History of Mrs Mary, Alias Mr George*[4] *Hamilton, who was Convicted of having Married a young Woman of Wells and Lived with her as her Husband. Taken from Her Own Mouth Since Her Confinement*, published anonymously on 12 November

1746.[5] Fielding's version of 'Mrs Mary, Alias Mr George Hamilton' tells the story of one of the three transgressive and unmentioned Mary Hamiltons who are invoked but never identified in *A Room*. The pamphlet, a hyper-enhanced and altered account of an actual criminal trial, verdict, and punishment, is itself a fine example of how whopping lies can be mixed with some truth. Fielding's choice to conceal his own authorial identity is echoed in Woolf's stance of anonymity in the narration of both *Orlando* and *A Room of One's Own*.

Marcus evokes the spectral nature of the Hamiltons, writing:

> The metaleptic echo of the absent name of Mary (Hamilton) is, in Jefferson Humphries' words, 'a haunted trope', a ghostly allusion to an absence, and it mirrors the primal absence in the text of women's books on the shelves of the British Museum. (1987: 163–4)

The invisibility of the Mary Hamiltons in the essay parallels Terry Castle's discussion of how the lesbian is occluded in literature. Although only one of the Mary Hamiltons qualifies as a lesbian, the relevance of Castle's contention is clear:

> The lesbian is never with us, it seems, but always somewhere else: in the shadows, the margins, hidden from history, out of sight, out of mind, a wanderer in the dusk, a lost soul, a tragic mistake, a pale denizen of the night. (1993: 2)

Woolf scholars have noted that the narrator of *A Room* deliberately omits one of four Marys or Maries associated with various versions of a Scottish ballad.[6] In most versions of the ballad, the historically ambiguous Mary Hamilton is identified as a lady-in-waiting to the Queen of Scots, who was purportedly charged with infanticide and executed (although, as Antonia Fraser notes, the 'Maries' of Mary, Queen of Scots were actually 'Mary Fleming, Mary Seton, Mary Beton and Mary Livingstone' [1969: 32]). Speculation suggests the fate of this fictional Mary Hamilton was informed by that of a historical Mary Hamilton, a descendant of a Scottish emigrant to Russia. Serving as lady-in-waiting to Catherine I of Russia in the early 1700s,[7] she became a mistress to the Peter the Great and was found guilty of drowning a newborn baby fathered by the Czar. Unlike the Mary Hamilton in the Scottish ballad who was supposedly hanged in the 1500s either in Edinburgh or Glasgow, this Mary Hamilton was found guilty on all charges in November 1718 and sentenced to death by decapitation on 14 March 1719 in St Petersburg.[8]

The third Mary Hamilton invoked in *A Room* was a polygamist who did the unthinkable: she actually married other women – and not just one but many of them. Furthermore, she was never burdened with a pregnancy. A vivid description of her flagrant behaviour, titled 'A Woman who was imprisoned and whipped for marrying Fourteen Women', is provided in a 1746 *Newgate Calendar* entry '(Mary Hamilton').[9] Mary Hamilton's heinous strategy for conducting these seductions is sartorial: she cleverly deceived her wives into marriage 'under the outward garb of a man'.[10] Written in the plural first person, the *Newgate* entry asserts that, at the trial, 'Mary Price, the fourteenth wife, appeared in evidence (in such a case as this we must be pardoned for ambiguity) against her female husband' ('Mary Hamilton'):

> [She] swore that she was lawfully married to the prisoner, and that they bedded and lived together as man and wife for more than a quarter of a year; during all which time, so well did the impostor assume the character of man, [Price] still actually believed she had married a fellow-creature of the right and proper sex.

The 'learned quorum of justices' was initially flummoxed, but decided nonetheless:

> That the he or she prisoner at the bar is an uncommon, notorious cheat, and we, the Court, do sentence her, or him, whichever he or she may be, to be imprisoned six months, and during that time to be whipped in the towns of Taunton, Glastonbury, Wells and Shepton Mallet.

The 'Mary Hamilton' entry concludes: 'Mary, the monopoliser of her own sex, was imprisoned and whipped accordingly, in the severity of the winter of the year 1746.'

The Female Husband significantly expands on this *Newgate* account. Fielding adds numerous fictitious details to augment the scandalous nature of Hamilton's activities while concealing his own identity as the author. As Castle observes, Fielding's narrative is not a 'lesbian picaresque' but a cautionary tale (1982: 605, 609) calculatedly intended to discourage women from passing as men or exploring same-sex relationships. Yet, as Castle also observes, using 'cross dressing was a direct if risky way for a woman to escape those constraints . . . imposed by rigid sex roles' (1982: 606).

It took more than a century for scholars to determine that Fielding was the author of the pamphlet. Fielding's biographer, Wilbur L. Cross, notes in the third volume of his 1918 *History of Henry Fielding*: 'No copy known. Included here on the authority of [Andrew] Millar's list[11] in 2d ed. of *Cleopatra and Octavia*, 1758, and because of the use made of the story in *The Lover's Assistant*, line 295 *et seq*' (313).[12] Despite identifying the pamphlet as Fielding's work via these obscure sources, Cross was unable to locate a copy of *The Female Husband*.

However, just prior to the publication of his 1920 article 'The Printing of Fielding's Works', J. Paul de Castro stumbled upon one of the four surviving copies. As he reports in a note:

> Since the above was written, I have discovered a copy of 'The Female Husband'. It consists of 23 pages, and is the report of a case heard at Wells Quarter Sessions. It is a vividly written account of a Manx girl who ... travelled through Devon and Somerset in male attire as a doctor. While in Devon she married two women consecutively and then decamped ... [I]n Wells she there married a young girl ... but was shortly after identified as a 'wanted person' [and] ... was committed to Bridewell. (1920: 270)

Having clarified and studied the now extant pamphlet, de Castro offered conjectures about its significance. Considering Fielding's motivation for writing the pamphlet, de Castro suggests that the author had seized the opportunity to monetise a scandal: 'There can be no doubt that the case created much excitement and enquiry, and Fielding, then a widower with children, probably saw in it an opportunity of re-imbursing himself for some of the expenses of travelling the circuit' (1921: 185). De Castro regards the narrative as mainly factual and interprets Fielding's mention in the pamphlet of 'Mr Gold, an eminent and learned counselor at law' (184) as a reference to the author's first cousin.[13] De Castro notes that Gold's 'graphic account of the examination of Mary Price, "the wife", leaves the impression Fielding was himself in Court seated among counsel', actually witnessing Mary Hamilton's testimony; therefore, 'as was stated on [Fielding's] title-page' of the publication, the information was 'taken from her [Mary Hamilton's] own mouth' (185). Summing up, de Castro writes, 'The story is vividly told, but the subject matter is unedifying despite the characteristic moral reflections, and some psychologic [*sic*] master strokes' (185). He seems to see sincerity in the moralising and does not comment on the scurrilous depiction of Mary Hamilton or Fielding's lascivious descriptions toward the end of the pamphlet of her being whipped for her crimes (see Finlay 2007: 159).

Sheridan Baker, in his landmark 1959 article, 'Henry Fielding's *The Female Husband*: Fact and Fiction', counters de Castro's somewhat naïve version.[14] Convinced that Fielding neither 'interview[ed] the prisoner' nor 'was ... present at the trial' (1959: 219), Baker also rigorously investigates the life of the historical Mary Hamilton, indicating that, 'at fourteen, leaving home in her brother's clothes, she entered a[n] ... apprenticeship as a quack doctor' (213). Continuing to wear men's clothing, she began her own business using the name Dr Charles Hamilton. Baker also identifies fabrications in the pamphlet. For instance: 'Immediately we notice that the factual *Charles* Hamilton has become Fielding's *George* – and Fielding's text continues to diverge.

"This heroine in iniquity", [Fielding] writes, "was born in the Isle of Man, on the 16th Day of August, 1721"' (213). As Baker points out, Hamilton was actually born in Somerset. Baker notes that one of four surviving copies of *The Female Husband* was in the British Museum catalogue. The pamphlet was accessioned by the Museum in 1926, just two years before Woolf published *Orlando* and three before she published *A Room*.[15] Since the pamphlet had been identified as Fielding's work, it would have been catalogued under his name.

Marcus seems to be the earliest Woolf scholar to refer to Fielding's pamphlet,[16] noting, 'There was, however, another historical Mary Hamilton, whose story may have surfaced during the meetings regarding the defence for the Radclyffe Hall trial, which both Virginia and Leonard attended' (1987: 179). Marcus does not speculate as to whether Woolf might have read *The Female Husband*, but since the British Museum acquired the document during the same period that Woolf herself (as distinct from the narrators in *Orlando* and *A Room*) was researching 'all that men have written about women' (*AROO*: 27), she may have requested and read Fielding's 23-page pamphlet and then integrated the narrative and stylistic elements of his brief but bold account of Dr George Hamilton's adventures into both in *Orlando* and *A Room*.[17]

Fielding deftly uses subversive techniques to reference forbidden topics in his pamphlet just as Woolf generally takes an oblique approach in the discussion of delicate matters. Anne Fernald observes, 'Subversion, rather than confrontation, is Woolf's preferred mode of argument throughout *A Room of One's Own*' (1994: 182) – and the same principle applies to *Orlando*. When the narrator of *A Room* claims that, with regard to women's writing, 'The weight, the pace, the stride of a man's mind are too unlike her own for her to lift anything substantial from him successfully' (*AROO*: 75), one must recall that, since 'lift' is a familiar synonym for the act of theft, the wording may be subterfuge, an act of absconding. Woolf may have filched elements of Fielding's version of Dr Hamilton, just as Fielding himself selectively pilfered material from the trial. Although Woolf never confesses to having repurposed the stylistic elements of *The Female Husband*, she writes *A Room* and *Orlando* using many of the same licentious but euphemistic techniques as Fielding himself and transforms Fielding's sensationally suggestive and highly sexualised misogynistic rhetoric sometimes almost word for word into a feminist argument.

Whereas Fielding takes pleasure from depicting a woman's humiliating punishment for daring to live as a man, Woolf does the reverse and reveals the ways women can evade patriarchal suppression and fulfil their desires. Emily Finlay, in her analysis of *The Female Husband*, emphasises how:

[Fielding's] narrator explicitly informs us that she is to be not merely 'publicly' whipped but 'severely', 'four [separate] times, in four market towns'. 'To wit, once in each market town', he adds, as though we may have missed it. Imprisonment is almost an afterthought: 'and to be imprisoned & c.' The description is then repeated in journalistic present-perfect tense, momentarily diverging from the narratorial past-perfect, to remind us again how 'very severely [the lashes have] been inflicted'. This uncharacteristically obsessive repetition is punctuated by a rare image of the victim: 'so lovely a skin scarified with rods, in such a manner that her back was almost flayed'. (2007: 160)

This same motif of a woman whipped is specifically referenced in *A Room* when the narrator states that she herself is 'afraid of the lash' (*AROO*: 89). She is also concerned for the safety and wellbeing of the fictional author, Mary Carmichael, fearing that the novelist might be caught in the act of expressing herself and be punished. While this phrase can be viewed metaphorically as, perhaps, an allusion to the public humiliation Radclyffe Hall experienced during the obscenity trial of *Well of Loneliness*, implicit in Woolf's choice of terminology is a reference to a very different kind of writing – specifically that of scarification, of writing on the body with a whip. As Emily Bowles argues:

Hamilton's body is overwritten with signs of transgression that, Fielding suggests, have aesthetic and erotic meaning to her readers . . . [S]he also literally transforms from a sexual agent into a text that corresponds to Fielding's ideas about poetic justice . . . The story written on her skin is not her own, impressed on her as it is by scarifying rods, but her body continues to write it. (2010: par. 15)

This act of whipping is comparable to inscribing graffiti on the female body, and indeed, the motif of graffiti appears when the narrator, while discussing women's desire for anonymity in *A Room*, points out that men have 'an irresistible desire to cut their names' into 'a tombstone or a signpost . . . as Alf, Bert or Chas. must do in obedience to their instinct, which murmurs if it sees a fine woman go by' (*AROO*: 50). The motif later morphs into a sartorial variant of men imposing their own interpretations on the bodies of women. The narrator notes that, though 'we must wait a little, for Mary Carmichael will still be encumbered with that self-consciousness in the presence of "sin" which is the legacy of our sexual barbarity', she will eventually be able to write about 'those small, scented rooms where sit the courtesan, the harlot and the lady with the pug dog' who 'sit in the rough and ready-made clothes that the male writer has had perforce to clap upon their shoulders. But Mary Carmichael will have out her scissors and fit them close to every hollow and angle' (*AROO*: 87).

The male palimpsest is also apparent in Fielding's use of crude sexual references in his wording of a letter purportedly written by the semi-literate Mary Price to her suitor, Dr Hamilton. As Finlay notes, the letter is not just rife with deliberate misspellings but 'is composed of puns, which contribute to the metaphorical chain [of sexual allusions in the narrative]. "Kan nut" and "Kuntry" instantly evoke "cunt", while "cummand" plays on "cum", designating the letter as the space of explicitly female sexuality' (2007: 164).

Fielding promises his readers a shocking narrative by supplementing the oxymoronic title of *The Female Husband* with an epigraph from Ovid which recounts the monstrous fate of a woman transformed into a man:

> *Quodque id Mirum Magis Esset in Illo;*
> *Faemina Natus Erat. Monstri Novitate Moventur,*
> *Quisquis Adest: Narretque Rogant.*
>
> Ovid *Metam*. Lib. 12[18]

Inverting Fielding's storyline, Woolf depicts the adventures of Orlando using similar wordplay and motifs of cross-dressing and gender-bending. She upends Ovid's version of metamorphosis and repurposes Fielding's narrative, celebrating the life of a human being born a man and trans-formed into a woman who, despite the social constraints imposed by a patriarchal culture that privileges the male, is just as capable as she had been when she possessed the attributes of a man's body. Ultimately, Orlando triumphs over the false dichotomy of the sexes and validates humanity.

Woolf's vision for her faux biography apparently came to her abruptly as she wrote in her diary on 5 October 1927:

> having done my last article for the Tribune, & now being free again ... instantly the usual exciting devices enter my mind: a biography beginning in the year 1500 and continuing to the present day, called Orlando: Vita; only with a change about from one sex to the other. (*D* 3: 161)

Woolf does not acknowledge what triggered the concept, but perhaps she had recently read of Mary Hamilton as described either in the 1746 *Newgate Calendar* or Fielding's version[19] and thus imagined a way to use Hamilton's rollicking adventures as the template for depicting Vita and her many lovers.

Orlando's adventures in England during the rowdy mid-eighteenth century coincide roughly with the time frame of Dr Hamilton's esca-pades. When Orlando begins to spend time with (self-)important men of letters including Addison, Dryden, Pope, and Swift, who variously display their contempt for women, she discovers that the sartorial is critical in defining social status. As the narrator[20] notes:

> Different though the sexes are, they intermix. In every human being a vacillation from one sex to the other takes place, and often it is only the clothes that keep the male or female likeness, while underneath the sex is the very opposite of what it is above. (O: 139; see also Burns 1994)

– a nod not only to Vita Sackville-West's own cross-dressing adventures (Blair 2004) but potentially an acknowledgement of Mary Hamilton's 'outward garb of a man' ('Mary Hamilton') and, by association, the cross-dressing motif in Fielding's *The Female Husband*.

The sartorial is particularly evident when the narrator quotes the final passage from Addison's essay, 'Trial of the Petticoat':

> I consider woman as a beautiful, romantic animal, that may be adorned with furs and feathers . . . The peacock, parrot and swan shall pay contributions to her muff; . . . [a]ll this, I shall indulge them in, but as for the petticoat . . . I neither can, nor will allow it. (O: 154)

The epigraph of Addison's essay is Ovid's *Pars minima est ipsa puella sui*, followed by the translation, 'the young Lady is the Least Part of herself'. The setting is a court of law and the ribald focus is on a woman's undergarment, which is subjected both to scientific dissection and to erotic opening and penetration (Lubey 2008: 431–2). The argument presented in defence of the garment is strongly commercial, emphasising revenues generated by vast quantities of materials including wool and whalebone, though the petticoat also is argued to be sexual protection for women. As Kimberly Chrisman points out, 'In the face of widespread and violent protest from men, women willingly adopted the hoop as a means of protecting, controlling, and, ultimately, liberating female sexuality' (1996: 7). In the end, the judge determines that the cost of the hoop petticoat is too great a financial burden for fathers and husbands and decrees that it be forfeited. The curious instance of an item of women's clothing going on trial invokes the sartorial crimes of Mary Hamilton, hinting that Henry Fielding, though never mentioned anywhere in *Orlando*, is anonymously present in much the same way that the Mary Hamiltons exist though unnamed in *A Room of One's Own*.

Additional nods in Fielding's direction may be derived from the playful Preface to *Orlando* where Woolf thanks both Daniel Defoe and Laurence Sterne. These near contemporaries of Addison and Fielding similarly experimented with randy elements of narration, Defoe being well known for his lurid picaresque novels including *Moll Flanders* and *Roxana: The Fortunate Mistress*, and Sterne for his extraordinary

Tristram Shandy: A Cock and Bull Story. While Defoe represents women in his works as remarkably resourceful and sexually adventurous, Fielding's salacious narrative of Dr Hamilton does not celebrate her resiliance or her derring-do ways. Instead, the narrator salivates over a scene of violation in which Dr Hamilton's shirt is torn open exposing her breasts and lubricates the narrative with details of her whippings. Woolf's triumphant narrative of Orlando's evolution from man to woman counters Fielding's crude, degrading depiction of all women.

By mentioning Sterne in the Preface to *Orlando*, Woolf reminds the reader of the trauma that occurs 'when Susannah, the nursemaid, urges the five-year-old Tristram to make water out of the nursery [*sic*] window (in the absence of a chamber pot), [and] the window-sash suddenly falls with what appear to be disastrous results for the little boy' (Towers 1957: 16). In contrast to Tristram's near-castration, the adult Orlando awakens from a long sleep and discovers that the male equipment bestowed biologically at birth exists no longer. Now lacking the phallus she once possessed, she is newly identified as 'Lady' Orlando and thus is stripped of her inheritance upon her return to England.

During one of her street-haunting adventures in London, Orlando, wearing men's clothing, is approached by a prostitute named Nell and accepts the invitation to accompany her to her room. Nell is delighted when Orlando 'fl[ings] off all disguise and admit[s] herself a woman' (159). Soon Orlando begins to engage in a series of deliciously Sapphic visits with the covey of prostitutes including Nell, Prue, Prue Kitty, and Kitty Rose (O: 160; Sproles 2006: 81–2; Parkes 1994: 453–4), women whose names are nearly as repetitive as those of the Four Maries – Beton, Seton, Carmichael, and Hamilton – in *A Room of One's Own*.

Since these women already 'ha[ve] a society of their own', they collectively decide Orlando may join them and 'they now elected her a *member*' (O: 60, my emphasis). The reference to 'member' may initially seem innocuous, an ordinary term for any affiliate of an organisation, but the word could readily be a pun on a sexual substitute for the male organ, a tool remarkably similar to the sexual device Dr Hamilton uses to please her multiple wives. Dr Hamilton's tool (though not her sole vehicle for providing pleasure) offers offers a satisfying alternative to the dangers of heterosexual intercourse, protecting her partners not only from unwanted pregnancies but also from most sexually transmitted diseases like syphilis and gonorrhea. Bonnie Blackwell describes Dr Hamilton's '"infallible nostrum"' (2002: 60; Fielding 2012), as a 'medicine of secret composition' (2002: 60), a prosthetic substitute for biological male genitalia. Possession of such a prothesis is punishable, as Castle observes: 'Hamilton's dildo – for that is what one must assume is

signified by the none-too-mysterious "wherewithal" . . . reappears later
on as "something of too vile, wicked, and scandalous a nature" to toler-
ate that is discovered in her "trunk" and produced in evidence against
her' (1982: 609).

Examining the covert suggestiveness of *Orlando*, Adam Parkes
focuses on an episode where Orlando and her friends are enjoying
each other's company immensely but must be constantly on alert to the
arrival of any male customer:

> many were the fine tales they told and many the amusing observations they
> made, for it cannot be denied that when women get together – but hist – they
> are always careful to see that the doors are shut and that not a word of it gets
> into print. All they desire is – but hist again – that not a man's step on the
> stair? (O: 160)

Parkes observes that, 'as if to suppress any randiness before it reaches
the wrong audience, the invisible biographer exercises a tactful censorship over the content of the women's conversations' (1994: 454; Fernald
2005: 177). The intrusion of a male client suddenly silences the women,
and the tone of narration shifts from gaiety to sardonic mockery, allowing the narrator to expose male ignorance regarding the real nature of
female desire and women's relations with one another:

> All they desire, we were about to say when the gentleman *took the very words
> out of our mouths*. Women have no desires, says this gentleman, coming
> into Nell's parlour; only affectations . . . and it is well known (Mr T. R. has
> proved it) 'that women are incapable of any feeling of affection for their own
> sex and hold each other in the greatest aversion'. (O: 160; my emphasis)

Woolf's wording 'took *the very words out of our mouths*' is remarkably similar to Fielding's '*Taken from Her Own Mouth Since Her
Confinement*', the last phrase in the title of *The Female Husband*, and
the passage above seems to offer an intentional counter-narrative. The
nameless customer who interrupts the conversation is convinced that
women in the sex-trade find pleasure in servicing their clients, but the
wording of Woolf's passage suggests otherwise. Men pride themselves
on performance and duration, but this visitor, who believes women have
no desires, is himself merely a fleeting parenthetical '(she has served him
and he is gone)' (O: 160). Woolf's narrator also mocks the very Fielding-
esque 'Mr. S. W.', who claims '"It is well known . . . that when women
lack the *stimulus* of the other sex, women can find nothing to say to each
other"' and the equally ludicrous opinions of 'Mr. T. R.' (O: 160; my
emphasis). Such insistence that women lack desire infers the obverse: a
surfeit of female randiness unknown to men. Further, the repetition of

'hist' here must considered as a multifaceted pun. 'Hist' is a caution-ary reminder for women to be silent; it curtails and even castrates their alternative and secret version of hist/ory.[21] Mr S. W. thinks 'that when [women] lack the stimulus of the other sex, [they] can find nothing to say to each other. When they are alone, they do not talk, they scratch' (*O*: 160). 'Hist' also evokes the defensive hiss of a cat, and thus a woman alerting her companions to imminent danger, not attacking each other.

The anonymous male narrator in *The Female Husband* claims that his writing techniques are meant to protect 'delicate ears' (2012), and proba-bly Fielding's coding was intended to deceive the censors. So too, Woolf's narrators in *Orlando* and *A Room* are not merely concerned about apparent propriety but about personal safety. This cautious sleight-of-hand in wording appears in the famous passage from *A Room* below:

> I turned the page and read . . . I'm sorry to break off so abruptly. Are there no men present? . . . We are all women you assure me? Then I may tell you that the very next words I read were these – 'Chloe liked Olivia . . . Do not start. Do not blush. Let us admit in the privacy of our own society that these things sometimes happen. Sometimes women do like women. (*AROO*: 80–1)

This reference to *The Well of Loneliness* obscenity trial has been dis-cussed at length elsewhere (Marcus 1987: 166; Parkes 1994: 457), but Marcus also highlights the seductive Sapphist quality of the narrator's wording that 'has us breathing heavily, as the erotic nature of her verbal enterprise becomes clear' (1987: 167).

While the 300-year span of *Orlando* adds an element of fantasy to the reality of Sackville-West's sexual adventures, the time frame also roughly aligns Orlando's adventures with the fates of the three Mary Hamiltons, though in reverse. The ill-fated Scottish Mary Hamilton is a contemporary of the unfettered male Orlando; Orlando's Russian love interest, Sasha, may potentially be seen as an inverted acknowledgement of the Mary Hamilton who was Peter the Great's lover; Dr Hamilton is equivalent to Orlando herself as she transitions from male to female but continues to pass as a man.

From a feminist perspective, the culminating event in Woolf's faux biography may well be Orlando safely giving birth to a child without drastic consequences. With the presence of Nick Greene in both *Orlando* and *A Room*, Judith Shakespeare becomes the obverse of Orlando. Marcus specifically links the fates of the heterosexual Mary Hamiltons to the fictitious Judith Shakespeare, three women who die because of their fecundity. Two are executed for committing infanticide, while Judith Shakespeare accelerates the inevitable by choosing suicide (and thereby feticide), skipping the fuss of murdering a newborn and being arrested, tried, convicted, and executed. These women – like untold millions of others – are destroyed by their embodied fertility. Christine Froula compares Woolf's tragically pregnant Judith Shakespeare to Orlando, who is safely married to an androgynous husband when she gives birth, and laments the 'other bodies in the woman poet's grave, for the children (who alter their mother's futures as Orlando's child does not) also die' (2007: 192).

Just as Woolf invents a Judith Shakespeare, Fielding tinkers with the facts in *The Female Husband*. For instance, he identifies the Isle of *Man* as Hamilton's place of of birth – the place where the genetically mutated Manx cat with no tail originates.[22] Even though it is unclear as to whether the Manx cat's peculiarity and apparent deformity was an established fact at the time *The Female Husband* was written, Fielding depicts Dr Hamilton as freakish due to her lack of the male genitals and the affectation of disguising herself as a man, and Roger Lund argues that, for Fielding, 'it is not simply deformity that is the source of the ridiculous, but rather the attempt to disguise deformity through some form of affectation' (2005: 106).

The ambiguous Manx cat in *A Room* may be Woolf's wink at Fielding's Dr Hamilton. After all, 'The tailless cat, though some are said to exist in the Isle of Man, is rarer than one thinks. It is a queer animal, quaint rather than beautiful. It is strange what a difference a tail makes' (*AROO*: 11). Fernald observes, 'It is not hard to see the tailless cat as a figure for gender difference' (1994: 182), and Sandra Gilbert claims the Manx cat is more than just a gender marker. The cat is a sign of liberation: 'To be different – that is to be female – is not to be castrated or deformed . . . it is simply to be in command of oneself and one's words' (1987: 222) and thus tail-less but not without a tale to tell.

Woolf's word choices are also of interest. According to Eric Partridge, a variant of the adjective 'queer' meaning 'base, criminal, counterfeit, very inferior' was in use from circa sixteenth to the twentieth centuries. The derivation of 'quaint' is from the fourteenth-century word *quentiye* or *quenynte*, meaning 'the female pudenda', and is related to *cunt* (Partridge 1984: 278). In the 1920s, the word 'quaint' also came to mean 'amusingly old-fashioned; entertainingly unusual, even occ. as funny in an odd way' in both middle- and upper-class circles (944–5). In Fielding's pamphlet, Dr Hamilton is depicted as base, criminal, counterfeit, and very inferior to men because she possesses the female gentialia associated with the older meaning of the word 'quaint'.

Fielding also exchanged Hamilton's name Charles for George. Perhaps he did so purely on a whim, but the name choice could represent a frisson of lexiconic excitement. Partridge indicates 'George' is a truncated version of 'St George' and 'for George', both variants of a mild swear word (Partridge 1984: 1006). Partridge notes that, from the late seventeenth to the mid-nineteenth centuries, the term 'riding St George' (also 'the dragon upon St George'), whether used as a noun and an adjective, meant '(The position of) the woman being on top in the sexual act' (975), a potential reference to Mary Hamilton's faux masculine role as 'George' in her sexual encounters with various deceived wives.

Orlando and *A Room* both seem to offer audacious rewritings and repurposings of Fielding's pamphlet, emphasising the exceptional privileges enjoyed by a motivated non-heterosexual woman. Orlando enjoys a spectrum of sexuality comparable to that of the cross-dressing eighteenth-century Dr Hamilton who, though publicly whipped for her transgressions, nonetheless thwarts even the remotest possibility of conception that dooms so many heterosexual women. When, according to Fielding, one of Dr Hamilton's recalcitrant wives tells her female husband, 'you have not – you have not – what you ought to have', Dr Hamilton, though ultimately unsuccessful in assuaging the spouse's anxiety, nevertheless is able to promise her that: 'she would have all the pleasures of marriage without the inconveniences' (Fielding 2012). Without a doubt, these unnamed 'inconveniences' are linked to the untimely deaths of the other two apparitional Mary Hamiltons (one of whom is historical) as well as Judith Shakespeare.

When the narrator of *A Room* says 'call me ... by any name you please' (5), she subtly suggests that re-naming oneself authorises re-gendering oneself for a public audience, a façade that is a serviceable strategy for survival. 'Any name' hints that sex and gender are equally malleable. In *Orlando*, the protagonist does not actually change names, but does change genders and thereby destablises the boundaries of sexual identity in patriarchal culture. Fielding mocks Dr Hamilton by using coded references to ridicule same-sex female desire. Woolf uses similar techniques to reveal obliquely the Sapphic elements in both *A Room of One's Own* and *Orlando*, thus authenticating women's desires and exposing male delusions.

Notes

1. There are two identified narrators in *A Room*. The initial narrator explicitly avoids accepting a singular identity or even a particular name ('Call me Mary Beton, Mary Seton, Mary Carmichael, or by any name you please', a list of names that, as will argued here, implicitly includes Mary Hamilton).

Similarly, the authorial voice that concludes the essay – although the voice could potentially be perceived as that of Virginia Woolf – is effectively anonymous and probably should not be identified directly with the actual writer. The primary narrator is named twice as 'Mary Beton'. The first instance occurs in the second chapter where this narrator, referencing her financial autonomy, observes that: 'Society gives me chicken and coffee, bed and lodging, in return for a certain number of pieces of paper which were left me by an aunt, for no other reason than that I share her name'; she then explicates the source of her inheritance, naming her generous deceased relative and specifying the cause of her demise: 'My aunt, Mary Beton, . . . died by a fall from her horse when she was riding out to take the air in Bombay. The news of my legacy reached me one night about the same time that the act was passed that gave votes to women' (*AROO*: 37). The second instance is in the final chapter where an unnamed authorial voice takes over the narrative and controls the last few pages of the essay, stating: 'Here, then, Mary Beton ceases to speak. She has told you how she reached the conclusion . . . that it is necessary to have five hundred a year and a room with a lock on the door if you are to write fiction or poetry' (103). These voices of the narrative speaker and the authorial speaker validate the multiple anonymities in the essay rather than functioning solely as Woolf's own compounded surrogate voice (see Neverow 1999; Marcus 1987: 172).

2. In 1563, Thomas Randolph, the English ambassador to Scotland, described Mary, Queen of Scots' ladies-in-waiting, as 'virgins, maids, *Maries*, demoiselles of honour, or the Queen's mignons, call them as you please, your Honour' (Marcus 1987: 179; my emphasis).

3. A search of the CD-ROM of *Major Authors: Virginia Woolf* (Hussey 1995) reveals that Woolf's recorded references to Fielding are very scarce.

4. Sheridan Baker notes the 'factual *Charles* Hamilton . . . become[s] Fielding's *George*' (1959: 213). Mary Hamilton's alternate identities listed in John Willcock's 1887 volume, *Legal Facetiæ* include '*alias* Charles Hamilton, *alias* George Hamilton, *alias* William Hamilton' (2010: 196).

5. See Baker 1959: 213 n.1.

6. See Tolman (1927) regarding the ballads themselves; see Hanley (1984), Colburn (1995), and Goldman (2006) regarding the Mary Hamilton of ballad fame in *A Room*. Marcus suggests that Woolf's invisible Mary Hamilton represents Mary Llewellyn, the lover of Stephen Gordon, Radclyffe Hall's lesbian protagonist. At the time Woolf was writing the lectures that became *A Room*, Vita Sackville-West was having an affair with another Mary, Mary Campbell (Marcus 1987: 209 n.1).

7. See Sargent and Kittredge 1904: 421.

8. See Massie regarding charges brought against Hamilton and details of her execution (1981: 812–13).

9. I would like to thank my colleague, June Dunn, for alerting me to online access of *The Newgate Calendar*.

10. Fraser points out that Mary, Queen of Scots, and her Maries sometimes wore male clothing (1969: 186); making reference to D. Hay Fleming's 1897 biography of Queen Mary, Marcus notes that the Queen's four Maries 'were fond of adopting male dress and the queen herself, like

Virginia Woolf's *Orlando*, dressed as a man to wander the streets incognito' (1987: 179).

11. Millar was Fielding's publisher. De Castro identifies the 'list' as 'Millar's advertisement attached to Sarah Fielding's "Cleopatra and Octavia", published by him in 1758, that is four years after [Fielding's] death' (1921: 184).

12. In *The Lover's Assistant*, a free translation of Ovid's *Ars Amatoria*, Fielding tells the story of Pasiphaë, the mythological mother of the Minotaur. He smugly observes that, 'I am very sorry to say . . . [she] conceived a passion worse, if possible, than that of Mrs Mary Hamilton, for this Bull', the father of her monstrous offspring (Fielding 2010). Simon Dickie pointedly calls Fielding's translation of Ovid 'boorish' (2010: 572).

13. Fielding's first cousin is variously identified as Henry Gold (de Castro 1920: 30; 1921: 84–5), Henry Gould (Castle 1982: 604), and David Gould (Donoghue 1993: 74).

14. Adrienne Eastwood, mistakenly claiming Baker was the first to discuss the pamphlet, compares Fielding's 1746 pamphlet and the 1813 variant 'published anonymously under the title *The Surprising Adventures of a Female Husband!*, [and] retain[ing] some of Fielding's prose, [though] many alterations have been made' (2007: 491; see Neverow 2012).

15. Confirmed in an email from the British Library Rare Books Reference Team on 2 June 2011.

16. Marcus (1987: 180; 213 n.23) relies on Lillian Faderman's inaccurate assertion that 'Fielding found [Hamilton] guilty of marriages to three woman and ordered her whipped publically' (Faderman 1983: 68). Recent scholarship does not support the view that Fielding tried, convicted, or sentenced Hamilton, nor that he was even present at the trial.

17. Woolf certainly would have had access to Cross's biography of Fielding, de Castro's articles on Fielding's pamphlet, and Tolman's article on the Scottish ballads while doing her research.

18. My colleague Joseph Solodow has kindly translated the passage from Ovid's *Metamorphoses* as: 'And, what was more astonishing in him, he was born a woman. All who were there were moved by the novelty of the monstrosity and asked him to tell the story.' Solodow observes: 'The precise lines quoted are 12.174–6. The words through *natus erat* are a quotation from a speaker; the remainder is said by the narrator.'

19. Carolyn Woodward references Susan S. Lanser's argument that Fielding, Samuel Richardson, and John Cleland deliberately attempted to '"reorient women's erotic and affectional desires"' expressed in contemporary works such as *The Travels and Adventures of Mademoiselle de Richelieu*, Charlotte Charke's *A Narrative of the Life of Mrs Rich*, and Eliza Haywood's *The British Recluse* (Lanser qtd in Woodward 2004: 575).

20. Karyn Z. Sproles identifies the narrator as male (2006: 76) but Susan Dick points out that 'the narrator even claims to have no gender, for biographers, like historians, enjoy immunity "from any sex whatever"', quoting a passage from *Orlando*. Dick continues: 'Yet, once Orlando becomes a woman, the distance between her and the narrator narrows and the narrator sees things more from a woman's point of view' (2000: 64–5).

21. Kathryn Simpson suggested this insightful interpretation.

22. Karen Commings says that 'whether the tailless gene was imported to the [Isle of Man] or occurred spontaneously among the feral cat population living there', the 'existence of Manx cats has been documented for at least 200 years ... [T]he English landscape artist Joseph Turner had seven tailless cats as early as 1810, all of which came from the Isle of Man' (1999: 9).

Bibliography

Baker, S. (1959), 'Henry Fielding's *The Female Husband*: Fact and Fiction': *Publications of the Modern Language Association of America*, 74(3): 213–24.

Blackwell, B. (2002), '"An Infallible Nostrum": Female Husbands and Greensick Girls in Eighteenth-Century England', *Literature and Medicine*, 21(1): 56–77.

Blair, K. (2004), 'Gypsies and Lesbian Desire: Vita Sackville-West, Violet Trefusis, and Virginia Woolf', *Twentieth-Century Literature*, 50(2): 141–66.

Bowles, E. (2010), 'You Have Not What You Ought: Gender and Corporeal Intelligibility in Henry Fielding's *The Female Husband*', *Genders OnLine Journal*, 5, 37 paragraphs, <http://www.genders.org/g52/g52_bowles.html> (last accessed 2 December 2010).

British Library Rare Books Reference Team (2011), email, 2 June.

Burns, C. L. (1994), 'Re-Dressing Feminist Identities: Tensions between Essential and Constructed Selves in Virginia Woolf's *Orlando*', *Twentieth-Century Literature*, 40(3): 342–64.

Castle, T. (1982), 'Matters Not Fit to Be Mentioned: Fielding's *The Female Husband*', *ELH: English Literary History*, 49(3): 602–22.

Castle, T. (1993), *The Apparitional Lesbian: Female Homosexuality and Modern Culture*, New York: Columbia University Press.

Chrisman, K. (1996), 'Unhoop the Fair Sex: The Campaign Against the Hoop Petticoat in Eighteenth-Century England', *Eighteenth-Century Studies*, 30(1): 5–23.

Colburn, K. (1995), 'Women's Oral Tradition and *A Room of One's Own*', in *Re: Reading, Re: Writing, Re: Teaching Virginia Woolf: Selected Papers from the Fourth Annual Conference on Virginia Woolf*, ed. E. Barrett and P. Cramer, New York: Pace University Press, pp. 59–63.

Commings, K. (1999), *Manx Cats*, Hauppauge, NY: Barron's.

Cross, W. L. (1918), *The History of Henry Fielding*, vol. 3, New Haven, CT: Yale University Press.

de Castro, J. P. (1920), 'The Printing of Fielding's Works', *The Library*, series 4–1(1): 257–70.

de Castro, J. P. (1921), 'Fielding's Pamphlet, "Female Husband"', *Notes and Queries*, series 12-VIII(151): 184–5.

Dick, S. (2000), 'Literary Realism in *Mrs Dalloway*, *To the Lighthouse*, *Orlando* and *The Waves*', in *The Cambridge Companion to Virginia Woolf*, ed. S. Roe and S. Sellers, Cambridge: Cambridge University Press, pp. 50–71.

Dickie, S. (2010), 'Fielding's Rape Jokes', *The Review of English Studies*, 61(251): 572–90.

Donoghue, E. (1993), *Passions Between Women: British Lesbian Culture*

1668–1801, New York: Harper Collins.

Eastwood, A. L. (2007), 'Surprising Histories: A Comparison of Two Pamphlets', *Notes and Queries*, 54(4): 490–6.

Faderman, L. (1983), *Scotch Verdict: Miss Pirie and Miss Woods V. Dame Cumming Gordon*, New York: Columbia University Press.

Fernald, A. (1994), '*A Room of One's Own*, Personal Criticism, and the Essay', *Twentieth-Century Literature*, 40(2): 165–89.

Fernald, A. (2005), 'A Feminist Public Sphere? Virginia Woolf's Revisions of the Eighteenth Century', *Feminist Studies*, 31(1): 158–82.

Fielding, H. [1760] (2010), *The Lovers Assistant, or New Art of Love*, ed. and intro. C. E. Jones, *Internet Archive.org*, <http://archive.org/stream/thelover sassista31036gut/pg31036.txt> (last accessed 25 August 2013).

Fielding, H. [1746] (2012), *The Female Husband: Or The Surprising History of Mrs Mary, Alias Mr George Hamilton, who was Convicted of having Married a young Woman of Wells and Lived with her as her Husband. Taken from Her Own Mouth Since Her Confinement*, <http://ebooks.ade laide.edu.au/f/fielding/henry/female-husband/> (last accessed 30 December 2013).

Finlay, E. (2007), '"So Lovely a Skin Scarified with Rods": Modern Notions in Fielding's *The Female Husband*', *Déjà Vu: antiTHESIS*, 17: 154–70.

Fraser, A. (1969), *Mary, Queen of Scots,* New York: Bantam.

Froula, C. (2007), *Virginia Woolf and Bloomsbury Avant-Garde: War, Civilization, Modernity*, New York: Columbia University Press.

Gilbert, S. M. (1987), 'Woman's Sentence, Man's Sentencing: Linguistic Fantasies in Woolf and Joyce', in *Virginia Woolf and Bloomsbury: A Centenary Celebration*, ed. J. Marcus, Bloomington: Indiana University Press, pp. 208–24.

Goldman, J. (2006), *The Cambridge Introduction to Virginia Woolf*, New York: Cambridge University Press.

Hanley, L. T. (1984), 'Virginia Woolf and the Romance of Oxbridge', *The Massachusetts Review*, 25(3): 421–36.

Hussey, M. ed (1995), *Major Authors: Virginia Woolf*, CD-ROM, Woodbridge, CT: Primary Source Media.

Lubey, K. (2008), 'Erotic Interiors in Joseph Addison's Imagination', *Eighteenth-Century Fiction*, 20(3): 415–44.

Lund, R. D. (2005), 'Laughing at Cripples: Ridicule, Deformity and the Argument from Design', *Eighteenth-Century Studies*, 39(1): 91–114.

Marcus, J. (1987), *Virginia Woolf and the Languages of Patriarchy*, Bloomington: Indiana University Press.

'Mary Hamilton', *The Newgate Calendar*, <http://www.exclassics.com/ newgate/ng217.htm> (last accessed 24 August 2013).

Massie, R. K. (1981), *Peter the Great: His Life and World*, New York: Random House.

Neverow, V. (1999), 'Thinking Back Through Our Mothers, Thinking in Common: Virginia Woolf's Photographic Imagination and the Community of Narrators in *Jacob's Room, A Room of One's Own*, and *Three Guineas*', in *Virginia Woolf and Communities*, ed. J. McVicker and L. Davis, New York: Pace University Press, pp. 65–90.

Neverow, V. (2012), 'Bi-sexing the Unmentionable Mary Hamiltons in *A Room of One's Own:* The Truth and Consequences of Unintended Pregnancies and Calculated Cross-Dressing', in *Contradictory Woolf: Selected Papers from the Twenty-First International Conference on Virginia Woolf*, ed. D. Ryan and S. Bolaki, Clemson: Clemson University Digital Press, pp. 134–41.

Parkes, A. (1994), 'Lesbianism, History, and Censorship: *The Well of Loneliness* and the Suppressed Randiness of Virginia Woolf's *Orlando*', *Twentieth-Century Literature*, 40(4): 434–60.

Partridge, E. (1984), *A Dictionary of Slang and Unconventional English*, 8th edn, ed. P. Beale, New York: Macmillan.

Sargent, H. C. and G. L. Kittredge, eds (1904), *English and Scottish Popular Ballads Edited from the Collection of Francis James Child*, New York: Houghton Mifflin.

Solodow, J. (2013), email, 31 August.

Sproles, K. Z. (2006), *Desiring Women: The Partnership of Virginia Woolf and Vita Sackville-West*, Toronto: University of Toronto Press.

Tolman, A. H. (1927), 'Mary Hamilton: The Group Authorship of Ballads': *Publications of the Modern Language Association of America*, 42(2): 422–32.

Towers, A. R. (1957), 'Sterne's Cock and Bull Story', *English Literary History*, 24: 12–29.

Willcock, J. [1887] (2010), *Legal Facetiae: Satirical and Humorous*, Internet Archive.org, <https://archive.org/details/cu31924021264209> (last accessed 27 February 2014).

Woodward, C. (2004), 'Crossing Borders with Mademoiselle de Richelieu: Fiction, Gender, and the Problem of Authenticity', *Eighteenth-Century Fiction*, 16(4): 573–601.

Woolf, V. (1980), *The Diary of Virginia Woolf,* vol. 3, ed. A. O. Bell and A. McNeillie, New York and London: Harcourt Brace Jovanovich.

Woolf, V. [1929] (2005), *A Room of One's Own*, intro. and ed. S. Gubar, New York: Harcourt.

Woolf, V. [1928] (2006), *Orlando*, intro. and annot. M. DiBattista, New York: Harcourt.

Chapter 11

Two-Spirits and Gender Variance in Virginia Woolf's *Orlando* and Louise Erdrich's *The Last Report on the Miracles at Little No Horse*

Kristin Czarnecki

Innovative concepts of gender abound in Virginia Woolf's *Orlando* (1928) and Louise Erdrich's *The Last Report on the Miracles at Little No Horse* (2001). In Woolf's novel, Orlando undergoes a seemingly unwilled biological change from male to female, while in *The Last Report on the Miracles at Little No Horse*, a white woman, Agnes DeWitt, adopts a life-long disguise as a Catholic priest at an Ojibwe outpost in North Dakota. At first glance, novels by a modernist English writer and a contemporary Native American one may seem unlikely bedfellows; indeed, there are significant differences between their explorations of gender identity. Each novel speaks to other important issues as well: *Orlando* is at once a new kind of biography, an homage to Vita Sackville-West, and a tour through (and parody of) English literary history. *The Last Report* interweaves Ojibwe history and culture to depict the devastating effects of colonisation upon the Ojibwe as well as their means of survival, including storytelling, along with an ability to integrate conflicting cultural mores. A closer look, however, reveals significant affinities between these works, whose cataclysmic weather events and protagonists' long, deep sleeps precipitate singular gender experiences over vast spans of time.

While this paper discusses Western gender theory, I wish to explore gender in *Orlando* and *The Last Report* primarily through my understanding of Native American gender traditions, particularly that of the two-spirit.[1] Coined in 1990 at the third Native American/First Nations gay and lesbian conference, the term two-spirit denotes Native American/First Nations individuals who elect not to live by strict gender binaries. Sue-Ellen Jacobs et al. note that in 'Native North America, there were and still are cultures in which more than two gender categories are marked' (1997: 2); in many instances, two-spirit people were highly valued for their unique capabilities and contributions to the tribe and for their heightened spirituality. Lang further explains, 'Two-spirit statuses and roles reflect worldviews found widely in Native American cultures, which appreciate and recognize ambivalence and change both in individuals and in the world at large' (Lang 1997: 103). Similarly, Jacobs et al. cite the importance of 'gender variance' to Native Americans, defined as '"cultural expressions of multiple genders (i.e. more than two) and the opportunity for individuals to change gender roles and identities over the course of their lifetimes"' (qtd in Jacobs et al. 1997: 4).

The concepts of two-spirit and gender variance resound strongly within *Orlando* and *The Last Report on the Miracles at Little No Horse*. Considering Orlando as a two-spirit who exhibits a purposeful change of gender shifts our consideration of this character from one upon whom biological and social forces act to an agent of his and her own performance of gender. Karen Kaviola sees Orlando undergoing an 'unanticipated, undesired' and 'spontaneous' change of sex (1999: 235, 240), and Elise Swinford views him as one 'who, by no effort of his own and with no apparent cause, transforms and metamorphoses' (2011: 196). Conversely, Lisa Rado sees Orlando 'changing his sex in order to escape it' (1997: 156). Establishing a critical discourse encompassing Native traditions, however, we might see Orlando's move into an alternative gender role as a means of rejecting Western gender dichotomy, rather than rejecting gender altogether, and embracing the variability of human experience. Maria DiBattista seems to suggest this as well in her reference to Orlando as a 'man-woman' (2006: li), while Esther Sánchez-Pardo González argues: 'Orlando was already a woman in his previous life, or at least a man-womanly' (2004: 77). A Native American two-spirit often becomes known as a 'man-woman' or 'woman-man', terms placing the person's gender of choice first and biological sex second (Lang 1998: xvi). This articulation of the two-spirit concept recalls *A Room of One's Own*, where Woolf famously writes, 'it is fatal for anyone who writes to think of their sex. It is fatal to be a man or woman pure and simple; one must be woman-manly or man-womanly' (*AROO*: 102–3). González concludes, apropos of Woolf's concept of androgyny in *A Room*, that 'if the feminine and the masculine have to coexist, and there is no prevalence of any of the two, one might infer that they either neutralize each other, or that one of the two is foregrounded' (2004: 77). I see this foreground at play in *Orlando* and *The Last Report*, in which the protagonists' 'feminine' and 'masculine' characteristics alternately appear. With the concept of two-spirit in mind, we can see how events in the first part of *Orlando* propel him towards a life better suited to his gender-variant inclinations.

Woolf evokes the ambiguous nature of gender in *Orlando's* opening sentence: 'He – for there could be no doubt of his sex, though the fashion of the time did something to disguise it – was in the act of slicing at the head of a Moor' (O: 11). With this statement, the narrator raises doubts rather than puts them to rest; indeed, Orlando's gender ambiguity soon manifests itself. The young aristocrat often prefers the company of characters on the outskirts of society, foreshadowing his later proclivity for becoming a female and also as someone outside the status quo. During these excursions, women 'perched on his knee, flung their arms round his neck and, guessing that something out of the common lay hid beneath his duffle cloak, were quite as eager to come at the truth of the matter as Orlando himself' (22). What exactly is 'out of the common' beneath his cloak? Orlando is similarly unsure of the Muscovite Sasha. When he first sees her ice-skating, he cannot discern whether she is male or female. Amid the fragments we might observe – height, weight, and clothing – exists something more powerful 'which issued from the whole person' (28). As Kaviola states, 'human subjectivity is not reducible to a noncontradictory whole or consistently expressive of the sexed body' (1999: 235), contrary to Western ideology, which insists on linking gender, sex, and sexuality. However:

> [w]hen the boy, for alas, a boy it must be – no woman could skate with such speed and vigour – swept almost on tiptoe past him, Orlando was ready to tear his hair with vexation that the person was of his own sex, and thus all embraces were out of the question. (28)

His response reveals his dissatisfaction with his gender because of societal taboos.

Orlando and Sasha nevertheless embark on an affair, and in the midst of it, Orlando, too, succumbs to socially encoded gender prejudices as Sasha's melancholy silences lead him to consider rumours about the Russians. He wonders whether

> she was ashamed of the savage ways of her people, for he had heard that the women in Muscovy wear beards and the men are covered with fur from the waist down; that both sexes are smeared with tallow to keep the cold out, tear meat with their fingers and live in huts where an English noble would scruple to keep his cattle. (35–6)

Kaviola concurs with Kari Weil's assertion that androgyny in *Orlando* is linked closely with race, nation, sexuality, and class – that 'gender cannot be isolated from other axes of identity' (Kaviola 1999: 239). Indeed, Orlando becomes increasingly disturbed not only by the supposed masculine slant of Russian females but also by the rustic lives of both sexes. Although he ultimately dismisses such rumours, his initial misgivings indicate his position in Western society as a privileged male.

London at this stage is in the midst of a deep freeze. Soon, people die in the 'riot and confusion' of the thaw (46), caught on floes and then swept into the rushing waters in a scenario rife with implications for Orlando's eventual change of sex and gender. Standing on shore, Orlando sees Sasha's ship heading out to sea. After cursing the fickleness and faithlessness of women, he resolves to live in solitude, his diatribe against women concomitant with his callous treatment of his fiancée, Lady Margaret; his revulsion at the thought of Sasha possessing 'male' characteristics; and his brutalisation of the severed head, a trophy of colonialism, in the attic of his ancestral home, all of which comprise a man unable to recognise injustice beyond that of his own thwarted desires. Brenda S. Helt believes that, contrary to many analyses of *A Room of One's Own*, Woolf does not advocate for a fully androgynous mind because she knows it takes a woman's perspective to understand 'a history of patriarchal subjection' (2010: 150). Thus while Orlando seems to consider his life as having ended or reached a new and unwanted stage upon Sasha's supposed betrayal, he in fact starts down the path towards attaining an outsider's perspective on gender dichotomy. Jane de Gay finds Woolf asserting anti-patriarchal stances at this juncture concerning not only sex and gender but also nature and literary history: 'Ruskin's devastating Renaissance frosts', de Gay states, 'are thus rewritten as the start of revival and reawakening, so that this linear historical model of decline is replaced with a cyclical one of natural renewal' (2007: 68).

This period of renewal apparently requires vast stores of energy. Retreating alone to his home, Orlando falls asleep and awakens seven days later with 'an imperfect recollection of his past life' (50). The narrator wonders whether such a sleep is palliative, eradicating traumatic memory. Does it gradually prepare us for death so that we are not shocked with it all in a moment? 'Had Orlando, worn out by the extremity of his suffering, died for a week, and then come to life again?' (51). Rado views Orlando's sleep as a means of sexual repression, for he sleeps when the body threatens to erupt – when he might have run away with Sasha; in fact Rado believes 'the empowerment [Woolf's 'trope of the androgyne' in *Orlando*] is designed to produce is predicated on the repression of her own female identity, her own female body' (150), a statement seemingly belied by Orlando's eventual change of sex.

Orlando's demoralising experience with the poet Nick Greene, whom Nicola Thompson deems 'the embodiment of patriarchal literary convention' (1993: 309), is another step towards what I suggest is Orlando's deliberate shift from male to female. After Greene mocks Orlando's poetry, Orlando determines to write solely to please himself, deciding that 'obscurity lets the mind take its way unimpeded' (76). While we might attribute his stance to that of one who craves fame and concedes the unlikelihood of attaining it, we also see that at this point in time, the person writing in obscurity is a woman. The female gender, therefore, is better suited to Orlando's literary aspirations. Soon, he takes a renewed interest in his house and throws himself into domestic activities, spending lavishly on décor while also continuing to write, and repeatedly unwrite, his poem. Literary ambition and domestic pursuits dovetail as Orlando increasingly manifests proclivities for the female gender, becoming 'excessively generous both to women and to poets' (82).[2]

Years later in Constantinople, where Orlando has been posted as a diplomat, rumours circulating about him and a peasant woman precede his next long sleep. As people search his room for a clue to his condition, they find a marriage licence among his papers. That Orlando's slumber follows his marriage is further evidence to Rado that he sleeps to repress his sexuality. Julia Briggs, however, notes that the palace revolution that occurs after the marriage links '[v]iolent change in the body politic' with 'the private body, as Orlando wakes to find himself transformed into a woman (his patriarchal honours preceding, and perhaps even precipitating, this event)' (2005: 201). Three spirits approach just before the change: the Ladies of Purity, Chastity, and Modesty, who try to thwart the emergence of a variant gender and cloak Orlando's altered body. Woolf's parody here of patriarchal expectations of women's behaviour, attendant with the novel's parody of male-oriented English literary history, evokes the three celestial beings in Christine de Pizan's *The Book of the City of Ladies* (1405) – Lady Reason, Lady Virtue, and Lady Rectitude – who visit Christine after she becomes demoralised by all she has read about women in books written by men. Internalising such misogyny, she repudiates God for making her female instead of male. The ladies tell Christine not to believe such works. They encourage her to believe in herself, and, by urging her to treat male literary authority with scepticism, to rewrite literary history from a female perspective and establish a City of Ladies, perhaps a precursor to the Society of Outsiders Woolf proposes in *Three Guineas*. While González views this 'theatrical scene' in *Orlando* as a 'sham castration' (2004: 77), I believe it suggests Orlando's growing understanding that life gendered male has become insupportable and heralds the intentionality of his change.

When Orlando finally awakens, the narrator proclaims, 'Orlando had become a woman – there is no denying it' (102), as if forestalling a reader's understandable scepticism. We also see a curious use of pronouns: 'The change of sex, though it altered their future, did nothing whatever to alter their identity' (102). González believes that 'with the use of the plurals [the narrator] is indeed pointing to an androgynous being who is now revealing the feminine side that Orlando the man had been concealing in his behavior' (2004: 78), a comment lending itself to an interpretation of Orlando as a two-spirit. The narrator then says that from now on, we will dispense with 'he' and use 'she' instead. Moreover, the alteration seems to have occurred 'in such a way that Orlando herself showed no surprise at it . . . no . . . signs of perturbation. All her actions were deliberate in the extreme, and might indeed have been thought to show tokens of premeditation' (O: 103). Orlando is fundamentally unchanged, moving seamlessly from 'he' to 'their' to 'she', wholly at ease with gender variance. Orlando at this moment embodies two-spirit characteristics, embracing change, ambiguity, and fluidity to live out an alternative gender role.[3]

We see similar two-spirited dynamics at play in *The Last Report on the Miracles at Little No Horse*, which opens in 1996 with an elderly priest, Father Damien Modeste, whom the narrator refers to as 'he' – casting no doubts, envisioning no dubious readers in need of assurance about the character's sex or gender. In addition to ministering to the Ojibwe at the mission of the Sacred Heart at Little No Horse, Damien has for decades been writing unacknowledged letters to the popes about events on the reservation, particularly those surrounding Sister Leopolda (born Pauline Puyat), whom the Church is investigating for possible sainthood. A moment after writing one such letter, Damien prepares for bed and unwraps the binding around his chest. 'His woman's breasts were small, withered, modest as folded flowers' (Erdrich 2001: 8), the narrative states, going back to 1910 when 'all that happened began with that flow of water' (11), a flooding river launching Agnes DeWitt into life as a man. Even before the flood, Agnes experiences gender variance, initially as a teenager when she becomes a Catholic nun, a time when she also had to bind her breasts. Failing to wholly suppress her sexuality, she realises she has forsaken God and leaves the convent, eventually stumbling upon the farm of Berndt Vogel, a young German bachelor. While Agnes resists their sexual attraction to each other, Berndt resolves to win her over, but, the narrator states: 'She had also learned her share of discipline and in addition – for the heart of her gender is stretched, pounded, molded, and tempered for its hot task from the age of two – she was a woman' (18), indicating the cultural construction of gender. Soon Agnes and Berndt become lovers until a bizarre chain of events leaves Berndt dead and Agnes with a bullet wound to the head and subsequent memory lapses. A young priest, Damien Modeste, visits her on his way to his new posting in North Dakota. After meeting him, Agnes considers a possible escape from her grief into missionary life.

With the nearby river overflowing, the town experiences a tremendous flood that blasts through a wall of Agnes's house and lifts her piano with Agnes upon it, for she is also a gifted musician. Decades later, Damien will write: 'Blessed One, I now believe in that river I drowned in spirit but revived. I lost an old life and gained a new' (41). Before the new life begins, however, Agnes falls into a long, deep sleep, and, as in *Orlando*: 'That cessation of awareness proved a bridge between her old life and her new life' (42). Before the sleep, we learn, she had practised her faith with no real sense of conviction. Upon waking, she has a vision of Christ offering her food and warmth. Wandering days later through the flood's wreckage, she, like Orlando, observes human lives reduced to soggy detritus, and she happens upon the body of Father Damien, drowned and then swept up and caught in the branches of a tree. Viewing it as a sign from God, Agnes pulls the body down, strips off the clothes, buries the priest, dons his attire, and makes her arduous way to Little No Horse to take up his position. Like Woolf, Erdrich appreciates the transformative capacities of water.

In the same way Orlando exhibits propensities for gender variance before her change of sex, so too does Agnes before becoming Father Damien. When she first meets Berndt, her voice is 'husky and bossy' (13). We learn that she 'had a square boy's chin' (19) and, again, that her 'speech had always been husky and low for a woman' (while later 'Father Damien's voice [is] musical, for a man') (76). She refuses to eradicate her sexuality as a nun, and in turn-of-the-century rural America, she lives with a man out of wedlock, both stances defying proscribed gender roles for women. Before exploring this character as a two-spirit, however, I wish to address Patrice Hollrah's argument that applying the term to Agnes is 'incorrect and inappropriate' (2011: 99), constituting non-Native appropriation of Native concepts. Hollrah states that for Native Americans, gender is tightly tied to 'Native struggles and de-colonization movements' and that 'scholars should think carefully before using the term to describe non-Native characters who exhibit G/L/B/T/Q etc. characteristics in a text by a Native author' (107). The term simply does not apply to Damien, Hollrah avers:

> Father Damien makes the decision to pass as a priest before he arrives at Little No Horse, as a person socialized in Catholicism and Western constructs of gender based on a binary system of man and woman. To call him Two-Spirit appropriates a pan-Native term that does not apply to him. From the beginning, Agnes considers her existence as Father Damien as 'the great lie that was her life' (61). A true Native Two-Spirit would not think of her life

as a lie . . . If Agnes were truly a Two-Spirit according to Ojibwe beliefs, she would not feel that she had betrayed her biological nature as a woman. She would understand that her alternative gender is acceptable in the community. (2011: 108)

Non-Native scholars must certainly be wary of propensities towards modern-day colonisation, yet Lang states:

'Two-spirit'/'two-spirited' originally referred to (1) those people referred to as 'berdaches' in the literature, (2) modern Native Americans who identify with these 'alternative' roles and gender statuses, and (3) contemporary Native American lesbians and gays . . . The term has meanwhile come to encompass an entire host of roles, gender identities, and sexual behaviors', including 'traditions of gender variance in other cultures'. (1998: xiii)

Jacobs et al. also explain that the term 'has come to refer to a number of Native American roles and identities past and present, including . . . traditions of gender diversity in other, Non-Native American cultures' (2). Moreover, following through on the quotation from *The Last Report* cited by Hollrah, we find that 'the great lie that was her life' is also 'the true lie . . . the most sincere lie a person could ever tell' (Erdrich 2001: 61). While 'there would be times she missed the ease of moving in her old skin . . . Agnes was certain now that she had done the right thing. Father Damien Modeste had arrived here. The true Modeste . . . none other. No one else' (65).

Deirdre Keenan considers Damien a two-spirit because he comes to embrace Ojibwe cultural and religious traditions. Keenan concurs with Hollrah that

the assertion of a genuine Two Spirit nature is problematic because Father Damien is born Agnes DeWitt, a white woman, into a culture of gender dichotomy . . . But Damien's refusal to conform to this cultural hegemony and his liberation under the influence of the Ojibwe people demonstrate gender alterity within a multiple sex-gender social system. (2006: 4–5)

In her study of gender and *The Last Report*, Pamela J. Rader also sees Damien as a two-spirit, particularly since upon his arrival at Little No Horse, he reminds Kashpaw, an Ojibwe elder, of 'a Wishkob, an Ojibwe two-spirit person . . . A biological male, this Wishkob assumed the gender role of a woman, as wife to the chief and as Kashpaw's grandmother' (2007: 226). Additionally, in his 'History of the Puyats', Father Damien relays a conflict that arises when Pauline's mother is a child. The event occurs as a party of Ojibwe, returning from a buffalo hunt, encounters 'a party of Bwaanag, a source of mortal hatred' (Erdrich 2001: 150). The scene culminates in Pauline's grandfather proposing to settle their differences by holding a footrace with one of the Bwaan men. His opponents choose 'an ikwe-inini, a woman-man called *winkte* by the Bwaanag, a graceful sly boy . . . Some of the Ojibwe, who judged his catlike stance too threatening, rejected him as a male runner on account of his female spirit' (153). They eventually decide, however, 'that as the *winkte* would run with legs that grew down along either side of a penis as unmistakable as his opponent's, he was enough of a male to suit the terms' (154). Keenan believes 'the inclusion of the Lakota term, *winkte*, and the Ojibwe term, *ikwe-inini*, shows that both cultures recognize a third gender category' (2006: 10). The *winkte* 'peered into the tortoiseshell hand mirror that hung around his neck' (Erdrich 2001: 153), removed his dress to prepare for the race, and 'stood, astonishingly pure and lovely, in nothing but a white woman's lace-trimmed pantalets' (154). As Keenan further states, the 'lack of reaction to the *winkte*'s appearance suggests the familiarity of cross-dressing in multiple gender practice' (2006: 10). I would also propose that the *winkte* episode nods towards Damien as a two-spirit.

Orlando's and Damien's experiences with gender variance reveal further similarities between the novels as well as bring Woolf's critique of Western gender norms into relief against the more inclusive concepts of gender found among the Ojibwe. Travelling back to England after the change, Orlando begins to learn Western gender norms first in terms of clothing. As DiBattista says, 'Clothes are invested with extraordinary novelistic value in *Orlando*. The history of Orlando's sexual and social identity is inseparable from the history of his, then her, attire' (2006: lxiii). In England again, Orlando, who 'up to this moment . . . had scarcely given her sex a thought' (*O*: 113), must now wear women's clothing, which constricts her movements and draws the gazes of men. Soon, Orlando realises she must revise her previous narrow notions about women. At the same time, her lamentation that 'Now she will only be able to do tedious things for which she is ill-suited' (116) could render problematic the notion of her as a two-spirit. Orlando's misgivings, however, reveal an inquisitive mind that questions gender dichotomy more than repudiates femaleness. In a rush of confusion, Orlando seems both to renounce and comprise two genders at once: 'she was man; she was woman; she knew the secrets, shared the weaknesses of each. It was a most bewildering and whirligig state of mind to be in' (117). Although she entertains thoughts of escaping her dilemma and running off with the gypsies again, 'it is plain that something had happened during the night to give her a push towards the female sex' (117). This push prompts her to reconsider her feelings for Sasha, for though she herself was a woman, it was still a woman she loved; and if the consciousness of being of the same sex had any effect at all, it was to quicken and deepen those feelings which she had had as a man. (119)

Swept up in her newfound understanding of Sasha, and a strong surge of passion for her, 'it was as if a cannon ball had exploded at her ear' when she suddenly hears a man's voice (117), similar to Clarissa's memory in *Mrs Dalloway* in which Peter's intrusion upon her and Sally after their kiss seems 'like running one's face against a granite wall in the darkness!' (2005: 35). As Orlando's ship approaches land, she hopefully considers how binaries might work in her favor: 'To refuse and to yield . . . to pursue and to conquer . . . to perceive and to reason . . . Not one of these words so coupled together seemed to her wrong' (120). Soon, though, she fears returning to England will mean living a lie, a sentiment that again might problematise attributing to her a two-spirit identity. Later, we will see Damien, too, experiencing doubts about his new gender role, yet such doubts, albeit painful at times, are precisely what Woolf and Erdrich explore and celebrate. To expect or hope for static, lifelong stances concerning one's own gender or that of another runs contrary to both authors' concepts of gender relativity and possibility.

Orlando's qualms regularly come to the fore, yet while she bemoans the fact that she will never again 'crack a man over the head, . . . or draw [her] sword and run him through the body' (O: 116), nowhere does the narrative indicate she had done any such things as a man. Life as a woman compels Orlando to become more mature and introspective while alternating between performing and resisting expected gendered behaviours. She cares little for clothing, and she 'detested household matters', but she is also 'excessively tender-hearted', with 'none of the formality of a man, or a man's love of power' (139). The Western mania for categories and binaries leads to consternation among those who observe her. Her biographer admits, 'Whether, then, Orlando was most man or woman, it is difficult to say and cannot now be decided' (140). Orlando herself refuses to choose between the two. Upon realising the extent of men's low opinion of women, she selects men's clothing from her closet one night for an outing into the streets. Soon she begins to change 'frequently from one set of clothes to another' (161) depending upon the activities she wishes to pursue, in true two-spirit fashion. In Native America, 'Becoming a "berdache" apparently is not a matter of sexual orientation but of occupational preferences and special personality traits' (Jacobs et al. 1997: 101). Orlando 'reaped a twofold harvest' by switching clothes and gender roles; 'the pleasures of life were increased and its experiences multiplied. From the probity of breeches she turned to the seductiveness of petticoats and enjoyed the love of both sexes equally' (O: 161).

Not until the Victorian Age does Orlando feel the full weight of social pressure to succumb to gender dichotomy, to go 'against her natural temperament' (O: 178) and wear a wedding ring, take a husband, and hide her writing. 'In *A Room of One's Own*, as in *Orlando*, gender is historically inflected: expressions of androgynous identity are more permissible in some historical contexts, less so in others', writes Kaviola (1999: 236). (In *The Last Report*, we will see that androgynous identity is more permissible in some *cultural* contexts than in others.) Even now, Orlando does not necessarily rue being female but buckles under the weight of constant scrutiny. In her mind, she still harbours resistance and a determination to fulfil her own wishes, which she does by beginning to write again. Kaviola believes Orlando fails to transcend gender (237). Reading *Orlando* alongside *The Last Report* shows that perhaps gender need not be transcended but rather conceived of more openly.

Damien, too, however, finds socially constructed gender norms at play at Little No Horse upon his arrival in 1912. Wearing the black robes of a Catholic priest, he experiences the privileges accorded to males. 'Ah, the priest's clothes!' Damien thinks. 'Even now, the driver treated her with much more respect as a priest than she'd ever known as a nun' (Erdrich 2001: 62). As we have seen, Kashpaw, the wagon driver taking Damien to his post, senses that the 'priest was clearly not right, too womanly' (64), likening him to Sweet, his Wishkob grandmother, and leaving it at that. Almost immediately, Agnes feels 'free to pursue all questions with frankness and ease' (62), losing the inhibitions she previously felt as a woman in male-dominated *milieus*. 'After donning the robes of a priest', Mark Shackleton writes, Agnes 'is immediately aware of the privileges and power allowed men but denied to women. The preferential treatment Damien experiences dressed as a priest even extends into being given more personal space, allowing greater freedom of physical and mental movement' (2011: 77) as opposed to the constraints Orlando feels as a woman. 'Put simply, donning robes or roles not only affects the way others see us but also affects the way we see ourselves' (77). This observation precisely describes Orlando's experience as Woolf and Erdrich dismantle Western gender norms, including the assumption that clothing indicates biological sex. As *Orlando*'s narrator states, 'In every human being a vacillation from one sex to the other takes place, and it is often only the clothes that keep the male or female likeness, while underneath the sex is the very opposite of what is above' (O: 139).

Like Orlando, Father Damien learns gender when he embarks upon life as a man. He composes 'Some Rules to Assist in My Transformation', which include: 'Make requests in the form of orders' and 'Ask questions in the form of statements' (Erdrich 2001: 74). Unfortunately, rule number five entails condescension towards females: 'Admire women's handiwork with copious amazement' (74). We learn that in the convent, Agnes had 'been taught to walk with eyes downcast. Now, Father Damien tipped his chin out and narrowed his gaze, focused straight ahead' (76). Furthermore, 'As a farm wife, Agnes had leaned out with a hand on her hip, carried things on her hip, nudged doors open and shut with her hip' (76). Realising that men carry themselves differently, 'Father Damien walked with soldierly directness and never swayed' (76). He asks: 'Between these two, where is the real self? It came to her that both Sister Cecilia and then Agnes were as heavily manufactured of gesture and pose as was Father Damien' (76). She resolves to 'make of Father Damien her creation . . . He would be Agnes's twin, her masterwork, her brother' (77).

Damien's new life comes not without its anguish, for '[s]he transformed herself each morning with a feeling of loss that she finally defined as the loss of Agnes' (76). While she may be seen as having had greater choice than Orlando in terms of gender change and should therefore be more at peace with her decision, that she becomes Father Damien due to a sense of vocation complicates notions of choice. Much of what occurs seems preordained or sanctioned. Agnes must hide evidence of her menstruation, for instance, 'the exasperating monthly flow that belonged to her past but persisted into the present' (78). When she prays for it to stop,

> [t]he heavy cramping faded until, stopping to change the cloth that she buried deep in snow, she found it barely spotted with darkness. No sooner had the evidence vanished than she felt a pang, a loss, an eerie rocking between genders. (78)

Others notice Damien's 'betweenness' as well. Just as people see feminine characteristics in Orlando when he is male and masculine ones when she is female, the Ojibwe note their new priest's gender ambiguity. When Damien visits a home decimated by disease and starvation, he encounters Fleur Pillager, who 'with a cold sarcasm laughed at the unmanly priest' (85), although they soon become close friends, and tribal elder Nanapush sees the priest as 'oddly feminine' (91).

As in *Orlando*, further moments in *The Last Report* might challenge the use of the term two-spirit. Damien considers his 'subterfuge' (Erdrich 2001: 267) and the 'long siege of deception' (342) that is his life. Despairing at times, he questions the faith that led to his decision to become Damien in the first place. As aforementioned, I believe such doubts illustrate the complex relationship between gender, culture, and vocation, for two-spirits and gender-variant individuals gravitate towards the tasks and activities to which they feel most suited. As Erdrich writes: 'Agnes and Father Damien became one indivisible person in prayer. That poor, divided human priest enlarged and smoothed into the person of Father Damien' (109). Moreover, Keenan points out, 'the representation of traditional gender variance . . . substantially depends on ways the Anishinaabeg at Little No Horse perceive [Damien] and recognize his Two Spirit status' (2006: 6). Several years into their friendship, during a game of chess, Nanapush asks Damien outright:

> 'What are you? . . . A man priest or a woman priest? . . . Why . . . are you pretending to be a man priest? . . . We used to talk of it, Kashpaw and myself . . . but when we noticed that you never mentioned it, we spoke of this to no one else.' (231)

Nanapush expresses his and Kashpaw's acceptance of Damien's choices along with their respect for him and his privacy. As Lang states, 'women-men and men-women were accepted in most Native American cultures', including Ojibwe, and 'to some extent, even highly respected' (1998: 313), although, Nanapush says, 'We don't get so many of those lately. Between us, Margaret and me, we couldn't think of more than a couple' (232), for the influx of white Christian mores suppressed gender variance in many Native American cultures. 'Still,' Nanapush says, 'that is what your spirits instructed you to do, so you must do it. Your spirits must be powerful to require such a sacrifice' (232). As tender and revealing as their discussion may be, Damien realises that Nanapush only raises the subject to distract him and gain the upper hand in their chess match.

Further examples illustrate the Ojibwes' acceptance of Damien's preferred gender role. The Ojibwe men in general grow 'accustomed . . . to the priest's combination of delicacy and shrewd toughness' (Erdrich 2001: 161–2) without necessarily knowing Damien is biologically female. Others do know, however. After breaking off a clandestine love affair with another priest sent by the diocese to Little No Horse, Damien in his grief sinks into another days-long sleep. His caretaker, Mary Kashpaw, sits vigil by his side and notices no beard growth. 'Every morning after that she heated a kettle of water, readied the mug of shaving soap, dipped in the brush, stropped the razor, and was seen, ostentatiously, to be putting these things aside just as Sister Hildegarde arrived' (212). Mary even sleeps in solidarity with Damien, guiding him back to his waking life when he becomes lost in his dreams' tunnels and mazes. 'Impossible to say how many dreams within the dream [Damien experienced] before he met the one who followed him in to guide him back: Mary Kashpaw' (213). Another woman respects Damien's secret as well. Looking thoughtfully at Fleur one day, Damien notes her 'fierce intelligence' and that 'nothing slipped by her, so he accepted that she'd known his secret from the beginning, and it hadn't mattered' (263–4).

Decades later, a priest sent to Little No Horse to research the life of Leopolda watches the elderly Damien, over 100 years old now,[4] and experiences the unsettling sensation that he is seeing an old woman; as a Westerner, he 'has no cultural frame of reference to absorb the gender alterity he too senses in Father Damien' (Keenan 2006: 7). Years earlier, Leopolda had spitefully called the priest '*Sister* Damien' (Erdrich 2001: 273). 'You are mannish', she says, 'unwomanly, yet your poor neck is scrawny ... It is obvious to me you wrap your chest. Apparent that you haven't a man's equipment, though that is useless anyway upon a priest. I am not as stupid as the others' (274). The others are not stupid, of course, but open-minded, loving, and respectful of Damien's gender variance. Having long ago repudiated her Native heritage, Leopolda has thoroughly imbibed Western prejudices and threatens to expose Damien, believing gender ambiguity to be shameful. 'Were he exposed', Damien thinks, 'were he known to have fooled, deceived, and hidden his most fundamental nature, all would be lost' (276), his fear again recalling Hollrah's assertion that Damien ought not be considered a two-spirit. More than anything, though, his thoughts depict 'the perils of mono-genderedness' (Barak 1996: 55), to borrow Julie Barak's phrase from her essay on 'berdaches' in Erdrich's earlier novels.

It is unsurprising to find gender variance in Erdrich's work given that many tribal women, including Ojibwe, 'have reportedly turned completely to masculine tasks, with or without cross-dressing' and without 'carry[ing] out a gender status change' in order to achieve maximum independence (Lang 1998: 268, 269). These women found an 'alternative *feminine role* that was culturally acceptable' (269). In addition to portraying the Ojibwes' acceptance of the womanly priest in their midst, *The Last Report* describes several Ojibwe women who blur gender norms, such as Mashkiigikwe, one of Kashpaw's wives and one of the few successful hunters during the punishing winters:

Mashkiigikwe's legs were oak fence posts and her neck, solid, was packed with a power that surged up through her body and flashed from the eyes. [Nanapush] drifted in admiration as she tore wolfishly at a piece of deer liver with strong little teeth ... Yet, when well fed, she could be very jolly, too. Her singing voice was of a surprising lilt and softness, and her songs were often children's games. It charmed Nanapush to watch her ... (91–2)

Mashkiigikwe's blending of masculine and feminine traits elicits delight in a man – a delight standing in stark contrast to the repugnance felt by Orlando regarding rumours of 'savagery' and masculinity in Sasha.[5] Mary Kashpaw is also described in largely masculine terms, with her powerful build and gruff manner, yet she displays tenderness toward Damien and becomes the object of a young man's fascination and ardour.

As the Ojibwe grow to love and accept Damien, he comes to love them and embrace their culture. He counters American governmental deception and obtains land for them, and 'render[s] into English certain points of their own philosophy that illuminate the precious being of the Holy Ghost' (Erdrich 2001: 49), as he writes to the Pontiff. He also becomes increasingly uneasy about converting the Ojibwe (although he still does) and horrified that Leopolda 'baptized their defenseless bodies' during times of sickness (122). He asks Margaret Kashpaw to add beadwork to his vestments, and he fills his cabin with Ojibwe bead-work and paintings. In addition, he becomes fluent in Ojibwemowin, even writing an Ojibwe grammar and dictionary. 'As I understand the place of the noun in the Ojibwe mind', he writes, 'it is unprejudiced by gender distinctions' (257). Moreover, F. David Peat explains that many Native languages, including Ojibwe, emphasise verbs rather than nouns and that such an emphasis 'perfectly reflects a reality of transformation and change' (2005: 237). For Damien, such transformation involves not only gender but also the blending of religious traditions. He comes to prefer 'the Ojibwe word for praying, anama'ay, with its sense of a great motion upward. She began to address the trinity as four and to include the spirit of each direction' (182). Thanks to Nanapush, Damien 'now practiced a mixture of faiths, kept the pipe, translated hymns or brought in the drum, and had placed in the nave of his church a statue of the Virgin' (276). He is accepted where no other white man is, and he is the only one, he believes, who would 'listen to the sins of the Anishinaabeg and forgive them – at least not as a mirthless trained puppet of the dogma, but in the spirit of the ridiculous and wise Nanabozho' (276), the traditional Ojibwe trickster figure. When he plans his own death and the disposal of his body in order to preserve his dignity, he determines to enter the Ojibwe heaven.[6] Damien lives out his preferred gender role among people open to life's possibilities.

Exploring *Orlando* and *The Last Report* with a focus on two-spirits and gender variance fosters an understanding of vibrant Native American traditions while bringing into even sharper focus Woolf's desire for greater gender inclusivity in Western society. While the Ojibwes' open-ness neither eradicates nor solves the problems encountered by those living out different or multiple genders, it allows readers to appreciate the dynamic nature of an individual's motivations and preferences not only in terms of gender identity but also the activities to which he or she feels most drawn. Perhaps, then, Woolf wishes neither to transcend nor neutralise gender but to enable additional gender categories along with unimpeded, lifelong manoeuvrability among them. She might have agreed that two-spirit sensibilities could bring such a vision to fruition.

Notes

1. It is important to explain the provenance and contested nature of the term 'two-spirit'. Jacobs et al. state that in past centuries, non-Native anthropologists, ethnographers, sociologists, sexologists, psychologists, and the like applied the term 'berdache' to males they saw in Native American cultures living as females: 'berdaches' were engaged in women's activities, such as pottery and basketry, and, at times, married to men. As Walter L. Williams explains, 'The word originally came from the Persian *bardaj*, and via the Arabs spread to the Italian language as *bardasso* and to the Spanish as *bardaxa* or *bardaje* by the beginning of the sixteenth century. About the same time the word appeared in French as *bardache*' (1986: 9). Seventeenth- and eighteenth-century Western publications describe the berdache variously as 'male prostitute', 'beautiful boy', 'passive homosexual partner', and a 'young man or boy who serves another's succubus, permitting sodomy to be committed on him' (qtd in Williams 1986: 9), exemplifying Western insistence on conflating sexuality and gender. Additionally, confounded by the sight of men dressed as women, whites began 'using the term *hermaphrodite* as a synonym for *berdache*' (10). Understandably, many Native Americans came to reject the term 'berdache' as 'inappropriate and insulting' and adopted the term two-spirit instead (Jacobs et al. 1997: 3). See Jacobs et al. (1997) for multiple views on the meaning and usage of 'berdache' and two-spirit.
2. It is of course problematic to link an interest in domesticity with women. I do so not in an essentialist manner but to highlight Western gender norms, particularly in the time of Orlando's change of sex, the late seventeenth century.
3. In terms of pronouns, *The Last Report* toggles smoothly between 'Agnes' and 'Father Damien' and 'she' and 'he'. I have paid close attention to whether the names and pronouns are juxtaposed with particular gendered behaviour but found no such pattern, indicating the shortcomings of trying to establish a critical apparatus for *The Last Report* based on Western gender norms.
4. Williams states that 'berdaches' 'were always believed to live longer than average men' (1986: 38), lending further credence to the concept of Damien as a two-spirit.
5. While gendered divisions of labour exist(ed) throughout many Native cultures, they did/do not stem from or result in the privileging of male endeavours or the denigration of women's. Rather, different gendered activities are believed to bring the entire community into harmony.

6. 'There is no way around the fact that beneath these clothes I am a shocking creature, to be prodded, poked, and marveled at when dead. Defenseless, that's how I picture it, and the prospect is so truly dreadful that I prefer to disappear', Damien writes (Erdrich 2001: 342; original emphasis).

Bibliography

Barak, J. (1996), 'Blurs, Blends, Berdaches: Gender Mixing in the Novels of Louise Erdrich', *Studies in American Indian Literatures*, 8(3): 49–62.

Briggs, J. (2005), *Virginia Woolf: An Inner Life*, New York: Harcourt.

de Gay, J. (2007), 'Virginia Woolf's Feminist Historiography in Orlando', *Critical Survey*, 19(1): 62–72.

de Pizan, C. [1405] (1998), *The Book of the City of Ladies*, New York: Persea Books.

DiBattista, M. (2006), Introduction, *Orlando: A Biography*, New York: Harcourt, pp. xxxv–lxvii.

Erdrich, L. (2001), *The Last Report on the Miracles at Little No Horse*, New York: Harper Perennial.

González, E. S. P. (2004), '"What Phantasmagoria the Mind Is": Reading Virginia Woolf's Parody of Gender', *Atlantis*, 26(2): 75–86.

Helt, B. S. (2010), 'Passionate Debates on "Odious Subjects": Bisexuality and Woolf's Opposition to Theories of Androgyny and Sexual Identity', *Twentieth-Century Literature*, 56(2): 131–67.

Hollrah, P. (2011), 'Love and the Slippery Slope of Sexual Orientation: L/G/B/T/Q etc. Sensibility in *The Last Report on the Miracles at Little No Horse*', in *Louise Erdrich: Tracks, The Last Report on the Miracles at Little No Horse, The Plague of Doves*, ed. D. Madsen, London and New York: Continuum, pp. 98–116.

Jacobs, S., W. Thomas, and S. Lang, eds (1997), *Two-Spirit People: Native American Gender Identity, Sexuality, and Spirituality*, Urbana and Chicago: University of Illinois Press.

Kaviola, K. (1999), 'Revisiting Woolf's Representations of Androgyny: Gender, Race, Sexuality, and Nation', *Tulsa Studies in Women's Literature*, 18(2): 235–61.

Keenan, D. (2006), 'Unrestricted Territory: Gender, Two Spirits, and Louise Erdrich's *The Last Report on the Miracles at Little No Horse*', *American Indian Culture and Research*, 30(2): 1–15.

Lang, S. (1997), 'Various Kinds of Two-Spirit People: Gender Variance and Homosexuality in Native American Communities', in *Two-Spirit People: Native American Gender Identity, Sexuality, and Spirituality*, ed. S. Jacobs, W. Thomas, and S. Lang, Urbana and Chicago: University of Illinois Press, pp. 100–18.

Lang, S. (1998), *Men as Women, Women as Men: Changing Gender in Native American Cultures*, trans. J. L. Vantine, Austin: University of Texas Press.

Peat, F. D. (2005), *Blackfoot Physics*, Newburyport, MA: Weiser Books.

Rader, P. J. (2007), 'Disrobing the Priest: Gender and Spiritual Conversions in Louise Erdrich's *The Last Report on the Miracles at Little No Horse*', in

The Catholic Church and Unruly Women Writers: Critical Essays, ed. J. Del Rosso, L. Eicke, and A. Kothe, New York: Palgrave Macmillan, pp. 221–35.

Rado, L. (1997), 'Would the Real Virginia Woolf Please Stand Up? Feminist Criticism, the Androgyny Debates, and *Orlando*', *Women's Studies*, 26: 147–69.

Shackleton, M. (2011), 'Power and Authority in the Realms of Racial and Gender Politics: Post-colonial and Critical Race Theory in *The Last Report on the Miracles at Little No Horse*', in *Louise Erdrich: Tracks, The Last Report on the Miracles at Little No Horse, The Plague of Doves*, ed. D. Madsen, London and New York: Continuum, pp. 67–81.

Swinford, E. (2011), 'Transforming Nature: *Orlando* as Elegy', in *Virginia Woolf and the Natural World: Selected Papers of the Twentieth Annual International Conference on Virginia Woolf*, ed. K. Czarnecki and C. Rohman, Clemson: Clemson University Digital Press, pp. 196–201.

Thompson, N. (1993), 'Some Theories of One's Own: *Orlando* and the Novel', *Studies in the Novel*, 25(3): 306–17.

Weil, K. (1992), *Androgyny and the Denial of Difference*, Charlottesville and London: University of Virginia Press.

Williams, W. L. (1986), *The Spirit and the Flesh: Sexual Diversity in American Indian Culture*, Boston, MA: Beacon Press.

Woolf, V. [1925] (2005a), *Mrs Dalloway*, New York: Harcourt.

Woolf, V. [1929] (2005b), *A Room of One's Own*, New York: Harcourt.

Woolf, V. [1928] (2006a), *Orlando: A Biography*, New York: Harcourt.

Woolf, V. [1938] (2006b), *Three Guineas*, New York: Harcourt.

Index